CALIFORNIA

McDougal Littell

MATH

Algebra 1

Larson   Boswell   Kanold   Stiff

California Standards Review and Practice

The California Standards Review and Practice book begins with in-depth review and practice of every California Algebra 1 Standard. This is followed by an intensive cumulative review with mixed practice. A pretest and posttest covering the Algebra 1 standards are included with the intensive review. All exercises are in multiple-choice format.

McDougal Littell
A DIVISION OF HOUGHTON MIFFLIN COMPANY
Evanston, Illinois • Boston • Dallas

Cover photo: © James Randklev/Photographer's Choice/Getty Images

ISBN 13: 978-0-618-89343-0
ISBN 10: 0-618-89343-1   9 10 11 12 13 14   0982   15 14 13 12 11
                                            4500310291

Contents

In-Depth Standards Review and Practice

Alg. 1.0   Arithmetic Properties..2

Alg. 1.1   Use Properties of Numbers 5

Alg. 2.0   Opposites, Reciprocals, Roots, and Exponents 7

Alg. 3.0   Absolute Value Equations and Inequalities 10

Alg. 4.0   Solve Equations and Inequalities...............................13

Alg. 5.0   Solve Problems Using Linear Equations and Inequalities...............15

Alg. 6.0   Graph Linear Equations and Inequalities 18

Alg. 7.0   Write and Interpret Linear Equations 22

Alg. 8.0   Parallel and Perpendicular Lines 24

Alg. 9.0   Solve Linear Systems.....................................27

Alg. 10.0   Monomials and Polynomials 31

Alg. 11.0   Factor Polynomials......................................36

Alg. 12.0   Simplify Rational Expressions 40

Alg. 13.0   Operations With Rational Expressions 42

Alg. 14.0   Solve Quadratic Equations.................................45

Alg. 15.0   Rate, Work, and Percent Mixture Problems......................48

Alg. 16.0   Relations and Functions...................................51

Alg. 17.0   Domain and Range 53

Alg. 18.0   Functions 56

Alg. 19.0   Quadratic Formula......................................58

Alg. 20.0   Use the Quadratic Formula 60

Alg. 21.0   Graphing Quadratic Functions...............................62

Alg. 22.0   Quadratic Functions and x-intercepts 66

Alg. 23.0   Using Quadratic Equations to Solve Problems 68

Alg. 24.1   Inductive and Deductive Reasoning 70

Alg. 24.2   Hypothesis and Conclusion 72

Alg. 24.3   Counterexamples 74

Alg. 25.1   Analyze Claimed Assertions 76

Alg. 25.2   Judge the Validity of an Argument............................78

Alg. 25.3   Determine When a Statement is True 80

Contents *(continued)*

Intensive Standards Review and Practice

Pretest 84

Properties of Numbers (Alg. 1.0, Alg. 1.1) 91

Opposites, Reciprocals, Roots, and Exponents (Alg. 2.0) 92

Absolute Value Equations and Inequalities (Alg. 3.0) 93

    Mixed Review 94

Expressions, Equations, and Inequalities (Alg. 4.0) 96

Problem Solving with Linear Equations (Alg. 5.0) 97

    Mixed Review 98

Logical Arguments (Alg. 24.1, Alg. 24.2, Alg. 24.3) 100

Analyze Results, Procedures, and Statements (Alg. 25.1, Alg. 25.2, Alg. 25.3) 101

    Mixed Review 102

Graph Linear Equations and Inequalities (Alg. 6.0) 104

Points, Lines, and Linear Equations (Alg. 7.0) 105

    Mixed Review 106

Parallel and Perpendicular Lines (Alg. 8.0) 108

Solve Linear Systems (Alg. 9.0) 109

    Mixed Review 111

Operations on Monomials and Polynomials (Alg. 10.0) 113

Factor Polynomials and Solve Quadratic Equations (Alg. 11.0, Alg. 14.0) 115

    Mixed Review 116

Quadratic Formula (Alg. 19.0, Alg. 20.0) 118

Graphs of Quadratic Functions (Alg. 21.0, Alg. 22.0) 119

Applications of Quadratic Equations (Alg. 23.0) 120

    Mixed Review 121

Simplify Rational Expressions (Alg. 12.0) 123

Operations With Rational Expressions (Alg. 13.0) 124

Rate, Work, and Percent Mixture Problems (Alg. 15.0) 125

    Mixed Review 126

Relations and Functions (Alg. 16.0, Alg. 18.0) 128

Domain and Range (Alg. 17.0) 129

    Mixed Review 130

Posttest 132

California Algebra 1
Mathematics Standards

As you read and study your mathematics textbook this year, you will be learning many of the ideas described in the California Mathematics Standards. The Algebra 1 Standards that you will concentrate on are listed below.

Following each standard is an explanation of what it means and how you will learn about it. Included are some real-world situations in the textbook to which you will apply the content in the standard. By the end of the year, you will have learned the content of these California Algebra 1 Standards.

Algebra 1 Standard		What It Means to You
1.0	Students identify and use the arithmetic properties of subsets of integers and rational, irrational, and real numbers, including closure properties for the four basic arithmetic operations where applicable:	You will learn how to use different properties to solve problems involving various types of numbers. You will use these properties to simplify numerical and algebraic expressions and to mathematically justify your steps.
1.1	Students use properties of numbers to demonstrate whether assertions are true or false.	You will learn to decide whether a mathematical statement is true or false. You will use properties of numbers to support your reasoning, such as properties of addition and multiplication, inverse properties, and identity properties.
2.0	Students understand and use such operations as taking the opposite, finding the reciprocal, taking a root, and raising to a fractional power. They understand and use the rules of exponents.	You will learn to subtract a number by adding its opposite. You will learn that dividing by a fraction is the same as multiplying by its reciprocal. You will expand on your knowledge of square roots by learning about fractional exponents and you will learn rules for performing operations on expressions with powers. You will use these skills to solve problems.
3.0	Students solve equations and inequalities involving absolute values.	The absolute value of a number is its distance from 0 on a number line. You will learn to use absolute value equations and inequalities to solve problems that involve a distance from another value, regardless of direction. For example, you will find the minimum, maximum, and acceptable range of air pressures for a basketball.

Algebra 1 Standard		What It Means to You
4.0	Students simplify expressions before solving linear equations and inequalities in one variable, such as $3(2x - 5) + 4(x - 2) = 12$.	You will learn that when solving an equation or inequality, it is best to first combine the like terms and simplify the expressions making up a statement. This allows you to rewrite the equation or inequality in a form that is easier to work with and solve.
5.0	Students solve multistep problems, including word problems, involving linear equations and linear inequalities in one variable and provide justification for each step.	You will learn to use properties to justify steps in solving equations and inequalities. You will apply these skills to solving multistep word problems. For example, you will write and solve an equation to find out when the number of new cars sold will equal twice the number of used cars sold.
6.0	Students graph a linear equation and compute the x- and y- intercepts (e.g., graph $2x + 6y = 4$). They are also able to sketch the region defined by linear inequalities (e.g., they sketch the region defined by $2x + 6y < 4$).	You will learn to use solutions of a linear equation to graph the equation and see that the graph is a line. You will also find where the graph intersects the axes. In addition, you will learn how to graph and interpret linear inequalities. You will see that the graph of a linear inequality with two variables is a region in a coordinate plane bounded by a line.
7.0	Students verify that a point lies on a line, given an equation of the line. Students are able to derive linear equations by using the point-slope formula.	You will learn how to use the x- and y-values of an ordered pair to determine if a point lies on the graph of an equation. You will also learn how to write the equation of a line knowing only the slope and the value of one point on the line. For example, you will write an equation modeling the cost of a gym membership over time.
8.0	Students understand the concepts of parallel lines and perpendicular lines and how their slopes are related. Students are able to find the equation of a line perpendicular to a given line that passes through a given point.	You will learn that the slope of a line describes how it slants and that parallel lines have the same slope. You will also learn that the product of the slopes of two perpendicular lines is -1. You will apply these skills to describe lines in objects, such as a state flag. You will also use these relationships to write equations of lines.

Algebra 1 Standard		What It Means to You
9.0	Students solve a system of two linear equations in two variables algebraically and are able to interpret the answer graphically. Students are able to solve a system of two linear inequalities in two variables and to sketch the solution sets.	A system of linear equations consists of two or more equations with the same variables. Solution(s) of a system of linear equations are ordered pair(s) that make each equation true. You will learn to use systems of linear equations and systems of inequalities to solve problems involving situations such as finding when the total cost of two different website hosting providers will be equal.
10.0	Students add, subtract, multiply, and divide monomials and polynomials. Students solve multistep problems, including word problems, by using these techniques.	A polynomial is a monomial or a sum of monomials. You will learn to add, subtract, multiply, and divide polynomials to solve problems such as finding the area of a skateboard park and analyzing costs associated with making and printing brochures.
11.0	Students apply basic factoring techniques to second- and simple third-degree polynomials. These techniques include finding a common factor for all terms in a polynomial, recognizing the difference of two squares, and recognizing perfect squares of binomials.	A polynomial is factored by writing it as a product of other polynomials. You will learn several methods of factoring to solve problems.
12.0	Students simplify fractions with polynomials in the numerator and denominator by factoring both and reducing them to the lowest terms.	A rational expression is an expression that can be written as a ratio of two polynomials where the denominator is not 0. You will use rational expressions to model quantities, such as the average cost of cell phone service, and use factoring techniques to write rational expressions in simplest form.
13.0	Students add, subtract, multiply, and divide rational expressions and functions. Students solve both computationally and conceptually challenging problems by using these techniques.	You will learn to add, subtract, multiply, and divide rational expressions, and will use operations involving rational expressions to solve problems such as finding the travel time of a boat or finding a baseball player's batting average.

Algebra 1 Standard	What It Means to You
14.0 Students solve a quadratic equation by factoring or completing the square.	You will learn to use factoring and completing the square to solve equations in the form $ax^2 + bx + c = 0$, where $a \neq 0$. You can use these techniques to solve problems such as finding the width of a banner, finding how long it takes a discus to hit the ground, and finding the distance it takes a car to come to a complete stop.
15.0 Students apply algebraic techniques to solve rate problems, work problems, and percent mixture problems.	You will write and solve systems of equations, and will use them to solve problems involving rates and times. You will also use systems of equations to solve problems about mixtures. You will use inverse variation equations and work rates to solve work problems, such as calculating how long it takes two workers to complete a task.
16.0 Students understand the concepts of a relation and a function, determine whether a given relation defines a function, and give pertinent information about given relations and functions.	A relation is a pairing of the elements of one set, called the domain, with the elements of another set, called the range. A function is a relation in which there is exactly one range element for each domain element. You will use this definition to determine if a relation is a function. You will also describe functions, such as the cost of concert tickets as a function of the number of tickets you buy.
17.0 Students determine the domain of independent variables and the range of dependent variables defined by a graph, a set of ordered pairs, or a symbolic expression.	You will identify the domain and range of functions, including functions represented by graphs, sets of ordered pairs, and symbolic expressions. Some of the functions you will analyze and describe include gas cost as a function of the amount purchased, and the elevation of a submersible as a function of the time since it began descending.
18.0 Students determine whether a relation defined by a graph, a set of ordered pairs, or a symbolic expression is a function and justify the conclusion.	You will decide whether a relation determined by a set of ordered pairs is a function. You will also determine whether a graph represents a function.
19.0 Students know the quadratic formula and are familiar with its proof by completing the square.	You will learn to solve quadratic equations by using the quadratic formula. You can use the method of completing the square and a property of radicals to derive the quadratic formula.

Algebra 1 Standard		What It Means to You
20.0	Students use the quadratic formula to find the roots of a second-degree polynomial and to solve quadratic equations.	The quadratic formula and properties of radicals can be used to find the roots of second-degree polynomials and to solve quadratic equations. Solving quadratic equations can help you predict the amount of money spent on advertising in the United States, or to find how far from the shore a water arc is when it reaches a height of 50 feet.
21.0	Students graph quadratic functions and know that their roots are the x-intercepts.	When you find the x-intercept(s) of the graph of a quadratic function, you find the value or values of x for which the function equals 0. You will learn to use x-intercepts to solve problems involving objects moving under the force of gravity, such as finding the amount of time a shotput is in the air.
22.0	Students use the quadratic formula or factoring techniques or both to determine whether the graph of a quadratic function will intersect the x-axis in zero, one, or two points.	The graph of a given quadratic function can intersect the x-axis at no point, or at one or two points. You will learn various methods for determining how many x-intercepts a graph has, including graphing, factoring, completing the square, and finding the discriminant.
23.0	Students apply quadratic equations to physical problems, such as the motion of an object under the force of gravity.	You will learn how to use quadratic equations to solve problems involving the motion of an object under the force of gravity, such as modeling the path of an arrow through the air.
24.0	Students use and know simple aspects of a logical argument:	You will learn to use properties of numbers and equations to show that mathematical statements are true.
24.1	Students explain the difference between inductive and deductive reasoning and identify and provide examples of each.	When you make a conjecture based on several examples, you are using inductive reasoning. Your conjecture may or may not be true. When you come to a conclusion based on statements that have been proven true, you are using deductive reasoning. You will make conjectures and use deductive reasoning to prove them.

California Standards Review and Practice
Grade 8 Standards   **ix**

Algebra 1 Standard		What It Means to You
24.2	Students identify the hypothesis and conclusion in logical deduction.	The statement "If a number is divisible by 10, then it is even" is an example of a conditional statement written in if-then form. The "if" part of the statement is called the hypothesis. The "then" part is called the conclusion. You will learn to identify the hypothesis and the conclusion in a statement and to write conditional statements in if-then form.
24.3	Students use counterexamples to show that an assertion is false and recognize that a single counterexample is sufficient to refute an assertion.	A counterexample is an example that shows that a statement is false. You will learn to find a counterexample to prove that a statement is false and understand that one counterexample is enough.
25.0	Students use properties of the number system to judge the validity of results, to justify each step of a procedure, and to prove or disprove statements:	You will learn important properties, such as the commutative and associative properties of addition and multiplication and the distributive property. You will learn to use these and other properties to justify your steps in performing mathematical operations and to prove or disprove statements.
25.1	Students use properties of numbers to construct simple, valid arguments (direct and indirect) for, or formulate counterexamples to, claimed assertions.	You can use properties, such as the distributive property and the addition property of equality, to demonstrate that a conjecture is true. You will learn to use counterexamples to prove that a statement is false. You will learn to use indirect proof to prove statements.
25.2	Students judge the validity of an argument according to whether the properties of the real number system and the order of operations have been applied correctly at each step.	You will learn to make a conjecture and to use the properties of real numbers and equations and the order of operations to prove that the conjecture is true for all real numbers. For example, you will learn to use number properties and properties of equations to show why a number trick works.
25.3	Given a specific algebraic statement involving linear, quadratic, or absolute value expressions or equations or inequalities, students determine whether the statement is true sometimes, always, or never.	You will learn to apply properties of real numbers to prove that a mathematical statement is true for all real numbers. You will also decide whether statements are always, sometimes, or never true.

California Standards Review
and Practice

In-Depth Review

Name _____   Date _____

California Standards

Algebra 1.0

Students identify and use the arithmetic properties of subsets of integers and rational, irrational, and real numbers, including closure properties for the four basic arithmetic operations where applicable.

Arithmetic Properties

Properties of Real Numbers
Commutative Property The order in which you add or multiply any two numbers a and b does not change the sum or product.
Algebra $a + b = b + a$ **Example** $(-7) + (-1) = (-1) + (-7)$ **Algebra** $a \cdot b = b \cdot a$ **Example** $5 \cdot (-3) = (-3) \cdot 5$
Associative Property The way you group any three numbers a, b, and c in a sum or product does not change the sum or product.
Algebra $(a + b) + c = a + (b + c)$ **Example** $(2 + 4) + 3 = 2 + (4 + 3)$ **Algebra** $(a \cdot b) \cdot c = a \cdot (b \cdot c)$ **Example** $(5 \cdot 6) \cdot 7 = 5 \cdot (6 \cdot 7)$
Identity Property The sum of a number n and 0 is that number n. The product of a number n and 1 is that number n.
Algebra $n + 0 = n$ **Example** $(-20) + 0 = -20$ **Algebra** $n \cdot 1 = n$ **Example** $275 \cdot 1 = 275$
Multiplication Property of -1 and 0 The product of a number n and -1 is the opposite of the number. The product of a number n and 0 is 0.
Algebra $n \cdot (-1) = -n$ **Example** $8 \cdot (-1) = -8$ **Algebra** $n \cdot 0 = 0$ **Example** $11 \cdot 0 = 0$
Inverse Property The sum of a number n and its opposite is 0. The product of a number n and its reciprocal is 1.
Algebra $n + (-n) = 0$ **Example** $6 + (-6) = 0$ **Algebra** $n \cdot \dfrac{1}{n} = 1$ **Example** $9 \cdot \dfrac{1}{9} = 1$
Distributive Property Let a, b, and c be real numbers. The product of a and $(b + c)$ is $ab + ac$. The product of a and $(b - c)$ is $ab - ac$.
Algebra $a(b + c) = ab + ac$ **Example** $6(3 + 2) = 6(3) + 6(2)$ **Algebra** $a(b - c) = ab - ac$ **Example** $5(8 - 2) = 5(8) - 5(2)$
Closure Properties A set of numbers is *closed* under addition or multiplication, respectively, if the sum or product of any two numbers in the set is also a number in the set.
Example Because whole numbers are closed under addition and multiplication, the sum $3 + 4$ and the product $3 \cdot 4$ are both whole numbers.

California Standard
Algebra 1.0

Properties of Equality

Reflexive Property A quantity is equal to itself.

  Algebra $a = a$ **Example** $5 = 5$

Symmetric Property If one quantity equals a second, then the second quantity equals the first.

  Algebra If $a = b$, then $b = a$ **Example** If $5 + 3 = 8$, then $8 = 5 + 3$

Transitive Property If one quantity equals a second and the second quantity equals a third, then the first quantity equals the third quantity.

  Algebra If $a = b$ and $b = c$,   **Example** If $5 + 2 = 6 + 1$ and $6 + 1 = 7$,
              then $a = c$ then $5 + 2 = 7$

Addition and Multiplication Properties of Equality Adding the same number to each side of an equation, or multiplying each side of an equation by the same nonzero number produces an equivalent equation.

  Algebra If $x - a = b$,   **Example** If $x - 6 = 2$,
              then $x - a + a = b + a$ then $x - 6 + 6 = 2 + 6$, or $x = 8$

  Algebra If $\frac{x}{a} = b$, then $a \cdot \frac{x}{a} = a \cdot b$ **Example** If $\frac{x}{3} = 4$, then $3 \cdot \frac{x}{3} = 3 \cdot 4$, or $x = 12$

The set of *real numbers* is the set of all rational and irrational numbers, as illustrated below.

Real Numbers

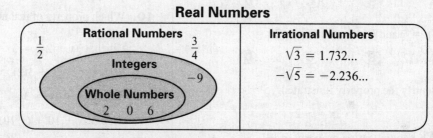

The set of *real numbers* is the set of all rational and irrational numbers, as illustrated below.

Example 1

Identify Arithmetic Properties

Identify the property used in the equation.

a. $7 + (x + 4) = 7 + (4 + x)$ **b.** $(x + y) + 0 = x + y$

c. $6 + (2 + z) = 8 + z$ **d.** $(-1) \cdot (3 - 4x + y) = -3 + 4x - y$

Solution

a.   The second and third terms are reversed.   **Commutative property of addition**

b.   Zero is added to $(x + y)$.   **Identity property of addition**

c.   The 6 and 2 are grouped to give 8.   **Associative property of addition**

d.   The sign of each term on the left side of the equation is reversed by multiplying by -1.   **Multiplication property of -1**

Example 2 Justify Steps of a Solution

Name the property that justifies each step in solving the equation $4x + 5 = 17$.

$4x + 5 = 17$	**Given.**
$4x + 5 + (-5) = 17 + (-5)$	**Addition property of equality**
$4x + [5 + (-5)] = 17 + (-5)$	**Associative property of addition**
$4x = 12$	**Inverse property of addition**
$\frac{1}{4} \cdot 4x = \frac{1}{4} \cdot 12$	**Multiplication property of equality**
$x = 3$	**Inverse property of multiplication**

Exercises

1. $7 + (-3) =$

Ⓐ 10   Ⓑ 4   Ⓒ -4 Ⓓ -10

2. $(-8) - (-6) =$

Ⓐ 14   Ⓑ 2   Ⓒ -2 Ⓓ -14

3. If $x = -2$ and $y = 5$, then $x + 3y =$

Ⓐ -11 Ⓑ -1 Ⓒ 13   Ⓓ 17

4. If $a = \frac{2}{5}$ and $b = \frac{7}{2}$, then $5a + 2b =$

Ⓐ 12   Ⓑ 9   Ⓒ -5 Ⓓ $-\frac{11}{10}$

5. Identify the property illustrated.

$$-1 \cdot 2x = -2x$$

Ⓐ Multiplication property of -1

Ⓑ Identity property of multiplication

Ⓒ Inverse property of addition

Ⓓ Multiplication property of equality

6. $-3(-1)(7) =$

Ⓐ 3   Ⓑ 10   Ⓒ 11   Ⓓ 21

7. Which of the following is an example of the inverse property of addition?

Ⓐ $8 - 9 = -1$ Ⓑ $9 - 8 = 1$

Ⓒ $(-8) + (-8) = -16$ Ⓓ $8 + (-8) = 0$

8. Which expression is equivalent to $(3a + 2b)(-4c)$?

Ⓐ $(4c)(3a + 2b)$ Ⓑ $-8bc - 12ac$

Ⓒ $-7ac - 6bc$ Ⓓ $3a(2b - 4c)$

9. Identify the property being illustrated.

$$-3a + 0 = -3a$$

Ⓐ Identity property of addition

Ⓑ Inverse property of addition

Ⓒ Inverse property of multiplication

Ⓓ Identity property of multiplication

10. Which property of real numbers is used in Step 3?

Given: $\left(\frac{1}{5}x + 2\right)5 = 3$

Step 1: $5 \cdot \frac{1}{5}x + 5(2) = 3$

Step 2: $x + 10 = 3$

Step 3: $x + 10 + (-10) = 3 + (-10)$

Step 4: $x = -7$

Ⓐ Symmetric property

Ⓑ Reflexive property

Ⓒ Addition property of equality

Ⓓ Identity property of addition

11. Simplify $6(a - b) + 7(b - 3a)$.

Ⓐ $13a - 27b$

Ⓑ $-15a + b$

Ⓒ $15a + b$

Ⓓ $3a - b$

12. Which statement is *false* for *all* values of a and b? Let $a < 0$ and $b > 0$.

Ⓐ $a - b < 0$ Ⓑ $ab < 0$

Ⓒ $ab > 0$ Ⓓ $a + b = 0$

Name _____ Date _____

California Standards
Algebra 1.1

Students use properties of numbers to demonstrate whether assertions are true or false.

Use Properties of Numbers

Example 1   ## Analyze a Mathematical Claim

Mary claims that $2(3x - 1) - 6x + 3 = 1$. Determine whether Mary's claim is *true* or *false*. *Justify* your answer.

Solution

Simplify the left side of the equation $2(3x - 1) - 6x + 3 = 1$

$2(3x - 1) - 6x + 3 = 6x - 2 - 6x + 3$	**Distributive property**
$= 6x - 6x - 2 + 3$	**Commutative property**
$= (6x - 6x) + (-2 + 3)$	**Associative property**
$= 0 + (-2 + 3)$	**Inverse property of addition**
$= 0 + 1$	**Add −2 and 3.**
$= 1$	**Identity property of addition**

Answer Mary's claim is true, $2(3x - 1) - 6x + 3 = 1$.

Example 2   ## Use the Closure Property

Is the set of negative integers *closed* under multiplication? Explain.

Solution

STEP 1 Assume that the set of negative integers is closed under multiplication and find a counterexample.

STEP 2 Multiplying a negative integer by another negative integer gives a positive integer.

   Example: $-2 \cdot (-4) = 8$

STEP 3 Because 8 is not a negative number, the set of negative integers is not closed under multiplication.

Answer No, the set of negative numbers is *not* closed under multiplication.

Exercises

1. Which step is incorrect?

Step 1: $3[-4x + \frac{x}{3}(3 - 7y)] =$

$$3(-4x) + 3\left(\frac{x}{3}\right)(3 - 7y)$$

Step 2: $3(-4x) + 3\left(\frac{x}{3}\right)(3 - 7y) =$

$$-12x + x(3 - 7y)$$

Step 3: $-12x + x(3 - 7y) = -12x + 3x - 7y$

Step 4: $-12x + 3x - 7y = -9x - 7y$

   (A) Step 3

   (B) Step 1

   (C) Step 2

   (D) Step 4

2. The steps Jessie took to simplify this expression are shown below.

$$\left(\frac{1}{3x}\right)(4x - 9)$$

Step 1: $\left(\frac{1}{3x}\right)(4x - 9) = 4x\left(\frac{1}{3x}\right) - 9\left(\frac{1}{3x}\right)$

Step 2: $4x\left(\frac{1}{3x}\right) - 9\left(\frac{1}{3x}\right) = \frac{4}{3}\left(x \cdot \frac{1}{x}\right) - \left(\frac{1}{9}\right)(3x)$

Step 3: $\frac{4}{3}\left(x \cdot \frac{1}{x}\right) - \left(\frac{1}{9}\right)(3x) = \frac{4}{3}(1) - \left(\frac{1}{3}\right)x$

Step 4: $\frac{4}{3}(1) - \left(\frac{1}{3}\right)x = \frac{4}{3} - \frac{1}{3}x$

In which step does an error occur?

   (A) Step 2

   (B) Step 4

   (C) Step 3

   (D) Step 1

3. Which set is *closed* under multiplication?

   (A) set of *all* integers

   (B) set of *odd negative* integers

   (C) set of *all negative* integers

   (D) set of *even negative* integers

4. Which statement is true about the set below?

$$S = \{\ldots, -6, -3, 0, 3, 6, \ldots\}$$

   (A) The set S is not closed under multiplication.

   (B) The set S is closed under addition and multiplication.

   (C) The set S is not closed under addition.

   (D) The set S is closed under addition, but not under multiplication.

5. Zoe told Angelina that the set

$$\left\{\ldots, \frac{1}{27}, \frac{1}{9}, \frac{1}{3}, 1, 3, 9, \ldots\right\}$$

is closed. Under which operation or operations is the set *not* closed?

   (A) Addition

   (B) Addition and multiplication

   (C) Multiplication

   (D) None of the above.

6. Which of the following is incorrect?

   (A) $(2 + 3)6 = 12 + 18$

   (B) $(8 - 5x) + 3 = 8 + (-5x + 3)$

   (C) $-6(9 + 8x) = -54 + 48x$

   (D) $-7 - x = -x - 7$

7. Which set is closed under addition, but not multiplication?

   (A) Negative integers

   (B) Rational numbers

   (C) Positive whole numbers

   (D) Positive rational numbers

California Standards
Algebra 2.0

Students understand and use such operations as taking the opposite, finding the reciprocal, taking a root, and raising to a fractional power. They understand and use the rules of exponents.

Opposites, Reciprocals, Roots, and Exponents

Terms to Know	Example
Opposites are two numbers that are the same distance from 0 on a number line but are on opposite sides of 0.	2 units 2 units 2 and -2 are *opposites*
The **reciprocal** of a nonzero real number a is $\frac{1}{a}$.	The *reciprocal* of $\frac{3}{4}$ is $\frac{4}{3}$.
A **power** is an expression that represents repeated multiplication of the same factor.	The 3rd *power* of 2 is 8, because $2^3 = 2 \cdot 2 \cdot 2 = 8$.
The **base** of a power is the number or expression that is used as a factor in a repeated multiplication.	The *base* of 2^3 is 2.
An **exponent** is the number or variable that represents the number of times a base of a power is used as a factor.	The *exponent* of 2^3 is 3.
If $b^2 = a$, then b is a **square root** of a. The square root of a is written with the radical sign, $\sqrt{a}$, or as a power of a, $a^{1/2}$.	The *square roots* of 9 are 3 and -3, because $3^2 = 9$ and $(-3)^2 = 9$. So, $\sqrt{9} = \pm 3$.
If $b^3 = a$, then b is the **cube root** of a, or $b = \sqrt[3]{a}$. The cube root of a can also be written as $a^{1/3}$.	The *cube root* of 8 is 2 because $2^3 = 8$. So, $\sqrt[3]{8} = 2$.

Properties of Exponents

Let a and b be real numbers, and let m and n be integers.

Product of Powers Property To multiply powers having the same base, add the exponents.

Algebra $a^m \cdot a^n = a^{m+n}$ **Example** $2^2 \cdot 2^5 = 2^7$

Power of a Power Property To find a power of a power, multiply exponents.

Algebra $(a^m)^n = a^{mn}$ **Example** $(5^3)^4 = 5^{12}$

Power of a Product Property To find a power of a product, find the power of each factor and multiply.

Algebra $(ab)^m = a^m b^m$ **Example** $(3 \cdot 7)^6 = 3^6 \cdot 7^6$

Quotient of Powers Property To divide powers having the same base, subtract exponents.

Algebra $\frac{a^m}{a^n} = a^{m-n}, a \neq 0$ **Example** $\frac{2^4}{2^{-2}} = 2^{4-(-2)} = 2^{4+2} = 2^6$

Power of a Quotient Property To find a power of a quotient, find the power of the numerator and the power of the denominator and divide.

Algebra $\left(\frac{a}{b}\right)^m = \frac{a^m}{b^m}, b \neq 0$ **Example** $\left(\frac{3}{5}\right)^2 = \frac{3^2}{5^2}$

Example 1   ## Solve an Equation Using Opposites and Reciprocals

Solve the equation.

a. $x + 8 = 12$

b. $2x = 6$

c. $\frac{2}{3}x - 5 = 3$

Solution

a. $x + 8 = 12$ **Write equation.**

   $x + 8 + (-8) = 12 + (-8)$ **Add the opposite of 8 to each side.**

           $x = 4$ **Simplify.**

b. $2x = 6$ **Write equation.**

   $\frac{1}{2} \cdot (2x) = \frac{1}{2} \cdot 6$ **Multiply each side by the reciprocal of 2.**

           $x = 3$ **Simplify.**

c. $\frac{2}{3}x - 5 = 3$ **Write equation.**

   $\frac{2}{3}x - 5 + 5 = 3 + 5$ **Add 5 to each side.**

           $\frac{2}{3}x = 8$ **Simplify.**

   $\frac{3}{2} \cdot \left(\frac{2}{3}x\right) = \frac{3}{2} \cdot 8$ **Multiply each side by the reciprocal of $\frac{2}{3}$.**

           $x = 12$ **Simplify.**

Example 2   ## Use Properties of Exponents

Simplify the expression.

a. $(x^2 \cdot y^6)^{1/2} \cdot xy^2$

b. $\left(\dfrac{a^2}{b^2}\right)^{1/2} \cdot \dfrac{5}{a^5}$

Solution

a. $(x^2 \cdot y^6)^{1/2} \cdot xy^2 = xy^3 \cdot xy^2$ **Power of a power property**

$= x^2y^5$ **Product of powers property**

b. $\left(\dfrac{a^2}{b^2}\right)^{1/2} \cdot \dfrac{5}{a^5} = \dfrac{(a^2)^{1/2}}{(b^2)^{1/2}} \cdot \dfrac{5}{a^5}$ **Power of a quotient property**

$= \dfrac{a}{b} \cdot \dfrac{5}{a^5}$ **Power of a power property**

$= \dfrac{5a}{a^5b}$ **Multiply fractions.**

$= \dfrac{5}{a^4b}$ **Quotient of powers property**

Answer **a.** $(x^2 \cdot y^6)^{1/2} \cdot xy^2 = x^2y^5$

b. $\left(\dfrac{a^2}{b^2}\right)^{1/2} \cdot \dfrac{5}{a^5} = \dfrac{5}{a^4b}$

Example 3   **Simplify Radical Expressions**

Simplify the radical expression.

a. $\sqrt{16} - \sqrt[3]{27}$ **b.** $2\sqrt{9} + 5\sqrt[3]{64}$

Solution

a. $\sqrt{16} - \sqrt[3]{27} = \sqrt{4^2} - \sqrt[3]{3^3}$ **Rewrite 16 and 27 as powers.**

$= 4 - 3$ **Use definition of square root and cube root.**

$= 1$ **Simplify.**

b. $2\sqrt{9} + 5\sqrt[3]{64} = 2\sqrt{3^2} + 5\sqrt[3]{4^3}$ **Rewrite 9 and 64 as powers.**

$= 2(3) + 5(4)$ **Use definition of square root and cube root.**

$= 26$ **Simplify.**

Exercises

1. If $-a = 3$, then $a =$

Ⓐ -3 Ⓑ $-\frac{1}{3}$ Ⓒ $\frac{1}{3}$ Ⓓ 3

2. Solve for x.

$$\frac{1}{3} + x = 1$$

Ⓐ $1\frac{1}{3}$ Ⓑ $\frac{2}{3}$ Ⓒ $\frac{1}{3}$ Ⓓ $-\frac{2}{3}$

3. Simplify $2\sqrt{9} - 5\sqrt[3]{8}$.

Ⓐ 22 Ⓑ -4 Ⓒ 16 Ⓓ -10

4. Solve the equation $\frac{1}{k} = \frac{3}{7}$ for k.

Ⓐ $\frac{3}{7}$ Ⓑ $\frac{7}{3}$ Ⓒ 3 Ⓓ 7

5. If $x^3 - 2 = -10$, then $x =$

Ⓐ 2 Ⓑ -2 Ⓒ -8 Ⓓ -12

6. The area of a square field is $\frac{1}{9}$ of a square mile. The formula for the area A of a square is $A = s^2$, where s is the side length of the square. What is the side length of the square field?

Ⓐ 9 miles   Ⓑ 3 miles

Ⓒ $\frac{2}{9}$ mile   Ⓓ $\frac{1}{3}$ mile

7. Which expression is equivalent to $\sqrt[4]{a^2b^7}$?

Ⓐ $b^3 \cdot \sqrt[4]{a^2b^4}$ Ⓑ $b^7 \cdot \sqrt[4]{a^2b^4}$

Ⓒ $b \cdot \sqrt[4]{a^2b^3}$ Ⓓ $b^3 \cdot \sqrt[4]{a^2b^3}$

8. If $x = 3^2 \cdot 4^{1/3}$, then $x^3 =$

Ⓐ $3^6 \cdot 4$ Ⓑ $3^5 \cdot 4$

Ⓒ $3^5 \cdot 4$ Ⓓ $3 \cdot 4$

9. Let $k = u^2 \cdot v^4$. Which of the following is equivalent to k^3?

Ⓐ $u^5 \cdot v^{12}$ Ⓑ $u^6 \cdot v^{12}$

Ⓒ $u^6 \cdot v^7$ Ⓓ $u^5 \cdot v^7$

10. Which expression is equivalent to $\left(\frac{2}{x}\right)^2 + \left(\frac{3}{y}\right)^3$?

Ⓐ $\frac{4}{x^2} + \frac{y^3}{9}$ Ⓑ $\frac{x^2}{4} + \frac{y3}{27}$

Ⓒ $\frac{4}{x^2} + \frac{27}{y^3}$ Ⓓ $\frac{x^2}{4} + \frac{9}{y^3}$

11. If $a = 2x^2$ and $b = 3x^4$, then $a^3 + b^2 =$

Ⓐ $2x^5 + 3x^6$ Ⓑ $8x^5 + 9x^6$

Ⓒ $2x^6 + 3x^8$ Ⓓ $8x^6 + 9x^8$

12. The surface area A of a cylinder is given by the formula $A = 2\pi rh$, where r is the radius of the cylinder and h is the height of the cylinder. If $A = 200$ cm^2 and $r = 10$ cm, what is the height of the cylinder?

Ⓐ $\frac{1}{\pi}$ cm   Ⓑ $\frac{2}{\pi}$ cm

Ⓒ $\frac{10}{\pi}$ cm   Ⓓ $\frac{20}{\pi}$ cm

13. Each equal side of an isosceles right triangle is 4 feet long. Find the length of the hypotenuse.

Ⓐ $2\sqrt{2}$ feet   Ⓑ 32 feet

Ⓒ $4\sqrt{2}$ feet   Ⓓ 16 feet

14. Which of the following is an example of the power of a power property?

Ⓐ $x^2 \cdot x^3 = x^5$ Ⓑ $(x^2)^3 = x^6$

Ⓒ $x^2 + 3x^2 = 4x^2$ Ⓓ $\frac{x^4}{x^5} = x^{-1}$

California Standards
Algebra 3.0

Students solve equations and inequalities involving absolute values.

Absolute Value Equations and Inequalities

Terms to Know	Example
The **absolute value** of a number a is the distance between a and 0 on a number line. The symbol $\vert a \vert$ represents the absolute value of a.	$\vert 7 \vert = 7$ $\vert -7 \vert = 7$
An **absolute value equation** is an equation that contains an absolute value expression.	$\vert 3x - 5 \vert = 25$ is an absolute value equation.
An **absolute value inequality** is an inequality that contains an absolute value expression.	$\vert y - 25 \vert \le 5$ is an absolute value inequality.

Example 1   ### Solve an Absolute Value Equation

Solve $\vert z - 5 \vert = 15$.

Solution

$\vert z - 5 \vert = 15$	Write original equation.
$z - 5 = 15 \; or \; z - 5 = -15$	Rewrite as two equations.
$z = 20 \; or \; z = -10$	Add 5 to each side.

Answer The solutions are $z = -10$ or $z = 20$. The solution set is $\{-10, 20\}$.

Example 2   ### Solve an Absolute Value Inequality

Solve $\vert a + 3 \vert \le 8$.

Solution

$\vert a + 3 \vert \le 8$	Write original inequality.
$a + 3 \ge -8 \; or \; a + 3 \le 8$	Rewrite as two inequalities.
$a \ge -11 \; or \; a \le 5$	Add -3 to each side.
$-11 \le a \le 5$	Rewrite as a compound inequality.

Answer The solutions are all real numbers greater than or equal to -11 *and* less than or equal to 5. The solution set is $\{a : -11 \le a \le 5\}$.

Example 3   ## Solve an Absolute Value Inequality

Solve $\frac{1}{2}|y + 2| - 3 < 2$.

Solution

$\frac{1}{2}|y + 2| - 3 < 2$	**Write original inequality.**
$\frac{1}{2}|y + 2| < 5$	**Add 3 to each side.**
$|y + 2| < 10$	**Multiply each side by 2.**
$-10 < y + 2 < 10$	**Rewrite as a compound inequality.**
$-12 < y < 8$	**Add -2 to each expression.**

Answer The solutions are all real numbers greater than -12 *and* less than 8. The solution set is $\{y : -12 < y < 8\}$.

Exercises

1. Solve for x.

$$|x - 3| = 5$$

(A) $x = -8$ or $x = 2$

(B) $x = -2$ or $x = 8$

(C) $x = -2$ or $x = 2$

(D) $x = -8$ or $x = 8$

2. What is the solution set of $2|y + 1| = 8$?

(A) $\{-4, 4\}$ (B) $\{-5, 4\}$

(C) $\{-5, 3\}$ (D) $\{3, 4\}$

3. What is the solution set of $|4x + 1| = 13$?

(A) $\{-\frac{7}{2}, 3\}$ (B) $\{-3, 3\}$

(C) $\{-\frac{7}{2}, \frac{7}{2}\}$ (D) $\{3, \frac{7}{2}\}$

4. Solve for x.

$$|4 + x| - 3 = 9$$

(A) $x = 2$ or $x = 10$ (B) $x = -16$ or $x = 8$

(C) $x = 8$ or $x = 16$ (D) $x = -10$ or $x = 2$

5. What is the solution set of $3\left|\frac{4}{3} - y\right| = 7$?

(A) $\{-1, \frac{11}{3}\}$ (B) $\{-\frac{1}{3}, 1\}$

(C) $\{-1, 1\}$ (D) $\{-\frac{11}{3}, \frac{11}{3}\}$

6. What is the solution set of $|5 - 2x| = 9$?

(A) $\{2, 7\}$ (B) $\{-2, 2\}$

(C) $\{-2, 7\}$ (D) $\{-7, 7\}$

7. Solve for y.

$$|7 - y| = 12$$

(A) $y = -5$ or $y = 5$

(B) $y = -5$ or $y = 19$

(C) $y = -5$ or $y = -19$

(D) $y = 5$ or $y = 19$

8. What is the solution set of $-3|y - 2| = 12$?

(A) The empty set, $\{\emptyset\}$

(B) $\{6, 6\}$

(C) $\{-2, -2\}$

(D) $\{2, 2\}$

9. What is the solution set of $3|3x - 1| - 2 = 10$?

(A) $\{-1, -\frac{5}{3}\}$

(B) $\{-\frac{5}{3}, -1\}$

(C) $\{1, \frac{5}{3}\}$

(D) $\{-1, \frac{5}{3}\}$

10. Solve for y.

$$|2 - 3y| + 4 = 7$$

(A) $y = \frac{1}{3}$ or $y = \frac{5}{3}$

(B) $y = -\frac{1}{3}$ or $y = \frac{5}{3}$

(C) $y = -\frac{1}{3}$ or $y = \frac{1}{3}$

(D) $y = \frac{1}{3}$ or $y = -\frac{5}{3}$

11. What is the solution set of $|x + 30| = 3$?

Ⓐ $\{-27, 33\}$

Ⓑ $\{-33, -27\}$

Ⓒ $\{-33, 27\}$

Ⓓ $\{27, 33\}$

12. What is the solution set of $\frac{1}{5}|2y - 5| = 3$?

Ⓐ $\{5, 10\}$

Ⓑ $\{-5, -10\}$

Ⓒ $\{-5, 10\}$

Ⓓ $\{-5, 5\}$

13. What is the solution set of $|y + 6| \leq 5$?

Ⓐ $\{y : 1 \leq y \leq 5\}$

Ⓑ $\{y : -5 \leq y \leq -1\}$

Ⓒ $\{y : -11 \leq y \leq -1\}$

Ⓓ $\{y : -11 \leq y \leq 5\}$

14. What is the solution set of $|4 - y| - 3 < 8$?

Ⓐ $\{y : y < 15\}$

Ⓑ $\{y : -7 > y > 15\}$

Ⓒ $\{y : y > -7\}$

Ⓓ $\{y : -7 < y < 15\}$

15. Solve $|5 - 2y| < 11$.

Ⓐ $6 < y < 8$

Ⓑ $3 < y < 16$

Ⓒ $-3 < y < 8$

Ⓓ $6 < y < 16$

16. What is the solution set of $\frac{1}{3} > |\frac{1}{2}y + 2|$?

Ⓐ $\left\{y : -\frac{10}{3} < y < \frac{10}{3}\right\}$

Ⓑ $\left\{y : -\frac{14}{3} < y < -\frac{10}{3}\right\}$

Ⓒ $\left\{y : -\frac{14}{3} < y < \frac{14}{3}\right\}$

Ⓓ $\left\{y : -\frac{14}{3} > y > -\frac{10}{3}\right\}$

17. What is the solution set of $|x + 2| > \frac{1}{2}$?

Ⓐ $-\frac{5}{2} < x < -\frac{3}{2}$

Ⓑ $x < -\frac{3}{2}$ or $x > \frac{5}{2}$

Ⓒ $x < -\frac{5}{2}$ or $x > -\frac{3}{2}$

Ⓓ $\frac{3}{2} < x < \frac{5}{2}$

18. What is the solution set of $|5 - y| \geq 3$?

Ⓐ $\{y : y \leq -2 \text{ or } y \geq -8\}$

Ⓑ $\{y : y \leq 2 \text{ or } y \geq 8\}$

Ⓒ $\{y : -8 \leq y \leq -2\}$

Ⓓ $\{y : 2 \leq y \leq 8\}$

19. What is the solution set of $\frac{2}{3}|2x - 3| + 4 > 6$?

Ⓐ $\{x : x < 0 \text{ or } x > 3\}$

Ⓑ $\{x : x < -6 \text{ or } x > 3\}$

Ⓒ $\{x : x < 0 \text{ or } x > 6\}$

Ⓓ $\{x : x < -6 \text{ or } x > 6\}$

20. What is the solution set of $\frac{1}{3}|x - 5| - \frac{4}{3} \geq 1$?

Ⓐ $\{x : x \leq -12 \text{ or } x \geq 12\}$

Ⓑ $\{x : x \leq -2 \text{ or } x \geq 12\}$

Ⓒ $\{x : x \leq 2 \text{ or } x \geq 12\}$

Ⓓ $\{x : x \leq -2 \text{ or } x \geq 2\}$

21. Which of the following is a solution of $|4x - 5| > 10$?

Ⓐ 3

Ⓑ 5

Ⓒ 0

Ⓓ -1

22. What is the solution set of $|5x - 13| = -3$?

Ⓐ $\{4, 3\}$

Ⓑ $\{-2, 2\}$

Ⓒ $\{-2, 3\}$

Ⓓ The empty set, $\{\emptyset\}$

California Standards
Algebra 4.0

Students simplify expressions before solving linear equations and inequalities in one variable, such as $3(2x - 5) + 4(x - 2) - 12$.

Solve Equations and Inequalities

Example 1   ### Simplify an Expression

Simplify $7(-4x + 3) + 9x$.

Solution

$7(-4x + 3) + 9x = -28x + 21 + 9x$	**Distributive property**
$= -28x + 9x + 21$	**Commutative property of addition**
$= -19x + 21$	**Combine like terms.**

Example 2   ### Solve an Equation

Solve the equation $3(2 - 4x) + 2(1 + 7x) = 18$.

Solution

$3(2 - 4x) + 2(1 + 7x) = 18$	**Write original equation.**
$6 - 12x + 2 + 14x = 18$	**Distributive property**
$2x + 8 = 18$	**Combine like terms.**
$2x = 10$	**Subtract 8 from each side.**
$x = 5$	**Divide each side by 2.**

Example 3   ### Solve an Inequality

Solve the inequality $4 - 3x \geq 2(x - 1)$.

Solution

$4 - 3x \geq 2(x - 1)$	**Write original inequality.**
$4 - 3x \geq 2x - 2$	**Distributive property**
$4 \geq 5x - 2$	**Add 3x to each side.**
$6 \geq 5x$	**Add 2 to each side.**
$\frac{6}{5} \geq x$	**Divide each side by 5.**

Exercises

1. Which equation is equivalent to
$2(x + 1) + 4(x - 3) = 12$?

    (A) $6x - 10 = 12$ **(B)** $6x + 13 = 12$

    (C) $6x + 14 = 12$ **(D)** $-2x + 14 = 12$

2. Which of the following is equivalent to
$3x = 6(x + 2)$?

    (A) $9x = 2$ **(B)** $-3x = 12$

    (C) $3x = 12$ **(D)** $9x = 12$

3. Which inequality is equivalent to
$4(x - 1) > 3 - 5x$?

    (A) $9x > 7$ **(B)** $9x > 4$

    (C) $x > 7$ **(D)** $x < -7$

4. Simplify $5(y - 1) - 6(y - 8)$.

    (A) $53 - 11y$ **(B)** $53 - y$

    (C) $11y + 43$ **(D)** $43 - y$

5. Simplify $\frac{1}{2}x - \frac{2}{3}(3x - 6)$.

    (A) $\frac{5}{2}x + 4$ **(B)** $-\frac{3}{2}x + 4$

    (C) $-\frac{3}{2}x - 4$ **(D)** $\frac{5}{2}x - 4$

6. Which inequality is equivalent to
$4(y - 1) \geq 3(2 - y)$?

    (A) $4y - 1 \geq 6 - y$

    (B) $4y - 4 \geq 6 - 3y$

    (C) $4y - 4 \geq 5 - 3y$

    (D) $4y - 4 \geq 6 - 6y$

7. Which equation is equivalent to $2y + 3 = y - 1$?

    (A) $y + 3 = -1$

    (B) $2y = y + 2$

    (C) $3y + 3 = -1$

    (D) $2y = -1$

8. What is the solution of this inequality?
$4 - 3x \geq 2(x - 1)$

    (A) $\frac{5}{6} \geq x$ **(B)** $\frac{6}{5} \geq x$

    (C) $\frac{6}{5} \leq x$ **(D)** $\frac{5}{6} \leq x$

9. Solve $7 - 14x < 3(6x - 2)$.

Step 1: $7 - 14x < 18x - 6$

Step 2: $7 < 4x - 6$

Step 3: $13 < 4x$

Step 4: $\frac{13}{4} < x$

Which is the first *incorrect* step in the solution shown above?

    (A) Step 1

    (B) Step 2

    (C) Step 3

    (D) Step 4

10. Which inequality could be Step 3 of the solution?

Step 1: $5x + 2(x + 10) = 15x$

Step 2: $5x + 2x + 20 = 15x$

Step 3: ?

Step 4: $20 = 8x$

    (A) $6x + 20 = 15x$

    (B) $10x + 20 = 15x$

    (C) $7x + 20 = 15x$

    (D) $7x + 10 = 15x$

11. Which equation is equivalent to
$3(x - 5) + 2 = 6(x - 1)$?

    (A) $9x = -19$

    (B) $3x = -7$

    (C) $3x = -19$

    (D) $9x = -7$

12. Which inequality could be Step 3 of the solution?

Step 1: $3x > 4(x - 1)$

Step 2: $3x > 4x - 4$

Step 3: ?

    (A) $7x > -4$

    (B) $-x > -4$

    (C) $4x > -4$

    (D) $-7x > -4$

California Standards
Algebra 5.0

Students solve multistep problems, including word problems,
involving linear equations and linear inequalities in one variable
and provide justification for each step.

Solve Problems Using Linear Equations and Inequalities

Example 1   ## Solve a Linear Equation

Solve $3(2y - 1) = 1 + 2(3 - y)$. Justify each step.

Solution

$3(2y - 1) = 1 + 2(3 - y)$	**Write original equation.**
$6y - 3 = 1 + 6 - 2y$	**Distributive property**
$6y - 3 = 7 - 2y$	**Simplify.**
$8y - 3 = 7$	**Add 2y to each side.**
$8y = 10$	**Add 3 to each side and simplify.**
$\frac{1}{8}(8y) = \frac{1}{8}(10)$	**Multiply both sides by the reciprocal of 8.**
$y = \frac{5}{4}$	**Simplify.**

Answer $y = \frac{5}{4}$

Example 2   ## Solve a Multistep Problem

For a class trip, 115 students and 4 teachers will ride buses to the science museum. If
each bus holds 18 passengers, how many buses are needed for the trip?

Solution

Let n represent the number of buses needed for the trip. The total number of
passengers on the trip is $115 + 4 = 119$. Write a verbal model. Then write and solve
the equation.

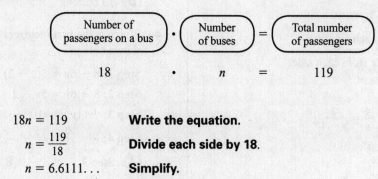

$18n = 119$	**Write the equation.**
$n = \frac{119}{18}$	**Divide each side by 18.**
$n = 6.6111\ldots$	**Simplify.**

Because n must be an integer, 7 buses will be needed for the trip.

Example 3

Solve a Problem Using a Linear Inequality

Allison takes her sister bowling. The rental fee for a pair of bowling shoes is $2.50 and the cost for each game is $3.00. If Allison has $37.00, how many games can they bowl?

Solution

STEP 1 Let g represent the total number of games played. Write a verbal model. Then write an inequality.

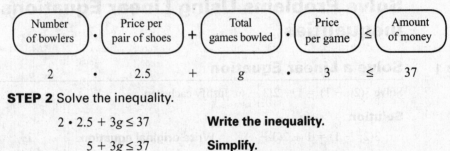

Number of bowlers		Price per pair of shoes		Total games bowled		Price per game		Amount of money
2	$\cdot$	2.5	$+$	g	$\cdot$	3	$\leq$	37

STEP 2 Solve the inequality.

$2 \cdot 2.5 + 3g \leq 37$	**Write the inequality.**
$5 + 3g \leq 37$	**Simplify.**
$3g \leq 32$	**Subtract 5 from each side.**
$g \leq 10.66\ldots$	**Divide each side by 3.**

They can bowl 10 games total.

Check $2 \cdot 2.5 + 10 \cdot 3 = 5 + 30 = 35;\ \$35.00 < \$37.00$

Answer Allison and her sister can bowl 10 games total, or 5 games each.

Exercises

1. Juan simplifies the inequality $2(x - 4) > 7x$ as shown.

   Given: $2(x - 4) > 7x$

   Step 1: $2x - 8 > 7x$

   Step 2: $-8 > 5x$

   Step 3: $\dfrac{-8}{5} > 5x$

   To get from Step 1 to Step 2, Juan . . .

   (A) adds 5 to each side.

   (B) subtracts 8 from each side.

   (C) adds $7x$ to each side.

   (D) subtracts $2x$ from each side.

2. Solve for y.

   $$\frac{4}{y} = \frac{3}{y - 1}$$

   (A) $y = 4$

   (B) $y = 1$

   (C) $y = -1$

   (D) $y = -4$

3. Brenda, Julie and Carlotta collect buttons. Together they have 78 buttons. Brenda has half as many buttons as Julie, and Carlotta has 3 times as many buttons as Brenda. How many buttons does Brenda have?

   (A) 7 buttons

   (B) 8 buttons

   (C) 9 buttons

   (D) 13 buttons

4. Which is the first *incorrect* step in the solution shown below?

   Step 1: $8 - 6y = 5(y - 2)$

   Step 2: $8 - 6y = 5y - 2$

   Step 3: $-11y = -10$

   Step 4: $y = \dfrac{10}{11}$

   (A) Step 3   (B) Step 2

   (C) Step 4   (D) Step 1

5. Solve $2y - 3 \leq 7(4 - y)$.

  (A) $y \leq \dfrac{31}{9}$ **(B)** $y \leq 31$

  (C) $y \leq \dfrac{14}{9}$ **(D)** $y \leq 14$

6. The formula for converting from Fahrenheit (F) degrees to Celsius (C) degrees is $C = \dfrac{5}{9}(F - 32)$. Find F if $C = 20$.

  (A) 340   **(B)** 68

  (C) $29\dfrac{3}{5}$ **(D)** $-6\dfrac{2}{3}$

7. The surface area of a rectangular shipping container must be less than 126 square feet. The formula for surface area S is $S = 2hl + 2lw + 2wh$, where h, l, and w are height, length, and width, respectively, of the container's edges. If the height of the container is 3 feet and the length is 5 feet, which inequality describes the container's width?

  (A) $w < 5$ feet   **(B)** $w < 6$ feet

  (C) $w < 7$ feet   **(D)** $w < 10$ feet

8. In the solution below, Step 2 is incorrect. What is the correct Step 2 in solving the equation?

Given: $4 + 5y = -2(y - 3)$

Step 1: $4 + 5y = -2y + 6$

Step 2: $3y = 2$

Step 3: $y = \dfrac{2}{3}$

  (A) $7y = -2$ **(B)** $3y = 10$

  (C) $7y = 2$ **(D)** $3y = 2$

9. What are the integer solutions of $4(3 - y) \leq 4y$?

  (A) $\{-1, -2, -3, \ldots\}$

  (B) $\{2, 3, 4, \ldots\}$

  (C) $\{\emptyset\}$

  (D) $\{1, 2, 3, \ldots\}$

10. The cost C of manufacturing a product is given by the formula $C = 300(N - 2) + 500N + 2000$, where N is the number of products made. What is the difference in cost between manufacturing 2 products and 5 products?

  (A) 2400   **(B)** 2500

  (C) 2200   **(D)** 2100

11. Which of the following could be the first step in solving the equation $4(2 - y) = 4 - 7y$?

  (A) $6 - y = 4 - 7y$ **(B)** $8 - y = 4 - 7y$

  (C) $8 - 4y = 4 - 7y$ **(D)** $6 - y = 4 - 7y$

12. Which pair of steps contains an error in solving the inequality $|7 - 6y| \geq 31$?

  (A) $-31 \geq 7 - 6y$; $7 - 6y \geq 31$

  (B) $-38 \geq -6y$; $-6y \geq 24$

  (C) $6y \leq 38$; $6y \leq -24$

  (D) $y \leq \dfrac{38}{6}$; $y \leq -4$

13. Solve for x.

$$-2(3 - x) = 4(2x - 5)$$

  (A) $x = \dfrac{14}{10}$ **(B)** $x = \dfrac{7}{3}$

  (C) $x = -\dfrac{13}{3}$ **(D)** $x = \dfrac{7}{6}$

14. Which value of x lies *between* the solutions of the equation $2x - 3 = 7$ and the equation $5 - 4x = 17$ on a number line?

  (A) $x = 3$ **(B)** $x = -3$

  (C) $x = -5$ **(D)** $x = 5$

15. Rena has to install fiber-optic cable between four switch boxes of a computer network. The boxes lie in a straight line, and it is 200 feet from the first to the last box. The distance from the first box to the second is 3 feet less than 2 times the distance from the second box to the third. The distance from the third box to the last box is 20 feet less than the distance from the second box to the third. Which equation could be used to find x, the distance between the second box and the third box?

  (A) $200 = (3 - 2x) + x + (x - 20)$

  (B) $200 = (2x - 3) + x + (20 - x)$

  (C) $200 = (2x + 3) + x + (20 - x)$

  (D) $200 = (2x - 3) + x + (x - 20)$

16. Which equation is equivalent to $6x - 3 = 12x + 4$?

  (A) $3x - 6 = 4(3x + 1)$

  (B) $9x - 3x - 3 = 12 + x + 4$

  (C) $3(2x - 1) = 2(6x + 1) + 2$

  (D) $3(x - 2) = 2(6x + 1) + 1$

California Standards
Algebra 6.0

Students graph a linear equation and compute the *x*- and *y*-intercepts (e.g., graph 2*x* + 6*y* = 4). They are also able to sketch the region defined by linear inequalities (e.g., they sketch the region defined by 2*x* + 6*y* < 4).

Graph Linear Equations and Inequalities

Terms to Know	Example
The ***x*-intercept** is the *x*-coordinate of a point where a graph crosses the *x*-axis.	The *x-intercept* is −6. The *y-intercept* is 4.
The ***y*-intercept** is the *y*-coordinate of a point where a graph crosses the *y*-axis.	
A **linear inequality in two variables** is the result of replacing the = sign in a linear equation with <, ≤, >, or ≥.	$x - 4y > 7$ is a *linear inequality*.

Example 1

Graph a Linear Equation

Graph the equation $3x - y = 2$. What are the *x*- and *y*-intercepts of the graph?

Solution

STEP 1 Solve the equation for *y*.

$$3x - y = 2$$
$$y = 3x - 2$$

STEP 2 Make a table by choosing a few values for *x* and finding the values of *y*.

x	−2	−1	0	1	2
y	−8	−5	−2	1	4

STEP 3 Plot the points. Notice that the points appear to lie in a straight line.

STEP 4 Connect the points by drawing a line through them. Use arrows to indicate that the graph goes on without end.

STEP 5 Notice that the graph intersects the *x*-axis at the point $\left(\frac{2}{3}, 0\right)$ and the *y*-axis at the point $(0, -2)$.

Answer The *x*-intercept is $\frac{2}{3}$. The *y*-intercept is -2.

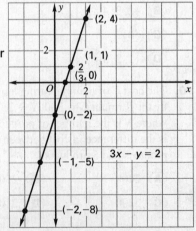

Name _____ Date _____

Example 2   ## Find Intercepts of an Equation

What are the x- and y-intercepts of the graph of $3x - 5y = 45$?

Solution

To find the x-intercept, substitute 0 for y and solve for x.

$3x - 5y = 45$ **Write the original equation.**

$3x - 5(0) = 45$ **Substitute 0 for y.**

$x = 15$ **Solve for x.**

To find the y-intercept, substitute 0 for x and solve for y.

$3x - 5y = 45$ **Write the original equation.**

$3(0) - 5y = 45$ **Substitute 0 for x.**

$y = -9$ **Solve for y.**

Answer The x-intercept is 15. The y-intercept is -9.

Example 3   ## Graph a Linear Inequality

Graph the inequality $y < -2x + 9$.

Solution

STEP 1 Graph the equation $y = -2x + 9$.

The inequality is $<$, so use a
dashed line.

STEP 2 Test $(0, 0)$ in $y < -2x + 9$.

$0 \overset{?}{<} -2(0) + 9$

$0 < 9$ ✓

STEP 3 Shade the half-plane that contains
$(0, 0)$, because $(0, 0)$ is a solution
of the inequality.

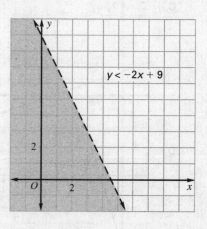

$y < -2x + 9$

Exercises

1. What is the y-intercept of the graph of
   $5x + 2y = 10$?

   Ⓐ $y = 5$ Ⓑ $y = 2$ Ⓒ $y = 0$ Ⓓ $y = -2$

2. Which equation is shown on the graph below?

   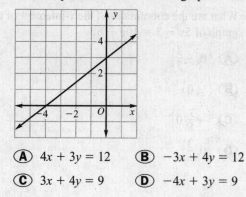

   Ⓐ $4x + 3y = 12$ Ⓑ $-3x + 4y = 12$
   Ⓒ $3x + 4y = 9$ Ⓓ $-4x + 3y = 9$

3. What are the coordinates of the y-intercept of the
   graph of $-9x + 2y = -4$?

   Ⓐ $(0, 2)$ Ⓑ $(0, -2)$
   Ⓒ $\left(\frac{4}{9}, 0\right)$ Ⓓ $\left(0, -\frac{4}{9}\right)$

4. What are the coordinates of the x-intercept of the
   graph of $-2x - 5y = 7$?

   Ⓐ $\left(-\frac{7}{5}, 0\right)$

   Ⓑ $\left(-\frac{7}{2}, 0\right)$

   Ⓒ $\left(0, \frac{7}{2}\right)$

   Ⓓ $\left(0, \frac{7}{5}\right)$

5. Which of the following is the graph of

$y = \frac{1}{3}x + 3$?

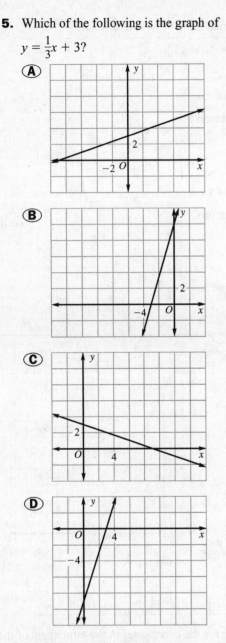

6. Which inequality is shown on the graph below?

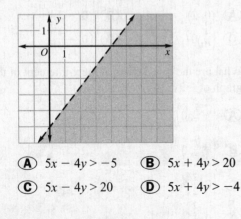

  Ⓐ $5x - 4y > -5$ Ⓑ $5x + 4y > 20$

  Ⓒ $5x - 4y > 20$ Ⓓ $5x + 4y > -4$

7. What is the y-intercept of the graph of $7x + 14y = -28$?

  Ⓐ 4   Ⓑ 2   Ⓒ -2 Ⓓ -4

8. What are the coordinates of the x-intercept of the graph of $y = \frac{4}{7}x$?

  Ⓐ $(0, 0)$ Ⓑ $(3, 0)$

  Ⓒ $(7, 0)$ Ⓓ $(0, 4)$

9. Which inequality is shown on the graph below?

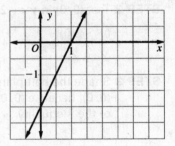

  Ⓐ $y < \frac{4}{5}x$ Ⓑ $y \le \frac{4}{5}x$

  Ⓒ $y > \frac{4}{5}x$ Ⓓ $y \ge \frac{4}{5}x$

10. Which equation is shown on the graph below?

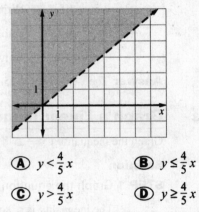

  Ⓐ $y = 2x + 1$

  Ⓑ $y = \frac{1}{2}x - 2$

  Ⓒ $y = \frac{1}{2}x + 1$

  Ⓓ $y = 2x - 2$

11. What are the coordinates of the x-intercept of the graph of $5x - 3 = 10y - 6$?

  Ⓐ $\left(0, -\frac{3}{5}\right)$

  Ⓑ $\left(\frac{3}{5}, 0\right)$

  Ⓒ $\left(-\frac{3}{5}, 0\right)$

  Ⓓ $\left(0, \frac{3}{5}\right)$

12. Which equation is shown on the graph below?

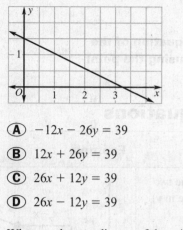

   Ⓐ $-12x - 26y = 39$

   Ⓑ $12x + 26y = 39$

   Ⓒ $26x + 12y = 39$

   Ⓓ $26x - 12y = 39$

13. What are the coordinates of the y-intercept of the graph of $y + 4 = 3x - 2$?

   Ⓐ $(0, -6)$

   Ⓑ $(-2, 0)$

   Ⓒ $(0, -2)$

   Ⓓ $(2, 0)$

14. Which set represents all values of y such that $(0, y)$ is a solution of $2x - 9y \le 15$?

   Ⓐ $\left\{ y : y \le -\dfrac{5}{3} \right\}$

   Ⓑ $\left\{ y : y \le \dfrac{5}{3} \right\}$

   Ⓒ $\left\{ y : y \ge -\dfrac{5}{3} \right\}$

   Ⓓ $\left\{ y : y \ge \dfrac{5}{3} \right\}$

15. Which equation is shown on the graph below?

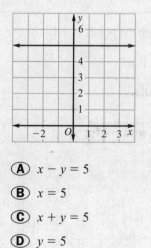

   Ⓐ $x - y = 5$

   Ⓑ $x = 5$

   Ⓒ $x + y = 5$

   Ⓓ $y = 5$

16. Which of the following is the graph of $y = -\dfrac{1}{5}x + 5$?

   Ⓐ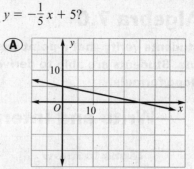

   Ⓑ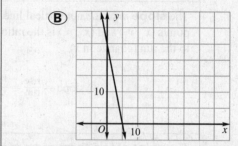

   Ⓒ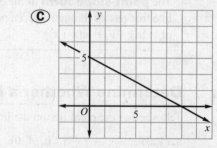

   Ⓓ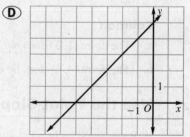

California Standards
Algebra 7.0

Students verify that a point lies on a line, given an equation of the line. Students are able to derive linear equations by using the point-slope formula.

Write and Interpret Linear Equations

Terms to Know	Example
The **slope** m of the nonvertical line passing through the two points (x_1, y_1) and (x_2, y_2) is the ratio of the rise (change in y) to the run (change in x). $$\text{slope} = \frac{\text{rise}}{\text{run}} = \frac{y_2 - y_1}{x_2 - x_1}$$	
The **point-slope form** of the equation of the nonvertical line that passes through a given point (x_1, y_1) and has a slope of m is $y - y_1 = m(x - x_1)$.	The equation $y - 2 = 5(x - 1)$ is in point-slope form.

Example 1

Determine Whether a Point Lies on a Line

Tell whether the point lies on the line $-x + y = -4$.

a. $(1, 3)$ **b.** $(4, 0)$

Solution

a. The point $(1, 3)$ does *not* lie on the line $-x + y = -4$ because $-(1) + 3 \neq -4$.

b. The point $(4, 0)$ does lie on the line $-x + y = -4$ because $-(4) + 0 = -4$.

Example 2

Use the Point-Slope Formula

Write an equation in point-slope form of a line that passes through the point $\left(\frac{2}{3}, -4\right)$ and has a slope of 2.

Solution

$$y - y_1 = m(x - x_1)$$ **Write the point-slope formula.**

$$y - (-4) = 2\left(x - \frac{2}{3}\right)$$ **Substitute 2 for m, $\frac{2}{3}$ for x_1, and -4 for y_1.**

$$y + 4 = 2\left(x - \frac{2}{3}\right)$$ **Simplify.**

Answer $y + 4 = 2\left(x - \frac{2}{3}\right)$

Name _____   Date _____

Exercises

1. Which point lies on the line defined by $-5x + 7y = 13$?

(A) $\left(-\frac{1}{5}, 2\right)$ (B) $\left(\frac{1}{5}, 2\right)$

(C) $\left(-\frac{34}{5}, 3\right)$ (D) $\left(2, \frac{3}{7}\right)$

2. Which point does *not* lie on the line defined by $x = 7$?

(A) $(7, \pi)$ (B) $(6, 7)$

(C) $(7, -1)$ (D) $(7, -\sqrt{11})$

3. Which *pair* of points lies on the line defined by $x - 3y = 6$?

(A) $(3, 1)$ and $(18, 4)$

(B) $(-1, 3)$ and $(1, -3)$

(C) $(3, -1)$ and $(9, 1)$

(D) $(9, 1)$ and $(9, 5)$

4. Which of the following equations represents a line that contains the following points?

x	?	3	5
y	2	?	1

(A) $x - y = 6$ (B) $y - x = 6$

(C) $x + y = 6$ (D) $x + y = 4$

5. Which of the following equations represents a line with a slope of $-\frac{1}{2}$ and y-intercept 5?

(A) $-x - 2y = 10$

(B) $x + 2y = 10$

(C) $x + 2y = -10$

(D) $x - 2y = 10$

6. Which point lies on the line defined by $3x - 6y = 2$?

(A) $(0, -1)$

(B) $(0, 1)$

(C) $\left(0, -\frac{1}{3}\right)$

(D) $\left(-1, \frac{5}{2}\right)$

7. What is the equation of the line that has a slope of 0 and passes through the point $(2, 3)$?

(A) $y = x + 3$ (B) $y = x - 3$

(C) $y = -3$ (D) $y = 3$

8. Which of the following points lies on *both* of the lines defined by $y = 2x + 1$ and $2y - x = -2$?

(A) $\left(\frac{4}{3}, -\frac{5}{3}\right)$ (B) $\left(\frac{4}{3}, \frac{11}{3}\right)$

(C) $\left(-\frac{4}{3}, -\frac{5}{3}\right)$ (D) $\left(-\frac{4}{3}, 0\right)$

9. What is the equation of the line that has a slope of -2 and passes through the point $(-5, 0)$?

(A) $2x + y = -10$

(B) $2x + y = 10$

(C) $2x + y = 7$

(D) $2x + y = -7$

10. The data in the table below shows the cost in dollars, C, of painting a wall and the number of cans of paint, n, needed to paint the wall.

n	1	2	3
C	42	49	56

If the number of cans of paint, n, were graphed on the horizontal axis and cost, C, were graphed on the vertical axis, what would be the equation of the line that fits the data?

(A) $C = 7n + 35$ (B) $C = -7n + 35$

(C) $C = 7n$ (D) $C = 35n$

11. Which of the following is *not* an equation for a line with a slope of 5?

(A) $-5x + y = 12$

(B) $5x + y = 9$

(C) $5x - y = -4$

(D) $-5x + y = 4$

12. Which of the following points lies on the line defined by $3y = 4x$?

(A) $(4, 3)$ (B) $(3, 4)$

(C) $(1, 1)$ (D) $\left(\frac{2}{3}, \frac{3}{4}\right)$

California Standards
Algebra 8.0

Students understand the concepts of parallel lines and perpendicular lines and how their slopes are related. Students are able to find the equation of a line perpendicular to a given line that passes through a given point.

Parallel and Perpendicular Lines

Terms to Know	Example
A linear equation of the form $y = mx + b$ is written in **slope-intercept form**, where m is the slope and b is the y-intercept of the equation's graph.	The equation $y = \frac{1}{4}x + 2$ is written in slope-intercept form, where $\frac{1}{4}$ is the slope and 2 is the y-intercept.
Parallel lines are two different lines in the same plane that have the same slope. Parallel lines do not intersect.	Lines a and b are parallel. Lines a and c are perpendicular.
Perpendicular lines are two different lines in the same plane that have slopes that are negative reciprocals. Perpendicular lines intersect to form a right angle.	

Example 1   **Write an Equation of a Parallel Line**

Write an equation of the line that passes through (2, 6) and is parallel to the line $y = -4x + 5$.

Solution

STEP 1 Identify the slope.

The graph of the given equation has a slope of -4. So, the parallel line passing through the point (2, 6) has a slope of -4.

STEP 2 Find the y-intercept. Use the slope and the given point.

$y = mx + b$	**Write the slope-intercept form.**
$6 = -4(2) + b$	**Substitute −4 for _m_, 2 for _x_, and 6 for _y_.**
$14 = b$	**Solve for _b_.**

STEP 3 Write the equation using the slope-intercept form.

$y = -4x + 14$ **Substitute using 14 for _b_ and −4 for _m_.**

Answer The equation of the line that passes through the point (2, 6) and is parallel to the line $y = -4x + 5$ is $y = -4x + 14$.

Check Compare the slopes and y-intercepts of $y = -4x + 5$ and $y = -4x + 14$. Because the lines have different y-intercepts and the same slope, the lines are parallel. Substitute $(2, 6)$ in $y = -4x + 14$.

$$6 \overset{?}{=} (-4)2 + 14$$

$$6 \overset{?}{=} -8 + 14$$

$$6 = 6 \checkmark$$

Example 2

Write an Equation of a Perpendicular Line

Which equation represents the line that passes through $(2, 6)$ and is perpendicular to the line $y = -4x + 5$?

(A) $y = 4x - 2$ **(B)** $y = \frac{1}{4}x + \frac{13}{2}$ **(C)** $y = \frac{1}{4}x + \frac{11}{2}$ **(D)** $y = 4x + 6$

Solution

STEP 1 Identify the slope.

The graph of the given equation has a slope of -4. The slopes of perpendicular lines are negative reciprocals. The negative reciprocal of -4 is $\frac{1}{4}$, so choices A and D can be eliminated.

STEP 2 Find the y-intercept. Use the slope and the given point.

$$y = mx + b \qquad \textbf{Write the slope-intercept form.}$$

$$6 = \frac{1}{4}(2) + b \qquad \textbf{Substitute } \frac{1}{4} \textbf{ for } m, \textbf{2 for } x, \textbf{ and 6 for } y.$$

$$5\frac{1}{2} = \frac{11}{2} = b \qquad \textbf{Solve for } b.$$

STEP 3 Write an equation.

$$y = mx + b \qquad \textbf{Write the slope-intercept form.}$$

$$y = \frac{1}{4}x + \frac{11}{2} \qquad \textbf{Substitute } \frac{1}{4} \textbf{ for } m \textbf{ and } \frac{11}{2} \textbf{ for } b.$$

Answer The correct choice is C: $y = \frac{1}{4}x + \frac{11}{2}$.

Check Because the lines have different y-intercepts and their slopes are negative reciprocals, the lines are perpendicular. Substitute $(2, 6)$ in $y = \frac{1}{4}x + \frac{11}{2}$.

$$y = \frac{1}{4}x + \frac{11}{2}$$

$$6 \overset{?}{=} \frac{1}{4}(2) + \frac{11}{2}$$

$$6 \overset{?}{=} \frac{1}{2} + \frac{11}{2}$$

$$6 \overset{?}{=} \frac{12}{2}$$

$$6 = 6 \checkmark$$

Exercises

1. What is the slope of a line perpendicular to the line $y = -5x - 2$?

   Ⓐ $\frac{1}{5}$ Ⓑ -5 Ⓒ $-\frac{1}{5}$ Ⓓ 5

2. Which of the following is a correct statement about the relationship between two parallel lines?

   Ⓐ They have the same slope, but different y-intercepts.

   Ⓑ They have opposite slopes.

   Ⓒ They have opposite slopes and different x-intercepts.

   Ⓓ They have reciprocal slopes and the same y-intercepts.

3. What is the equation of the perpendicular line that intersects the graph of $y = 2x - 5$ at $(1, -3)$?

   Ⓐ $x - 2y = 5$ Ⓑ $x + 2y = 5$

   Ⓒ $x - 2y = -5$ Ⓓ $x + 2y = -5$

4. Which of the following equations represents a line parallel to the line defined by the equation $x - y = 1$?

   Ⓐ $5x + 5y = 6$

   Ⓑ $4x - 4y = 3$

   Ⓒ $7x + 7y = 11$

   Ⓓ $-8x - 8y = 3$

5. The slope of line A is $\frac{1}{3}$. Which of the following equations represents a line perpendicular to line A?

   Ⓐ $3x + y = -2$

   Ⓑ $3x - y = 2$

   Ⓒ $3x + 2y = 1$

   Ⓓ $3x - 2y = -1$

6. Which of the following equations represents a line perpendicular to the line $y - 2x = 5$?

   Ⓐ $x - \frac{1}{2}y = -10$

   Ⓑ $x + \frac{1}{2}y = 10$

   Ⓒ $x + 2y = 10$

   Ⓓ $-x + 2y = 10$

7. Which of the following equations represents a line that is parallel to the line $y = -2$?

   Ⓐ $x = -2$

   Ⓑ $y = x$

   Ⓒ $y = 2$

   Ⓓ $x = 2$

8. Which of the following represents the slope, m, and y-intercept, b, of a line perpendicular to $y = -\frac{1}{3}x + 6$?

   Ⓐ $m = 3$ and $b = 6$

   Ⓑ $m = -3$ and $b = 1$

   Ⓒ $m = -3$ and $b = 6$

   Ⓓ $m = \frac{1}{3}$ and $b = 3$

9. What is the equation of the perpendicular line that intersects the graph of $y = x$ at $(0, 0)$?

   Ⓐ $x - y = 1$

   Ⓑ $y = -2x$

   Ⓒ $y = -x$

   Ⓓ $x + y = 1$

10. The equation of line A is $3x + 2y = 8$, and the equation of line B is $2x - 3y = 18$. Which statement about the two lines is true?

   Ⓐ Lines A and B are perpendicular.

   Ⓑ Lines A and B are parallel.

   Ⓒ Lines A and B have the same x-intercept.

   Ⓓ Lines A and B have the same y-intercept.

11. Which of the following equations represents a line that is *not* parallel to the line $-4x + y = -5$?

   Ⓐ $-20x + 5y = -250$

   Ⓑ $-12x + 3y = -15$

   Ⓒ $-8x + y = 56$

   Ⓓ $-6x + \frac{3}{2}y = 162$

Name _____   Date _____

California Standards
Algebra 9.0

Students solve a system of two linear equations in two variables algebraically and are able to interpret the answer graphically. Students are able to solve a system of two linear inequalities in two variables and to sketch the solution sets.

Solve Linear Systems

Terms to Know	Example
A **system of linear equations** in two variables, or simply a *linear system*, consists of two or more linear equations in the same variables.	$x - 5y = 12$ $-3x + 2y = 5$
A **system of linear inequalities** in two variables, or simply a *system of inequalities*, consists of two or more linear inequalities in the same variables.	$-7a + 6b \geq 10$ $-3a - 5b < 20$

Example 1   ## Solve a System of Equations

Solve the linear system: $x + 3y = 9$ **Equation 1**

$\qquad\qquad\qquad\qquad -2x + y = -4$ **Equation 2**

Solution

STEP 1 Multiply Equation 1 by 2.

$\qquad x + 3y = 9 \qquad$ ✕ 2 $\qquad 2x + 6y = 18$

$\qquad -2x + y = -4 \qquad\qquad\qquad \underline{-2x + y = -4}$

STEP 2 Add the equations. $\qquad\qquad\qquad\qquad 7y = 14$

STEP 3 Solve for y. $\qquad\qquad\qquad\qquad\qquad y = 2$

STEP 4 Substitute 2 for y in either equation and solve for x.

$\qquad\qquad x + 3y = 9 \qquad$ **Write Equation 1.**

$\qquad\qquad x + 3(2) = 9 \qquad$ **Substitute 2 for y.**

$\qquad\qquad\qquad x = 3 \qquad$ **Solve for x.**

Answer The solution is (3, 2).

Check Plot the points containing the x- and y-intercepts of the two equations.

Equation 1: (0, 3) and (9, 0)

Equation 2: (0, −4) and (2, 0)

The two lines appear to intersect at the point (3, 2).

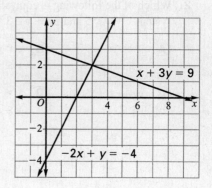

Example 2

Graph a System of Inequalities

Graph the system of inequalities: $x - y > 5$ **Inequality 1**

$2x + y < 4$ **Inequality 2**

Solution

Graph both inequalities in the same coordinate plane. The graph of the intersection of the two half-planes is the darker shaded region.

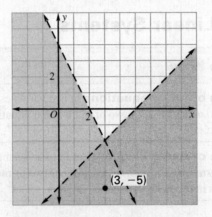

Answer The solution to the system of inequalities $x - y > 5$ and $2x + y < 4$ is the intersection of the two half-planes shown above.

Check Choose a point in the darker shaded region, such as $(3, -5)$. To check the solution, substitute 3 for x and -5 for y into each inequality.

$$x - y > 5 \qquad\qquad\qquad 2x + y < 4$$

$$3 - (-5) \overset{?}{>} 5 \qquad\qquad 2(3) + (-5) \overset{?}{<} 4$$

$$8 > 5 \checkmark \qquad\qquad\qquad 1 < 4 \checkmark$$

Exercises

1. What is the solution of the system shown below?

$$2x - y = 7$$
$$y = -3x + 5$$

A $(12, 17)$

B $\left(\dfrac{12}{5}, \dfrac{11}{5}\right)$

C $\left(\dfrac{12}{5}, -\dfrac{11}{5}\right)$

D $\left(\dfrac{12}{5}, -\dfrac{59}{5}\right)$

2. Which of the following is equivalent to the system $x + y < 5$ and $2x - y \geq 3$?

A $y < -x + 5$
$y \leq 2x - 3$

B $y < x + 5$
$y \leq -2x - 3$

C $y < -x + 5$
$y \geq 2x - 3$

D $y > -x + 5$
$y \leq 2x - 3$

3. What is the solution of the system shown below?

$$3x + 2y = 6$$
$$4x + 2y = 9$$

A $\left(-3, \dfrac{3}{2}\right)$

B $\left(3, -\dfrac{3}{2}\right)$

C $\left(-3, -\dfrac{3}{2}\right)$

D $\left(3, \dfrac{3}{2}\right)$

4. Which of the following points is *not* in the solution set of the system shown below?

$$3x - y > 12$$
$$x + y \geq 6$$

A $(7, 5)$

B $(1, 5)$

C $(9, 1)$

D $(5, 1)$

5. What is the solution of the system shown below?

$$y = 2x + 5$$
$$y = -x + 11$$

Ⓐ (4, 13)   Ⓑ (−4, 7)

Ⓒ (2, 9)   Ⓓ (−2, 13)

6. Which graph best represents the solution to this system of inequalities?

$$y > 3x - 1$$
$$y \le -2x + 5$$

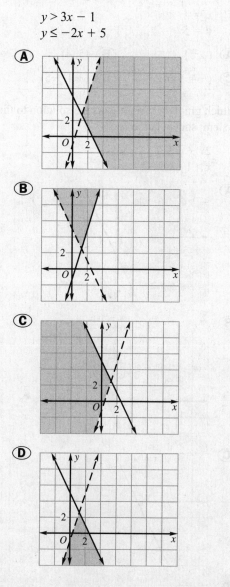

Ⓐ

Ⓑ

Ⓒ

Ⓓ

7. What is the solution of the system shown below?

$$y = 2x - 9$$
$$y = 4 + 3x$$

Ⓐ (5, 19)   Ⓑ (−5, −11)

Ⓒ (−13, −35)   Ⓓ (13, 42)

8. The solution to a system of equations is (7, −9). One of the equations in the system is $y = 5 - 2x$. Which of the following is the other equation in the system?

Ⓐ $x - 7y = 70$ Ⓑ $y = -\frac{1}{7}x - 10$

Ⓒ $y = \frac{1}{7}x + 10$ Ⓓ $x + 7y = 10$

9. What is the solution of the system $7x - 2y = 5$ and $-3x - 4y = 7$?

Ⓐ $\left(\frac{3}{17}, -\frac{32}{17}\right)$ Ⓑ $\left(-\frac{3}{17}, -\frac{32}{17}\right)$

Ⓒ $\left(\frac{3}{17}, \frac{32}{17}\right)$ Ⓓ $\left(-\frac{3}{17}, \frac{32}{17}\right)$

10. Which graph represents the system of equations shown below?

$$y = -3x - 5$$
$$y = 3x + 7$$

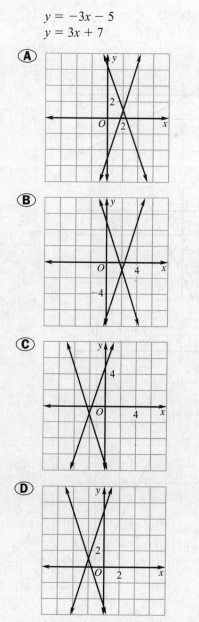

Ⓐ

Ⓑ

Ⓒ

Ⓓ

11. What is the solution of the system shown below?

$$y = -9x + 4$$
$$x = -3$$

Ⓐ no solution   Ⓑ $(-3, 31)$

Ⓒ infinite solutions   Ⓓ $(-3, -23)$

12. What is the solution of the system shown below?

$$y = 25x - 36$$
$$y = 25x - 72$$

Ⓐ no solution   Ⓑ $\left(\dfrac{108}{25}, 0\right)$

Ⓒ $\left(\dfrac{36}{25}, 0\right)$ Ⓓ infinite solutions

13. Which graph represents the system shown below?

$$y = 2x - 5$$
$$y = 3$$

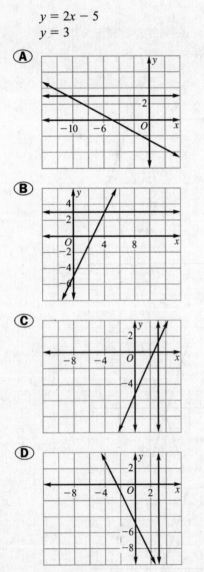

14. What is the solution of the system shown below?

$$5x + y = 3$$
$$\frac{1}{2}y = \frac{3}{2} - \frac{5}{2}x$$

Ⓐ infinite solutions   Ⓑ $(2, -7)$

Ⓒ $(1, -2)$ Ⓓ no solution

15. What is the solution of the system shown below?

$$x = 4$$
$$y = 5$$

Ⓐ $(4, 5)$ Ⓑ $(5, 4)$

Ⓒ $(-4, 5)$ Ⓓ $(-4, -5)$

16. Which graph best represents the solution to the system shown below?

$$2x - y \le 3$$
$$x > 1$$

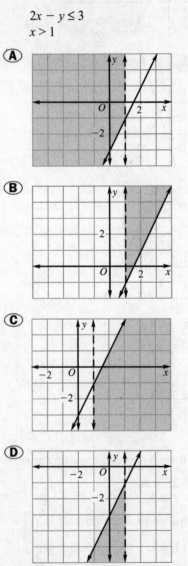

California Standards
Algebra 10.0

Students add, subtract, multiply, and divide monomials and polynomials. Students solve multistep problems, including word problems, by using these techniques.

Monomials and Polynomials

Terms to Know	Example
A **monomial** is a number, variable, or the product of a number and one or more variables with whole number exponents.	34, $-2x$, and $\frac{1}{3}xy^4$ are monomials.
A **polynomial** is a monomial or a sum of monomials, each of which is called a term of the polynomial.	-0.73, $-2a^3 + 4b^2$, and $xy^3 - 3x^3y$ are polynomials.
Like terms are terms that have the same variable parts. Constant terms are also like terms.	In the expression $5x + 2 - 3x - 4$, $5x$ and $-3x$ are like terms, and 2 and -4 are like terms.

Example 1   ## Add and Subtract Polynomials

Find the sum or difference.

a. $25a^3 + 24a^3$

b. $4 + 3m - (5 + 2m)$

c. $4xy^3 + 3x^3y - 3xy^3 - 4x^3y$

Solution

a. $25a^3 + 24a^3 = 49a^3$ **Combine like terms.**

b. $4 + 3m - (5 + 2m)$

$= 4 + 3m - 5 - 2m$ **Distributive property**

$= (4 - 5) + (3m - 2m)$ **Group like terms.**

$= -1 + m$ **Simplify.**

c. $4xy^3 + 3x^3y - 3xy^3 - 4x^3y$

$= (4xy^3 - 3xy^3) + (3x^3y - 4x^3y)$ **Group like terms.**

$= xy^3 - x^3y$ **Simplify.**

California Standard
Algebra 10.0

Example 2

Multiply Polynomials

a. What is the product of $5a^2(3ab^2 - 2a^5 + ba^3)$?

b. What is the product of $(4x^2 + 1)(2x^2 - 3x + 4)$?

Solution

a. $5a^2(3ab^2 - 2a^5 + ba^3)$ **Write product.**

    $= 5a^2(3ab^2) + 5a^2(-2a^5) + 5a^2(ba^3)$ **Distributive property**

    $= 15a^3b^2 - 10a^7 + 5a^5b$ **Product of powers property**

b. $(4x^2 + 1)(2x^2 - 3x + 4)$ **Write product.**

    $= (4x^2)(2x^2 - 3x + 4) + 1(2x^2 - 3x + 4)$ **Distributive property**

    $= 8x^4 - 12x^3 + 16x^2 + 2x^2 - 3x + 4$ **Distributive property**

    $= 8x^4 - 12x^3 + 18x^2 - 3x + 4$ **Simplify.**

Answer a. $5a^2(3ab^2 - 2a^5 + ba^3) = 15a^3b^2 - 10a^7 + 5a^5b$

      b. $(4x^2 + 1)(2x^2 - 3x + 4) = 8x^4 - 12x^3 + 18x^2 - 3x + 4$

Example 3

Solve a Multistep Problem

Use the formula for the area of a triangle, $A = \frac{1}{2}bh$, where
b is the length of the base and h is the length of the height,
to write an expression for the area of the triangle shown at
the right.

Solution

Substitute $2x - 9$ and $x + 2$ into the formula for the area of
a triangle.

    $A = \frac{1}{2}bh$ **Write the formula.**

    $= \frac{1}{2}(2x - 9)(x + 2)$ **Substitute $2x - 9$ for b and $x + 2$ for h.**

    $= \frac{1}{2}[2x(x + 2) - 9(x + 2)]$ **Distributive property**

    $= \frac{1}{2}(2x^2 + 4x - 9x - 18)$ **Distributive property**

    $= \frac{1}{2}(2x^2 - 5x - 18)$ **Combine like terms.**

    $= x^2 - \frac{5}{2}x - 9$ **Simplify.**

Name _____ Date _____

Example 4 **Divide a Polynomial by a Monomial**

Divide $3xy^2 - 9x^2y + 21x^3y^3$ by $3xy$.

Solution

$$(3xy^2 - 9x^2y + 21x^3y^3 \div 3xy) = \frac{3xy^2 - 9x^2y + 21x^3y^3}{3xy}$$ Write as a fraction.

$$= \frac{3xy^2}{3xy} - \frac{9x^2y}{3xy} + \frac{21x^3y^3}{3xy}$$ Divide each term by **3xy**.

$$= y - 3x + 7x^2y^2$$ Simplify.

Answer $(3xy^2 - 9x^2y + 21x^3y^3 \div 3xy) = y - 3x + 7x^2y^2$

Check

Check to see if the product of $3xy$ and $y - 3x + 7x^2y^2$ is $3xy^2 - 9x^2y + 21x^3y^3$.

$$3xy(y - 3x + 7x^2y^2) = 3xy(y) - 3xy(3x) + 3xy(7x^2y^2)$$
$$= 3xy^2 - 9x^2y + 21x^3y^3 \checkmark$$

Example 5 **Divide a Polynomial by a Binomial**

Divide $4a^2 + 6ab - 12b^2$ by $2a - 3b$.

Solution

To divide a polynomial by a binomial, use long division.

$$2a - 3b \overline{\smash{\big)}\ 4a^2 + 6ab - 12b^2}$$
quotient $2a + 6b$

$\underline{4a^2 - 6ab}$ Multiply **2a − 3b** by **2a**.

$12ab - 12b^2$ Subtract **4a² − 6ab**. Bring down **−12b²**.

$\underline{12ab - 18b^2}$ Multiply **2a − 3b** by **6b**.

$6b^2$ Subtract **12ab − 18b²**.

Answer $(4a^2 + 6ab - 12b^2) \div (2a - 3b) = 2a + 6b + \dfrac{6b^2}{2a - 3b}$

Exercises

1. $(x^2 - 2x + 4) - (3x^2 - 2x + 7) =$

(A) $-3x^2 - 3$

(B) $-2x^2 - 3$

(C) $2x^2 - 3$

(D) $-2x^2 - 4x - 3$

2. $\dfrac{27x^2}{72x^9} =$

(A) $\dfrac{27}{8x^7}$ (B) $\dfrac{3}{72x^7}$

(C) $\dfrac{3}{8x^7}$ (D) $\dfrac{3x^7}{8}$

3. Which polynomial represents the shaded area below?

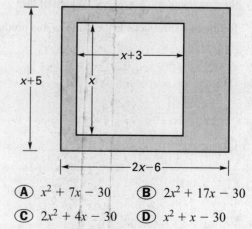

(A) $x^2 + 7x - 30$ (B) $2x^2 + 17x - 30$

(C) $2x^2 + 4x - 30$ (D) $x^2 + x - 30$

4. Simplify.

$$\frac{8x^4 + 2x^3 - 12x^2}{2x^2}$$

Ⓐ $6x^2 - 6$ Ⓑ $4x^2 - x$

Ⓒ $4x^2 + x - 6$ Ⓓ $4x^2 + x - 10$

5. Which expression is equivalent to $x(3x - 1)(2x^2 + 1)$?

Ⓐ $6x^3 - 2x^2 - x + 3$

Ⓑ $6x^4 - 2x^3 + 3x^2 - x$

Ⓒ $6x^3 - 2x^3 + 4x - 1$

Ⓓ $6x^4 - 2x^3 - x + 3$

6. Simplify $2x^2 - x + 3(x^2 + x)$.

Ⓐ $5x^2$ Ⓑ $5x^2 + 2x$

Ⓒ $5x^2 - 4x$ Ⓓ $x^2 + 2x$

7. $-x^2 - 2x + 4 - (x^2 + 2x - 4) =$

Ⓐ $-2x^2 - 4x + 8$ Ⓑ $-2x^2 - 4x$

Ⓒ $-4x + 8$ Ⓓ $-4x$

8. $\dfrac{18x^2y^3}{90x^5y} =$

Ⓐ $\dfrac{y^2}{5x^3}$ Ⓑ $\dfrac{y^3}{5x^3}$

Ⓒ $\dfrac{2x^3y^2}{5}$ Ⓓ $\dfrac{2y^2}{5x^3}$

9. The probability of winning a contest is represented by $\dfrac{1}{x}$. If you enter the contest a second time, your probability of winning is given by the expression $\dfrac{1}{2x - 7}$. The probability of winning *both* times is given by the product of the two fractions, $\dfrac{1}{x} \cdot \dfrac{1}{2x - 7}$. Which of the following expressions is the same as this product?

Ⓐ $\dfrac{1}{2x^2 - 7x}$

Ⓑ $\dfrac{1}{3x - 7}$

Ⓒ $\dfrac{1}{x} + \dfrac{1}{2x - 7}$

Ⓓ $\dfrac{1}{2x^2 - x - 7}$

10. $\dfrac{2x^2 - 7x + 4}{x^5} =$

Ⓐ $2x^3 - 7x^4 + 4x^5$

Ⓑ $\dfrac{2}{x^3} - \dfrac{7}{x^4} + \dfrac{4}{x^5}$

Ⓒ $\dfrac{2}{x^3} - \dfrac{7}{x^4} + 4$

Ⓓ $\dfrac{2}{x^3} - \dfrac{3}{x^5}$

11. $2(x^4 - 2x) - 6(x^4 + 3x) =$

Ⓐ $-4x^4 - 22x$ Ⓑ $-4x^4 - 14x$

Ⓒ $4x^4 - 22x$ Ⓓ $4x^4 + 22x$

12. What are the values of A, B, and C in the equation below?

$$8x^4 - 3x^2 + 2 - (Ax^4 + Bx^2 + C) = 3x^4 + 6$$

Ⓐ $A = 5, B = 3, C = 4$

Ⓑ $A = 5, B = 3, C = -4$

Ⓒ $A = 5, B = -3, C = -4$

Ⓓ $A = 5, B = -3, C = 4$

13. $\dfrac{(2x^3)^2}{3(5x)^2} =$

Ⓐ $\dfrac{4}{75}x^4$ Ⓑ $\dfrac{4}{15}x^4$

Ⓒ $\dfrac{4}{15}x^2$ Ⓓ $\dfrac{4}{15}x^3$

14. Simplify.

$$\frac{4x^5 - 10x^3 + 20x^2 - 5x}{6x}$$

Ⓐ $\dfrac{2}{3}x^5 - \dfrac{5}{3}x^2 + \dfrac{10}{3}x - \dfrac{5}{6}$

Ⓑ $\dfrac{2}{3}x^5 - \dfrac{5}{3}x^2 + \dfrac{10}{3}x$

Ⓒ $\dfrac{2}{3}x^4 - \dfrac{5}{3}x^2 + \dfrac{10}{3}x - \dfrac{5}{6}$

Ⓓ $\dfrac{2}{3}x^4 - \dfrac{5}{3}x^2 + \dfrac{10}{3}x$

15. $2x^3 - 4x^2 - (6x^2 + 3x^3) =$

Ⓐ $-4x^3 - 7x^2$ Ⓑ $-x^3 - x^2$

Ⓒ $-5x^2$ Ⓓ $-x^3 - 10x^2$

16. Ravi buys a second parcel of land for his avocado farm as shown below.

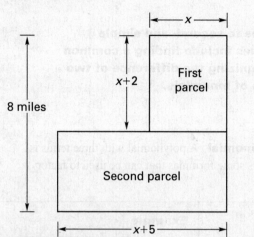

Which of the following expressions gives the area of *both* parcels?

Ⓐ $3x + 30$ square miles

Ⓑ $8x + 40$ square miles

Ⓒ $x^2 + 2x$ square miles

Ⓓ $2x^2 - 3x + 30$ square miles

17. $\dfrac{2x^3y^3}{8xy^2} =$

Ⓐ $\dfrac{x^3y}{4}$

Ⓑ $\dfrac{x^2y}{4}$

Ⓒ $\dfrac{x^2y}{6}$

Ⓓ $\dfrac{x^4y^5}{6}$

18. Simplify.

$$\frac{2x^3y^2 - 3x^2y^3 + 8xy^4}{2xy}$$

Ⓐ $x^2y - 3xy^2 + 4y^2$

Ⓑ $x^2y - \dfrac{3}{2}xy^2 + 4y^3$

Ⓒ $x^2y^2 - 3xy^2 + 6xy^3$

Ⓓ $2x^2y - 3xy^2 + 8y^2$

19. Multiply $(3xy^3)(3x^3y)(2xy)$.

Ⓐ $18x^3y^3$

Ⓑ $8x^3y^3$

Ⓒ $8x^5y^5$

Ⓓ $18x^5y^5$

20. The area of the triangle shown below is given by $x^2 + \dfrac{7}{2}x + 3$. What is the length of the base b if the height h is given by $x + 2$?

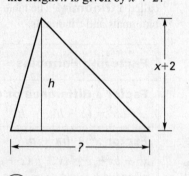

Ⓐ $2x - 3$

Ⓑ $x + \dfrac{1}{2}$

Ⓒ $2x + 3$

Ⓓ $2x - 1$

21. When $7x^2 - 4x + A$ is divided by $x - 3$, the remainder is -3. What is the value of A?

Ⓐ -54

Ⓑ 48

Ⓒ -48

Ⓓ 54

22. Divide $-2x^2 + 3x + 9$ by $3 - x$.

Ⓐ $3 - 2x$

Ⓑ $2x - 3$

Ⓒ $-3 - 2x$

Ⓓ $2x + 3$

California Standards
Algebra 11.0

Students apply basic factoring techniques to second- and simple third-degree polynomials. These techniques include finding a common factor for all terms in a polynomial, recognizing the difference of two squares, and recognizing perfect squares of binomials.

Factor Polynomials

A polynomial with two terms is called a **binomial**. A polynomial with three terms is called a **trinomial**. The table below shows some formulas that can be used to factor binomials and trinomials.

Factoring Formulas	Example
Factor a difference of two squares. $a^2 - b^2 = (a + b)(a - b)$	$x^2 - 16 = (x - 4)(x + 4)$ $9 - 4x^2 = (3 + 2x)(3 - 2x)$
Factor $x^2 + bx + c$. $x^2 + bx + c = (x + p)(x + q)$ provided $b = p + q$ and $c = pq$.	$m^2 - 6m - 16 = (m - 8)(m + 2)$, because $-6 = -8 + 2$ and $-16 = (-8)(2)$.
Factor a perfect square trinomial. $a^2 \pm 2ab + b^2 = (a \pm b)^2$	$x^2 + 6x + 9 = (x + 3)^2$

Example 1

Find the Greatest Common Factor

Factor out the greatest common factor.

a. $6a^3 - 9a^4b^2$

b. $13n(m + 1)^2 - 31(m + 1)$

Solution

a. The greatest common factor of 6 and 9 is 3. The greatest common factor of a^3 and a^4b^2 is a^3. Therefore, the greatest common factor of $6a^3 - 9a^4b^2$ is $3a^3$.

$$6a^3 - 9a^4b^2 = 3a^3(2 - 3ab^2)$$

b. The greatest common factor of 13 and 31 is 1. The factor $m + 1$ is common to both of the terms, $13n(m + 1)^2$ and $-31(m + 1)$.

Therefore, the greatest common factor of $13n(m + 1)^2 - 31(m + 1)$ is $1(m + 1)$, or $m + 1$.

$$13n(m + 1)^2 - 31(m + 1) = (m + 1)[13n(m + 1) - 31]$$

Name _____ Date _____

Example 2

Factor $x^2 + bx + c$

a. Factor $x^2 + 9x + 14$.

Find the positive factors of 14 whose sum is 9. Make an organized list.

Factors of 14	Sums of factors	
14, 1	$14 + 1 = 15$	✗
7, 2	$7 + 2 = 9$	← Correct sum

The factors 7 and 2 have a sum of 9, so they are the correct values of p and q.

$$x^2 + 9x + 14 = (x + 7)(x + 2)$$

b. Factor $x^2 - 2x - 15$.

Because $c = -15$, p and q must have different signs.

Factors of −15	Sums of factors	
−15, 1	$-15 + 1 = -14$	✗
15, −1	$15 + (-1) = 14$	✗
−5, 3	$-5 + 3 = -2$	← Correct sum
5, −3	$5 - 3 = 2$	✗

The factors −5 and 3 have a sum of −2, so they are the correct values of p and q.

$$x^2 - 2x - 15 = (x - 5)(x + 3)$$

Example 3

Factor $ax^2 + bx + c$

Factor $4x^2 + 8x - 5$.

Solution

Because b is positive and c is negative, the factors of c have different signs. You must consider the order of the factors of 4 and −5, because the x-terms of the possible factorizations are different. The table below shows some of the possible combinations.

Factors of 4	Factors of −5	Possible Factorization	Middle Term	
1, 4	1, −5	$(x + 1)(4x - 5)$	$-5x + 4x = -x$	✗
4, 1	−1, 5	$(4x - 1)(x + 5)$	$20x + (-1)x = 19x$	✗
2, 2	−1, 5	$(2x - 1)(2x + 5)$	$10x + (-2)x = 8x$	← Correct
2, 2	1, −5	$(2x + 1)(2x - 5)$	$-10x + 2x = -8x$	✗

$$4x^2 + 8x - 5 = (2x - 1)(2x + 5)$$

California Standard
Algebra 11.0

Example 4   ## Factor a Perfect Square and a Difference of Two Squares

Factor the polynomial.

a. Factor $9y^2 - 12y + 4$.

b. Factor $25a^2 - 36b^2$.

Solution

a.   **Perfect Square**   **b.**   **Difference of Two Squares**

$$a^2 \pm 2ab + b^2 = (a \pm b)^2$$ $$a^2 - b^2 = (a + b)(a - b)$$

$$9y^2 - 12y + 4 = (3y)^2 - 2(3 \cdot 2)y + 2^2$$ $$25a^2 - 36b^2 = (5a)^2 - (6b)^2$$

$$= (3y - 2)^2$$ $$= (5a + 6b)(5a - 6b)$$

Exercises

1. What is the factored form of $4x^3 - 2x^2 + 8x$?

(A) $x(4x^2 - 2x + 8)$

(B) $2x(2x^2 - x - 8)$

(C) $2x(x^2 - 4)(x + 1)$

(D) $2x(2x^2 - x + 4)$

2. Which of the following expresses $4(x - 2) - x(x - 2)$ as the product of two factors?

(A) $(x - 2)(4 - x)$

(B) $-8 + 6x - x^2$

(C) $x^2 - 6x + 8$

(D) $(x - 2)(x - 4)$

3. Which is a factor of $x^2 - 9$?

(A) $x + 6$

(B) $x - 3$

(C) $x - 9$

(D) $x^2 + 3$

4. Factor $4x^2 - 9$.

(A) $(x - 3)(2x + 3)$

(B) $(2x - 3)(2x + 3)$

(C) $(3x - 2)(3x + 2)$

(D) $(x - 2)(3x + 2)$

5. Which of the following shows $9x^4 + 24x^2y^2 + 16y^4$ factored completely?

(A) $(3x^2 + 4y^2)^2$

(B) $(3x^2 + 4y^2)(3x^2 - 4y^2)$

(C) $(3x^2 + y^2)(x^2 + 4y^2)$

(D) $9x^4 + 24x^2y^2 + 16y^4$

6. What is the factored form of $y^3 - 6y^2 - 4y + 24$?

(A) $(y - 4)(y - 2)$

(B) $(y + 2)(y + 4)$

(C) $(y + 2)(y + 4)(y - 2)$

(D) $(y - 2)(y + 2)(y - 6)$

7. What is the factored form of $8a^2 - 14ab + 3b^2$?

(A) $(2a + 3b)(4a - b)$

(B) $(8a - 2b)(a + 2b)$

(C) $(8a + 2b)(a - b)$

(D) $(2a - 3b)(4a - b)$

8. Which of the following is *not* a common factor for all terms of the polynomial $4x^3y^2 + 16x^5y^5 - 8x^4y^3$?

(A) $4xy$

(B) $4x^3y^2$

(C) x^5y^6

(D) x^3y

9. What is the factored form of $25x^2y^2 - 36a^2$?

  Ⓐ $(5x + 6a)^2$

  Ⓑ $(5xy - 6a)(5xy + 6a)$

  Ⓒ $(5xy - 6a)^2$

  Ⓓ $(5x^2y^2 - 6a)(5 + 6a)$

10. Which is *not* a factor of $3x^2 - 12$?

  Ⓐ $x + 2$ Ⓑ $x - 2$

  Ⓒ x Ⓓ 3

11. What is the factored form of $1 - 6x + 9x^2$?

  Ⓐ $(1 - 3x)(1 + 3x)$

  Ⓑ $(3x - 1)(3x + 1)$

  Ⓒ $(1 - 3x)^2$

  Ⓓ $(3x + 1)^2$

12. Which is a factor of $-4x^2 + 24x - 36$?

  Ⓐ $4x + 3$

  Ⓑ $4x - 3$

  Ⓒ $x + 3$

  Ⓓ $x - 3$

13. Which of the following shows $4a^2 - 8a - 12$ factored completely?

  Ⓐ $(a - 2)(4a - 12)$

  Ⓑ $4(a^2 - 2a - 3)$

  Ⓒ $4a(a - 2) - 12$

  Ⓓ $4(a + 1)(a - 3)$

14. Which of the following is the greatest common factor of $2x^6 + 4x^5 - 3x^4$?

  Ⓐ x^4 Ⓑ x^5

  Ⓒ $2x^4$ Ⓓ $2x^5$

15. Which of the following is a factor of $4a^2 - 9b^2$?

  Ⓐ $a - 3b$

  Ⓑ $2a - b$

  Ⓒ $3a - 3b$

  Ⓓ $2a - 3b$

16. Which of the following is a factor of $9x^2 - 30x + 25$?

  Ⓐ $3x + 5$ Ⓑ $3x - 5$

  Ⓒ $3x + 3$ Ⓓ $3x - 3$

17. What is the factored form of $8a^3b^2c^4 - 16a^5bc^7$?

  Ⓐ $8abc(a^2c^3 - a^4bc^6)$

  Ⓑ $8a^3bc^3(ab - 2ac)$

  Ⓒ $8a^2b^2c(ac^3 - a^3bc^6)$

  Ⓓ $8a^3bc^4(b - 2a^2c^3)$

18. Which of the following is a factor of $\frac{1}{4}x^2 + \frac{1}{3}xy + \frac{1}{9}y^2$?

  Ⓐ $\frac{1}{2}x + \frac{1}{3}y$ Ⓑ $\frac{1}{3}x - \frac{1}{2}y$

  Ⓒ $\frac{1}{2}x - \frac{1}{3}y$ Ⓓ $\frac{1}{3}x + \frac{1}{2}y$

19. Factor $x^3 - y^3$.

  Ⓐ $(x - y)^3$

  Ⓑ $3(x - y)^3$

  Ⓒ $(x + y)(x^2 - xy - y^2)$

  Ⓓ $(x - y)(x^2 + xy + y^2)$

20. Which gives the factor(s) for $8 - 12y + 6y^2 - y^3$?

  Ⓐ $2 - y, 2 + y$

  Ⓑ $2 - y, 2 + y$, and $3 - y$

  Ⓒ $2 + y$

  Ⓓ $2 - y$

21. What are two factors of $8a^3 - 27$?

  Ⓐ $2a - 3$ and $2a + 3$

  Ⓑ $2a - 3$ and $4a^2 + 6a + 9$

  Ⓒ $8a - 3$ and $a + 9$

  Ⓓ $8a + 3$ and $a - 9$

22. Which of the following is a factor of $x^3 - 2x^2 - 4x + 8$?

  Ⓐ $x - 1$

  Ⓑ $x + 1$

  Ⓒ $x - 2$

  Ⓓ $x + 3$

California Standards
Algebra 12.0

Students simplify fractions with polynomials in the numerator and denominator by factoring both and reducing them to the lowest terms.

Simplify Rational Expressions

Terms to Know	Example
A **rational expression** is an expression that can be written as a ratio of two polynomials where the denominator is not 0.	$\dfrac{x^2 - x - 2}{x^2 - 4}$ and $\dfrac{10}{4a^3 - b^3}$ are rational expressions.
A rational expression is in **lowest terms** if the numerator and denominator have no factors in common other than 1.	The rational expression $\dfrac{(x-2)(x+1)}{(x+4)x}$ is in lowest terms.

Example 1

Simplify an Expression by Dividing Out a Monomial

Simplify. $\dfrac{4x^4 + 2x^3 - 2x^2}{8x^3 - 12x^2 + 4x}$

Solution

$$\dfrac{4x^4 + 2x^3 - 2x^2}{8x^3 - 12x^2 + 4x} = \dfrac{2x^2(2x^2 + x - 1)}{4x\,(2x^2 - 3x + 1)}$$ Factor out monomials.

$$= \dfrac{2x^2(2x - 1)(x + 1)}{4x\,(2x - 1)(x - 1)}$$ Factor numerator and denominator.

$$= \dfrac{x(x + 1)}{2(x - 1)}$$ Divide out common factors and simplify.

Example 2

Simplify a Rational Expression

Simplify $\dfrac{2x^2 - 7x - 15}{x^2 - 25}$ to lowest terms.

Solution

$$\dfrac{2x^2 - 7x - 15}{x^2 - 25} = \dfrac{(2x + 3)(x - 5)}{(x + 5)(x - 5)}$$ Factor numerator and denominator.

$$= \dfrac{(2x + 3)(x - 5)}{(x + 5)(x - 5)}$$ Divide out common factors.

$$= \dfrac{(2x + 3)}{(x + 5)}$$ Simplify.

Name _____   Date _____

Exercises

1. Simplify $\dfrac{x^2 + x}{x^2 - x - 2}$ to lowest terms.

   Ⓐ $\dfrac{1}{x - 2}$ Ⓑ $\dfrac{x}{x - 2}$

   Ⓒ $\dfrac{1}{x(x + 1)}$ Ⓓ $\dfrac{x}{x + 1}$

2. What is $\dfrac{4a^2 - 9b^2}{2a - 3b}$ reduced to lowest terms?

   Ⓐ 0 Ⓑ 1

   Ⓒ $2a - 3b$ Ⓓ $2a + 3b$

3. Simplify $\dfrac{y^3}{12y^4 + 26y^3 - 10y^2}$ to lowest terms.

   Ⓐ $\dfrac{2y}{(3y - 1)(2y + 5)}$ Ⓑ $\dfrac{y}{(3y - 1)(2y + 5)}$

   Ⓒ $\dfrac{1}{2(3y - 1)(2y + 5)}$ Ⓓ $\dfrac{y}{2(3y - 1)(2y + 5)}$

4. Simplify $\dfrac{9x^2 - 6x + 1}{1 - 6x + 9x^2}$.

   Ⓐ $3x - 1$ Ⓑ 1

   Ⓒ -1 Ⓓ $(3x - 1)^2$

5. Which of the following rational expressions is reduced to lowest terms?

   Ⓐ $\dfrac{4y^2 - 9x^2}{4y^2 - 6xy}$ Ⓑ $\dfrac{x}{x^3 - 2x^2 + x}$

   Ⓒ $\dfrac{x}{x^2 - 2x + 1}$ Ⓓ $\dfrac{a^2 + b^2}{3a^3 + 3ab^2}$

6. Simplify $\dfrac{x - 4}{x^2 - 2x - 8}$.

   Ⓐ $\dfrac{1}{x - 2}$ Ⓑ $\dfrac{1}{x + 4}$

   Ⓒ $\dfrac{1}{x + 2}$ Ⓓ 0

7. What is $\dfrac{ab^2c^3}{a^3bc - ab^3c}$ reduced to lowest terms?

   Ⓐ $\dfrac{c^2}{ab(a - b)(a + b)}$ Ⓑ $\dfrac{abc}{(a - b)(a + b)}$

   Ⓒ $\dfrac{bc^2}{(a - b)(a + b)}$ Ⓓ $\dfrac{a}{bc\,(a - b)(a + b)}$

8. What is $\dfrac{(x - 1)^2(1 - x)^5}{(1 - x)^3(x - 1)^4}$ reduced to lowest terms?

   Ⓐ $\dfrac{(1 - x)^7}{(x - 1)^7}$ Ⓑ -1

   Ⓒ 1 Ⓓ $\dfrac{(1 - x)^2}{(x - 1)^2}$

9. Simplify $\dfrac{2500a^2 - 3600b^2}{25a^2 - 36b^2}$ to lowest terms.

   Ⓐ 100 Ⓑ $100a^2 - 100b^2$

   Ⓒ $10a^2 - 10b^2$ Ⓓ $10(a - b)$

10. What is $\dfrac{2x^2 + x - 1}{4x^2 - 4x + 1}$ reduced to lowest terms?

   Ⓐ $\dfrac{2x - 1}{x + 1}$ Ⓑ $\dfrac{x + 1}{2x - 1}$

   Ⓒ 0 Ⓓ $\dfrac{x + 1}{(2x - 1)^3}$

11. Simplify $\dfrac{a^2 - b^2}{(a + b)^2}$.

   Ⓐ $a - b$ Ⓑ $\dfrac{a - b}{a + b}$

   Ⓒ $\dfrac{a + b}{a - b}$ Ⓓ $a + b$

12. What is $\dfrac{\frac{1}{4}x - \frac{1}{2}y}{\frac{1}{16}x^2 - \frac{1}{4}xy + \frac{1}{4}y^2}$ reduced to lowest terms?

   Ⓐ $\dfrac{1}{4}x - \dfrac{1}{2}y$ Ⓑ $\dfrac{1}{4}x + \dfrac{1}{2}y$

   Ⓒ $\dfrac{4}{x + 2y}$ Ⓓ $\dfrac{4}{x - 2y}$

13. Two rectangles have areas given by the polynomials $x^2 - x$ and $x^2 + 3x - 4$. What is the ratio of the areas of the rectangles reduced to lowest terms?

   Ⓐ $\dfrac{x - 1}{x + 4}$ Ⓑ $\dfrac{x}{x + 4}$

   Ⓒ $\dfrac{x}{x - 1}$ Ⓓ $\dfrac{1}{(x - 1)(x + 4)}$

14. What is $\dfrac{x^3 - 3x^2 + 3x - 1}{x^2 + x - 2}$ reduced to lowest terms?

   Ⓐ $\dfrac{x - 1}{x + 2}$ Ⓑ $\dfrac{x - 1}{(x + 2)^2}$

   Ⓒ $\dfrac{(x - 1)^3}{(x - 2)^2}$ Ⓓ $\dfrac{(x - 1)^2}{x + 2}$

15. The steps to reducing $\dfrac{2x^2 - x - 1}{x^2 + 2x + 1}$ to lowest terms are shown below.

Step 1: $\dfrac{2x^2 - x - 1}{x^2 + 2x + 1} = \dfrac{(2x - 3)(x + 1)}{x^2 + 2x + 1}$

Step 2: $= \dfrac{(2x - 3)(x + 1)}{(x + 1)(x + 1)}$

Step 3: $= \dfrac{(2x - 3)}{(x + 1)}$

Which is the first incorrect step?

   Ⓐ Step 1   Ⓑ Step 2

   Ⓒ Step 3   Ⓓ All steps are correct.

California Standards
Algebra 13.0

Students add, subtract, multiply, and divide rational expressions and functions. Students solve both computationally and conceptually challenging problems by using these techniques.

Operations With Rational Expressions

The **least common denominator (LCD)** of two or more rational expressions is the same as the least common multiple of the denominators of the rational expressions. You can add and subtract rational expressions by finding the LCD.

Example 1

Add and Subtract Rational Expressions

Find the sum or difference.

a. $\dfrac{3}{2x^2} + \dfrac{4}{3x^4}$

b. $\dfrac{2x-1}{x^2+2x-3} - \dfrac{x-5}{x^2+x-6}$

Solution

a. $\dfrac{3}{2x^2} + \dfrac{4}{3x^4} = \dfrac{3 \cdot 3x^2}{2x^2 \cdot 3x^2} + \dfrac{4 \cdot 2}{3x^4 \cdot 2}$ **Rewrite each fraction using the LCD, $6x^4$.**

$= \dfrac{9x^2}{6x^4} + \dfrac{8}{6x^4}$ **Simplify numerators and denominators.**

$= \dfrac{9x^2 + 8}{6x^4}$ **Simplify numerator.**

b. $\dfrac{2x-1}{x^2+2x-3} - \dfrac{x-5}{x^2+x-6}$

$= \dfrac{2x-1}{(x-1)(x+3)} - \dfrac{x-5}{(x+3)(x-2)}$ **Factor denominators.**

$= \dfrac{(2x-1)(x-2)}{(x-1)(x-2)(x+3)} - \dfrac{(x-5)(x-1)}{(x-1)(x-2)(x+3)}$ **Rewrite fractions using the LCD, $(x-1)(x-2)(x+3)$.**

$= \dfrac{(2x-1)(x-2) - (x-5)(x-1)}{(x-1)(x-2)(x+3)}$ **Combine fractions.**

$= \dfrac{(2x^2 - 5x + 2) - (x^2 - 6x + 5)}{(x-1)(x-2)(x+3)}$ **Find products in numerator.**

$= \dfrac{x^2 + x - 3}{(x-1)(x-2)(x+3)}$ **Simplify.**

Example 2   ## Divide Rational Expressions

Find the quotient. $\dfrac{2x^2 + 6x}{x^2 + 4x - 5} \div \dfrac{4x^3 + 12x^2}{x^2 + 3x - 10}$

Solution

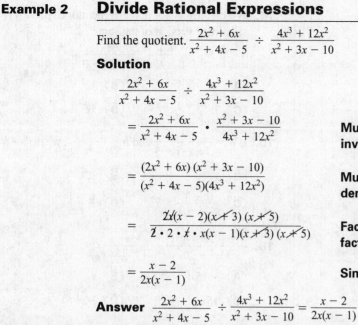

$$\dfrac{2x^2 + 6x}{x^2 + 4x - 5} \div \dfrac{4x^3 + 12x^2}{x^2 + 3x - 10}$$

$$= \dfrac{2x^2 + 6x}{x^2 + 4x - 5} \cdot \dfrac{x^2 + 3x - 10}{4x^3 + 12x^2}$$ **Multiply by the multiplicative inverse.**

$$= \dfrac{(2x^2 + 6x)\,(x^2 + 3x - 10)}{(x^2 + 4x - 5)(4x^3 + 12x^2)}$$ **Multiply numerators and denominators.**

$$= \dfrac{2x(x - 2)(x + 3)\,(x + 5)}{2 \cdot 2 \cdot x \cdot x(x - 1)(x + 3)\,(x + 5)}$$ **Factor and divide out common factors.**

$$= \dfrac{x - 2}{2x(x - 1)}$$ **Simplify.**

Answer $\dfrac{2x^2 + 6x}{x^2 + 4x - 5} \div \dfrac{4x^3 + 12x^2}{x^2 + 3x - 10} = \dfrac{x - 2}{2x(x - 1)}$

Exercises

1. Which of the following rational expressions is equivalent to $\dfrac{4}{x + 1} + \dfrac{2x - 1}{x}$?

   (A) $\dfrac{2x^2 + 12x + 1}{x^2 + x}$

   (B) $\dfrac{2x^2 + 5x - 1}{x^2 + x}$

   (C) $\dfrac{2x^2 + 5x}{x^2 + x}$

   (D) $\dfrac{2x^2 + 5x + 1}{x^2 + 1}$

2. Solve for x. $\dfrac{1}{2} + \dfrac{3}{x - 2} = \dfrac{3}{2}$

   (A) -5 (B) 3 (C) 5 (D) 7

3. Which fraction equals the product?

$$\dfrac{x^2 - 1}{x^2 + 2x} \cdot \dfrac{x^2 - x - 6}{x^2 - 2x - 3}$$

   (A) $\dfrac{x + 2}{x - 1}$ (B) $\dfrac{2x + 1}{x}$

   (C) $\dfrac{x - 1}{x + 1}$ (D) $\dfrac{x - 1}{x}$

4. $\dfrac{x^2 - 4}{x - 1} \div \dfrac{x + 2}{x^2 - 2x + 1} =$

   (A) $x - 1$ (B) $(x - 1)(x - 2)$

   (C) $\dfrac{x - 1}{x - 2}$ (D) $x - 2$

5. $\dfrac{4}{x} + \dfrac{2 - x}{x + 2} =$

   (A) $\dfrac{x^2 + 6x + 8}{x^2 + 2x}$

   (B) $\dfrac{-x^2 + 6x + 8}{x^2 + 2x}$

   (C) $\dfrac{x^2 + 6x}{x^2 + 2x}$

   (D) $\dfrac{-x^2 + 6x}{x^2 + 2x}$

6. $\dfrac{2x - 5}{x + 1} - \dfrac{x - 3}{3x + 1} =$

   (A) $\dfrac{5x^2 - 19x - 2}{3x^2 + 4x + 1}$

   (B) $\dfrac{6x^2 - 9x + 8}{3x^2 + 4x + 1}$

   (C) $\dfrac{5x^2 - 11x - 2}{3x^2 + 4x + 1}$

   (D) $\dfrac{5x^2 - 9x - 8}{x^2 + 4x + 1}$

7. Which fraction equals the product $\left(\dfrac{2}{3}\right) \cdot \left(\dfrac{1}{x} + \dfrac{1}{y}\right)$?

   (A) $\dfrac{4x - 4y}{3xy}$

   (B) $\dfrac{x + y}{6xy}$

   (C) $\dfrac{2x + 2y}{3xy}$

   (D) $\dfrac{2x - 2y}{3xy}$

8. $\dfrac{3 + 2x - x^2}{4x} \div \dfrac{x^2 - 2x - 3}{-2x^3} =$

Ⓐ $-\dfrac{x^2}{2}$ Ⓑ $-\dfrac{2x^2}{3}$

Ⓒ $\dfrac{x^2}{2}$ Ⓓ $\dfrac{2x^2}{x - 3}$

9. $\dfrac{2x + 1}{x - 5} + \dfrac{x + 5}{2x - 1} =$

Ⓐ $\dfrac{26 - 5x^2}{2x^2 - 11x + 5}$

Ⓑ $\dfrac{4x^2 - 25}{2x^2 - 11x + 5}$

Ⓒ $\dfrac{x^2 - 25}{2x^2 - 10x + 5}$

Ⓓ $\dfrac{5x^2 - 26}{2x^2 - 11x + 5}$

10. $\dfrac{x - 3}{x + 3} - \dfrac{2x}{3 - x} =$

Ⓐ $\dfrac{9 - 3x^2}{9 - x^2}$

Ⓑ $\dfrac{3x^2 - 9}{x^2 - 9}$

Ⓒ $\dfrac{3x^2 + 9}{x^2 - 9}$

Ⓓ $\dfrac{3x^2 - 9}{9 - x^2}$

11. Simplify $\dfrac{a + b}{a^2 - ab} \cdot \dfrac{3a^4 - 2a^3b - a^2b^2}{3a^2 + 4ab + b^2}$.

Ⓐ $(a - b)$

Ⓑ $a(a - b)$

Ⓒ a

Ⓓ $a(3a + b)$

12. Solve for x. $\dfrac{1}{4} + \dfrac{1}{x + 3} = \dfrac{5}{12}$

Ⓐ -1 Ⓑ 3

Ⓒ 4 Ⓓ 9

13. $\dfrac{x - 3}{4 - x^2} \cdot \dfrac{2x + 4}{3x - x^2} =$

Ⓐ $\dfrac{2}{2 - x^2}$

Ⓑ $\dfrac{2(x - 3)}{3 - x}$

Ⓒ $\dfrac{2(x - 3)}{x(2 - x)}$

Ⓓ $-\dfrac{2}{x(2 - x)}$

14. Which term is *not* in the numerator of the simplified version of the sum?

$$\dfrac{x + 1}{x - 3} + \dfrac{2x^2 + 5x + 2}{x^2 - 2x - 3}$$

Ⓐ $7x$ Ⓑ $3x^2$

Ⓒ 3 Ⓓ $5x$

15. If $a = \dfrac{x + 1}{2x^2 - x - 3}$ and $b = \dfrac{2x - 3}{x}$, what is $a \cdot b$?

Ⓐ $\dfrac{1}{x}$ Ⓑ $\dfrac{1}{2x - 3}$

Ⓒ $\dfrac{x + 1}{x(2x - 3)}$ Ⓓ $\dfrac{x + 1}{x}$

16. $\dfrac{41x - 28 - 15x^2}{15x^2 - 20x} \cdot \dfrac{15x^2}{21 - 15x} =$

Ⓐ $-15x^2$ Ⓑ x

Ⓒ $15x$ Ⓓ $-x^2$

17. Which of the following is equivalent to the fraction?

$$\dfrac{4x^2 - 81y^2}{8x^3 - 36x^2y}$$

Ⓐ $\dfrac{1}{4x^2}$ Ⓑ $\dfrac{2x - 9y}{4x^2}$

Ⓒ $\dfrac{2x + 9y}{4x^2}$ Ⓓ $-\dfrac{1}{4x^2}$

18. $\dfrac{x^2 - 9}{25 - 4x^2} \cdot \dfrac{5 + 3x - 2x^2}{x^2 - 3x} =$

Ⓐ $\dfrac{(x + 1)(x + 3)}{x(2x + 5)}$

Ⓑ $\dfrac{(x + 1)(x - 3)}{x(2x + 5)}$

Ⓒ $\dfrac{(x + 1)(x + 3)}{x(5 - 2x)}$

Ⓓ $\dfrac{x - 3}{x(2x + 5)}$

19. Which fraction equals the product?

$$(x^2 - 6x - 7) \cdot \dfrac{1}{21 + 4x - x^2}$$

Ⓐ $\dfrac{x + 1}{x + 3}$

Ⓑ $-\dfrac{x + 1}{x + 3}$

Ⓒ $\dfrac{x + 1}{x - 3}$

Ⓓ $-\dfrac{1 - x}{x + 3}$

California Standards
Algebra 14.0

Students solve a quadratic equation by factoring or completing the square.

Solve Quadratic Equations

Terms to Know	Example
A **quadratic equation** is an equation that can be written in the standard form $ax^2 + bx + c = 0$, where $a \neq 0$.	The equations $3y^2 = 5$ and $4t^2 + 2t = 11$ are quadratic equations.

For any real numbers a and b, if $ab = 0$, then $a = 0$, or $b = 0$. This is called the **zero-product property**. The zero-product property is used to solve an equation when one side is zero and the other side is a product of polynomial factors.

Example 1   ## Solve by Factoring

Solve by factoring.

a. $3y^2 = -27y$ **b.** $4n^2 + 19n = 5$ **c.** $36x^2 - 48x + 16 = 0$

Solution

a.
$3y^2 = -27y$	Write the original equation.
$3y^2 + 27y = 0$	Add $27y$ to each side.
$3y(y + 9) = 0$	Factor the left side.
$3y = 0 \; or \; y + 9 = 0$	Zero-product property
$y = 0 \; or \; y = -9$	Solve for y.

b.
$4n^2 + 19n = 5$	Write the equation.
$4n^2 + 19n - 5 = 0$	Add -5 to each side.
$(4n - 1)(n + 5) = 0$	Factor the left side.
$4n - 1 = 0 \; or \; n + 5 = 0$	Zero-product property
$n = \frac{1}{4} \; or \; n = -5$	Solve for n.

c.
$36x^2 - 48x + 16 = 0$	Write the equation.
$4(9x^2 - 12x + 4) = 0$	Factor out 4.
$9x^2 - 12x + 4 = 0$	Divide both sides by 4.
$(3x - 2)(3x - 2) = 0$	Factor and rewrite the left side.
$3x - 2 = 0 \; or \; 3x - 2 = 0$	Zero-product property
$x = \frac{2}{3}$	Because both factors are the same, solve one of them for x.

Example 2   ## Solve by Completing the Square

Solve $2a^2 - 6a + 2 = 0$ by completing the square.

Solution

$2a^2 - 6a + 2 = 0$	**Write the equation.**
$2a^2 - 6a = -2$	**Subtract 2 from each side.**
$a^2 - 3a = -1$	**Divide each side by 2.**
$a^2 - 3a + \left(-\frac{3}{2}\right)^2 = -1 + \left(-\frac{3}{2}\right)^2$	**Add $\left(-\frac{3}{2}\right)^2$, or $\frac{9}{4}$, to each side.**
$\left(a - \frac{3}{2}\right)^2 = -\frac{4}{4} + \frac{9}{4}$	**Write the left side as a square; simplify the right side.**
$a - \frac{3}{2} = \pm\sqrt{\frac{5}{4}}$	**Take the square root of each side.**
$a = \frac{3}{2} \pm \frac{\sqrt{5}}{2}$	**Add $\frac{3}{2}$ to each side.**

Answer The solutions are $\frac{3}{2} + \frac{\sqrt{5}}{2}$ and $\frac{3}{2} - \frac{\sqrt{5}}{2}$.

Exercises

1. What quantity should be added to both sides of the equation $x^2 - 8x = -6$ to complete the square?

   (A) 4   (B) 16   (C) 8   (D) 6

2. Solve $3 + 5x - 2x^2 = 0$ by factoring.

   (A) $x = -\frac{1}{2}$ or $x = 3$

   (B) $x = \frac{1}{2}$ or $x = 3$

   (C) $x = -\frac{1}{2}$ or $x = -3$

   (D) $x = \frac{1}{2}$ or $x = -3$

3. What is the first step to take in completing the square of $2x^2 - 8x = 4$?

   (A) Take one-half of -8.

   (B) Divide each side by 2.

   (C) Add -8 to each side.

   (D) Divide each side by 4.

4. If $4x$ is subtracted from x^2, the difference is 12. Which of the following could be the value of x?

   (A) 2   (B) 4   (C) -6 (D) -2

5. Supply the missing term to complete the square.

$$x^2 - \frac{1}{4}x + \underline{\ ?\ } = \frac{1}{2} + \underline{\ ?\ }$$

   (A) $\frac{1}{4}$ (B) $\frac{1}{8}$ (C) $\frac{1}{64}$ (D) $\frac{1}{16}$

6. What is the solution set of $4x^2 - 25 = 0$?

   (A) $\left\{-\frac{2}{5}, \frac{2}{5}\right\}$ (B) $\{-2, 5\}$

   (C) $\left\{-\frac{5}{2}, \frac{5}{2}\right\}$ (D) $\{2, -5\}$

7. If x^3 is added to $(-x^2 - 2x)$, the sum is 0. Which of the following is *not* a value for x?

   (A) 0   (B) 2   (C) -1 (D) -2

8. Solve $2x^2 + 8x = -8$ by completing the square.

   (A) $x = \pm 2$

   (B) $x = 4$

   (C) $x = 0$ or 2

   (D) $x = -2$

9. Solve $x^3 + x^2 - 2x = 0$ by factoring.

   (A) $x = -2$ or $x = 1$

   (B) $x = -2, x = 0$, or $x = 1$

   (C) $x = 2, x = 0$, or $x = -1$

   (D) $x = 2$ or $x = -1$

10. What value should the coefficient of x be to make the left side of the equation below a perfect square?

$$x^2 + \underline{\ ?\ }x + 81 = 93$$

   (A) 3   (B) -18 (C) -9 (D) 12

11. Which of the following quadratic equations has the solutions $x = 2 \pm 6$?

(A) $x^2 - 4x = 16$

(B) $x^2 - 4x - 32 = 0$

(C) $x^2 - 4x = -32$

(D) $x^2 - 4x + 16 = 0$

12. Where does the graph of $\dfrac{x^3 + 5x^2 - 14x}{x + 3}$ intersect the x-axis?

(A) $x = -3$

(B) $x = 3$

(C) $x = 0, x = 2, x = -7$

(D) $x = 0, x = -2, x = 7$

13. Which quantity should be added to both sides of the equation to complete the square?

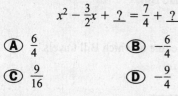

(A) $\dfrac{6}{4}$

(B) $-\dfrac{6}{4}$

(C) $\dfrac{9}{16}$

(D) $-\dfrac{9}{4}$

14. Which is the first *incorrect* step in completing the square of $9a^2 - 6a - 3 = 0$?

(A) **Step 1:** $9a^2 - 6a = 3$

(B) **Step 2:** $9a^2 - 6a + 9 = 3 + 9$

(C) **Step 3:** $9a^2 - 6a + 9 = 12$

(D) **Step 4:** $(3a + 3)^2 = 9$

15. What are the solutions of the quadratic equation $x^2 - 4x + 2 = -5$?

(A) $-3, 1$

(B) $3, -3$

(C) no solution

(D) $0, 3$

16. If x^2 is added to $4x$, the sum is 5. Which of the following is a possible value for x?

(A) 11   (B) -1 (C) -5 (D) -7

17. Ani solves the quadratic equation $x^2 + \dfrac{1}{3}x = 0$ by completing the square. Which choice below could be Step 2?

Step 1: $x^2 + \dfrac{1}{3}x + \dfrac{1}{36} = \dfrac{1}{36}$

Step 2: ?

(A) $x + \dfrac{1}{3} = \dfrac{1}{18}$

(B) $\left(x + \dfrac{1}{6}\right)^2 = \dfrac{1}{36}$

(C) $x + \dfrac{1}{6} = \pm\dfrac{1}{36}$

(D) $\left(x + \dfrac{1}{6}\right)^2 = \dfrac{1}{6}$

18. What are the solutions for the quadratic equation $15x^2 = 2x + 8$?

(A) $\dfrac{4}{5}, \dfrac{2}{3}$

(B) $-\dfrac{2}{3}, -\dfrac{4}{3}$

(C) $\dfrac{4}{5}, -\dfrac{2}{3}$

(D) $-\dfrac{4}{5}, \dfrac{2}{3}$

19. Which term can be added to each side of the quadratic equation $x^2 + Ax = 0$ to complete the square?

(A) $\dfrac{1}{2}A$

(B) $\dfrac{1}{4}A^2$

(C) $\dfrac{1}{2}A^2$

(D) $\dfrac{1}{4}A$

20. Solve for x. $\dfrac{x^2 - 9}{x + 3} = \dfrac{20}{x + 5}$

(A) $x = -7$ or $x = 5$

(B) $x = -37$ or $x = 35$

(C) $x = 37$ or $x = -35$

(D) $x = 7$ or $x = -5$

California Standards
Algebra 15.0

Students apply algebraic techniques to solve rate problems, work problems, and percent mixture problems.

Rate, Work, and Percent Mixture Problems

Example 1   ## Solve a Rate Problem

CYCLING Two cyclists, Jane and Bill, leave a ranger station at the same time and cycle in opposite directions. Jane travels 5 kilometers per hour faster than Bill. After two hours, they are 50 kilometers apart. What is Jane's speed?

Solution

STEP 1 Identify relationships.

Time: The cyclists ride for two hours.

Distance: The cyclists are 50 kilometers apart after two hours.

Rate: Jane travels 5 kilometers per hour faster than Bill.

STEP 2 Write a linear system.

Let d be the distance Jane travels, and let r be the rate at which Bill travels.

Equation 1: Distance Jane travels

$$\boxed{\text{Jane's distance}} = \boxed{\text{Jane's rate}} \cdot \boxed{\text{Jane's time}}$$

$$d \quad = \quad (r+5) \quad \cdot \quad 2$$

Equation 2: Distance Bill travels

$$\boxed{\text{Bill's distance}} = \boxed{\text{Bill's rate}} \cdot \boxed{\text{Bill's time}}$$

$$50 - d \quad = \quad r \quad \cdot \quad 2$$

The system of equations is $d = 2r + 10$

$$50 - d = 2r.$$

STEP 3 Solve the system of equations to find Jane's rate.

$$d = 2r + 10 \qquad \textbf{Write Equation 1.}$$

$$50 - d = 2r \qquad \textbf{Write Equation 2.}$$

$$50 = 4r + 10 \qquad \textbf{Add equations to eliminate } d.$$

$$r = 10 \qquad \textbf{Solve for } r.$$

Substitute 10 for r in the expression for Jane's rate, $r + 5$.

$$r + 5 = 10 + 5 = 15$$

Answer Jane traveled at a rate of 15 kilometers per hour.

Example 2   ## Solve a Work Problem

PAINTING Andre can paint a wall in 30 minutes. It takes Colin 45 minutes to do the same job. How long would it take them to paint the wall together?

Solution

STEP 1 Find the work rates for Andre and Colin.

Because Andre can do the entire job in 30 minutes, his rate is $\frac{1}{30}$ job per minute.

Colin's work rate is $\frac{1}{45}$ job per minute.

STEP 2 Find the part of the job done by each person.

Let t be the time (in minutes) they take to complete the job together.

Andre's work done: $\frac{1}{30} \cdot t = \frac{t}{30}$

Colin's work done: $\frac{1}{45} \cdot t = \frac{t}{45}$

STEP 3 Write an equation for the total work done. Then solve the equation.
The parts of the job found in Step 2 must add up to 1 whole job.

$\frac{t}{30} + \frac{t}{45} = 1$ **Write equation.**

$3t + 2t = 90$ **Multiply each side by LCD, 90.**

$t = 18$ **Solve for t.**

Answer It will take Andre and Colin 18 minutes to paint the wall together.

Example 3   ## Solve a Percent Mixture Problem

AGRICULTURE Selena and Suki picked tangerines in their family orchard. One percent of Selena's fruit was ripe, and 3.5 percent of Suki's fruit was ripe. Together they picked 50 baskets of fruit, and 2.5 percent of the fruit was ripe. How many baskets of fruit did Selena pick?

Solution

STEP 1 Write an equation for how much fruit Selena and Suki picked.

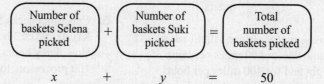

Number of baskets Selena picked	+	Number of baskets Suki picked	=	Total number of baskets picked
x	+	y	=	50

STEP 2 Write an equation for how much ripe fruit Selena and Suki picked.

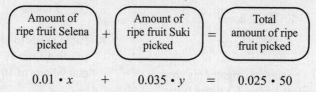

Amount of ripe fruit Selena picked	+	Amount of ripe fruit Suki picked	=	Total amount of ripe fruit picked
$0.01 \cdot x$	+	$0.035 \cdot y$	=	$0.025 \cdot 50$

STEP 3 Solve the system of linear equations.

$$x + y = 50$$ **Write the equation from Step 1.**

$$0.01x + 0.035y = 1.25$$ **Write the equation from Step 2.**

$$0.01x + 0.01y = 0.5$$ **Multiply the equation from Step 1 by 0.01.**

$$\underline{0.01x + 0.035y = 1.25}$$ **Write the equation from Step 2.**

$$-0.025y = -0.75$$ **Subtract the equations.**

$$y = 30$$ **Solve for y.**

Substitute 30 for y in $x + y = 50$ and solve for x.

$$x + 30 = 50$$

$$x = 20$$

Answer Selena picked 20 baskets of fruit.

Exercises

1. Butch can assemble 6 patio tables per hour. Jose can assemble 4 patio tables per hour. How many hours will it take them working together to assemble 60 tables?

   (A) 3 hours   **(B)** 4 hours

   (C) 6 hours   **(D)** 7 hours

2. How much 5% maple syrup and water mixture must be added to 100% pure maple syrup to produce 5 quarts of syrup that is 10% maple syrup?

   (A) $3\frac{1}{7}$ quarts   **(B)** $4\frac{14}{19}$ quarts

   (C) $4\frac{2}{7}$ quarts   **(D)** $5\frac{15}{19}$ quarts

3. A 3,000-mile cross-country airplane flight takes 7 hours. If the plane flies at 500 miles per hour for part of the flight and for 400 miles per hour for the rest of the flight, how many hours does the airplane fly at the faster speed?

   (A) 4 hours   **(B)** 2 hours

   (C) 5 hours   **(D)** 3 hours

4. Oscar wants to fill a pond that irrigates his crops. One water source fills the pond 1.5 times faster than a second source. When both sources are used together, the pond is filled in 6 hours. Which equation describes how fast both sources can fill the pond together?

   (A) $\frac{1}{r} + \frac{2}{3r} = \frac{1}{6}$ **(B)** $\frac{1}{r} - \frac{3}{2r} = \frac{1}{6}$

   (C) $6 = 1.5r + r$ **(D)** $6 = r + \frac{1}{2}r$

5. The Oxnard Juice Works makes a mango fruit drink from two types of mangoes. One type costs $3.50 per gallon and the other costs $4.25 per gallon. How many gallons of each are needed to make 100 gallons of juice that cost $4.00 per gallon?

   (A) 25 gallons of $3.50 juice and 75 gallons of $4.25 juice.

   (B) 40 gallons of $3.50 juice and 60 gallons of $4.25 juice.

   (C) $33\frac{1}{3}$ gallons of $3.50 juice and $66\frac{2}{3}$ gallons of $4.25 juice.

   (D) 50 gallons of each type of juice.

6. Calandra checks 50 processors in 2 hours. Krystal takes 3 hours to check 45 processors. How many hours will it take for them to check 100 processors together?

   (A) 2.5 hours   **(B)** 3.5 hours

   (C) 5 hours   **(D)** 2 hours

7. Pablo needs to produce 10 liters of a 15% solution from 10% and 25% solutions. How many liters of 10% solution does he need?

   (A) $6\frac{2}{3}$ L   **(B)** 5 L

   (C) $3\frac{1}{3}$ L   **(D)** 1 L

Name _____   Date _____

California Standards
Algebra 16.0

Students understand the concepts of a relation and a function, determine whether a given relation defines a function, and give pertinent information about given relations and functions.

Relations and Functions

Terms to Know	Example
A **relation** is any pairing of a set of inputs with a set of outputs.	The pairing in the table below is a *relation*, but it is not a function.

Input	1	2	2	3	5
Output	0	3	5	6	7

Terms to Know	Example
A **function** is: • a pairing of inputs with outputs such that each input is paired with exactly one output. • a set called the *domain* containing numbers called inputs, and a set called the *range* containing numbers called outputs.	The pairing in the table below is a *function*, because each input is paired with exactly one output.

Input	1	2	3	4	5
Output	3	5	6	8	9

The *domain* is the set of inputs: 1, 2, 3, 4, and 5.
The *range* is the set of outputs: 3, 5, 6, 8, and 9.

Example

Determine Whether a Relation is a Function

Which of the following relations is a function?

Ⓐ $\{(-5, 5), (0, 3), (0, -5), (5, 4)\}$ Ⓑ $\{(3, 4), (3, 5), (3, 6), (3, 7)\}$

Ⓒ $\{(-2, 1), (0, 1), (2, 5), (4, 5)\}$ Ⓓ $\{(3, 2), (5, 4), (5, 6), (7, 8)\}$

Solution

A relation is a function if each domain element is paired with exactly one range element.

In choice A, 0 is paired with 3 and -5. In choice B, 3 is paired with 4, 5, 6, and 7. In choice D, 5 is paired with 4 and 6. Choices A, B, and D are not functions.

In choice C, each domain element is paired with exactly one range element.

Answer Choice C is the only relation that is a function.

Exercises

1. When the input is 0, what is the output?

$\{(-5, 0), (1, -3), (1, 0), (0, -3)\}$

Ⓐ -5 Ⓑ -3

Ⓒ 0   Ⓓ -5 or 1

2. Which of the following is *not* in the range of the set?

$\{(5, -3), (-3, 6), (6, -3), (6, -8)\}$

Ⓐ -8 Ⓑ -3 Ⓒ 5   Ⓓ 6

California Standard
Algebra 16.0

3. Which of the following statements about a relation is *not always* true?

    Ⓐ It has a domain.

    Ⓑ It has a range.

    Ⓒ Elements in the domain are paired with elements in the range.

    Ⓓ Each element in the domain is paired with exactly one element in the range.

4. Which statement below correctly justifies whether the table below represents a function?

Input	5	−3	6	−3	6
Output	−1	6	−5	5	−8

    Ⓐ Yes, because each output occurs exactly once.

    Ⓑ No, because each output occurs exactly once.

    Ⓒ Yes, because exactly one input is repeated.

    Ⓓ No, because one input is paired with two outputs.

5. Which of the following is *not* in the domain of the set?

$$\{(8, -4), (1, 1), (-2, 8), (0, 0)\}$$

    Ⓐ −4   Ⓑ −2   Ⓒ 0   Ⓓ 1 and 0

6. Which of the following statements is *true*?

    Ⓐ Any set of ordered pairs is a relation.

    Ⓑ Any set of ordered pairs is a function.

    Ⓒ Any set of ordered pairs is both a relation and a function.

    Ⓓ No set of ordered pairs can be both a relation and a function.

7. When the input is 6, what is the output?

$$\{(5, -1), (-3, 6), (6, -5), (6, -8)\}$$

    Ⓐ 5   Ⓑ −5 or −3

    Ⓒ −3   Ⓓ −8 or −5

8. Which of following is *not* in the domain of the set?

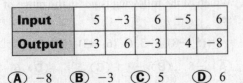

Input	5	−3	6	−5	6
Output	−3	6	−3	4	−8

    Ⓐ −8 Ⓑ −3 Ⓒ 5   Ⓓ 6

9. Which statement about functions is *true*?

    Ⓐ Every element in the range is paired with exactly one element in the domain.

    Ⓑ Every function is a relation.

    Ⓒ Any set of ordered pairs is a function.

    Ⓓ The set of outputs is called the domain.

10. Which of the following represents the relationship between functions and relations?

    Ⓐ A function is a relation if every element in the domain is paired with at least one element in the range.

    Ⓑ A function is a relation if every element in the range is paired with exactly one element in the domain.

    Ⓒ A relation is a function if every element in the domain is paired with exactly one element in the range.

    Ⓓ A relation is a function if every element in the range is paired with at least one element in the domain.

11. Which of the following is *not* in the range of the set?

$$\{(8, -4), (1, 1), (-2, 8), (0, 0)\}$$

    Ⓐ −4   Ⓑ −2   Ⓒ 0   Ⓓ 1 and 0

12. Which statement about relations is *false*?

    Ⓐ The set of inputs is called the range.

    Ⓑ A relation pairs elements in different sets.

    Ⓒ Some relations are functions.

    Ⓓ A relation can be represented by a single ordered pair.

13. Which statement below correctly justifies whether or not the table below represents a function?

Input	8	−9	2	−2	1	0
Output	−4	1	−2	1	0	0

    Ⓐ Yes, because each input occurs exactly once.

    Ⓑ Yes, because each ordered pair occurs once.

    Ⓒ No, because one output is repeated.

    Ⓓ No, because one input and output are the same.

Name _____   Date _____

California Standards
Algebra 17.0

Students determine the domain of independent variables and
the range of dependent variables defined by a graph, a set of
ordered pairs, or a symbolic expression.

Domain and Range

Terms to Know	Example
The **independent variable** is the input variable of a function.	In the function $y = 2x^2$, x is the *independent variable*.
The **dependent variable** is the output variable of a function.	In the function $y = 2x^2$, y is the *dependent variable*.
The **domain** of a function is the set of all inputs of a function.	Because x can be any real number, the *domain* of $y = 2x^2$ is the set of all real numbers.
The **range** of a function is the set of all outputs of a function.	Because y cannot be negative, the *range* of $y = 2x^2$ is the set of all real numbers greater than or equal to 0.

Example 1   **Find Domain and Range**

Find the domain and range of the function below.

$$\{(-6, 6), (-1, 0), (0, -8), (3, -9), (4, -3), (7, -1)\}$$

Solution

The domain is the set of all inputs of a function. Domain: $\{-6, -1, 0, 3, 4, 7\}$

The range is the set of all outputs of a function. Range: $\{-9, -8, -3, -1, 0, 6\}$

Example 2   **Find the Range of a Function**

Find the range of the function $y = -2x + 3$ when the domain is $\{-1, 0, 1, 2, 3\}$.

Solution

Use the domain values as inputs to find the range values.

Domain	$y = -2x + 3$	Range
-1	$y = -2(-1) + 3 = 5$	5
0	$y = -2(0) + 3 = 3$	3
1	$y = -2(1) + 3 = 1$	1
2	$y = -2(2) + 3 = -1$	-1
3	$y = -2(3) + 3 = -3$	-3

Example 3   ## Find Domain and Range from a Graph

Find the domain and range of the function whose graph is given below.

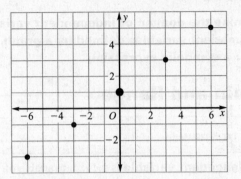

Solution

The independent variable is represented on the horizontal axis. Because the independent variable is x, the domain is the set of x values.

Domain: $\{-6, -3, 0, 3, 6\}$

The dependent variable is represented on the vertical axis. Because the dependent variable is y, the range is the set of y values.

Range: $\{-3, -1, 1, 3, 5\}$

Check Represent the points on the graph as a list of ordered pairs.

$\{(-6, -3), (-3, -1), (0, 1), (3, 3), (6, 5)\}$

The domain is $\{-6, -3, 0, 3, 6\}$ and the range is $\{-3, -1, 1, 3, 5\}$. ✓

Exercises

1. Which of the following best defines the domain of a function?

Ⓐ The set of all inputs

Ⓑ The set of all outputs

Ⓒ The set of all independent variables

Ⓓ The set of all dependent variables

2. Which of the following statements about the domain of a function is false?

Ⓐ It contains the set of all inputs.

Ⓑ It contains the set of independent variables.

Ⓒ It does not include every input.

Ⓓ It does not include every output.

3. What is the domain of the function graphed below?

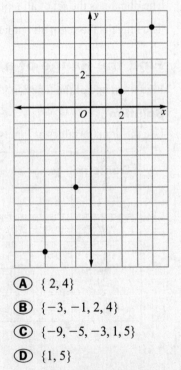

Ⓐ $\{2, 4\}$

Ⓑ $\{-3, -1, 2, 4\}$

Ⓒ $\{-9, -5, -3, 1, 5\}$

Ⓓ $\{1, 5\}$

4. Which of the following best defines the range of a function?

Ⓐ The set of all inputs

Ⓑ The set of all outputs

Ⓒ The set of all independent variables

Ⓓ The set of all dependent variables

5. What is the range of $y = x^2$ when $x = -5, -4, 0, 3,$ and 4?

Ⓐ $\{0, 9, 16, 25\}$

Ⓑ $\{2, 3\}$

Ⓒ $\{-25, -16, 0, 9, 16\}$

Ⓓ $\{-5, -4, 0, 2, 3\}$

6. Which of the following relations has a range of $\{-4, -1, 0, 1\}$ when $x = -3, 0, 1,$ and 2?

Ⓐ $y = -x - 1$ Ⓑ $y = x - 1$

Ⓒ $y = -x + 1$ Ⓓ $y = x + 1$

7. What is the domain of the function?

$\{(0, 0), (1, 0), (2, 0), (3, 0), (4, 0)\}$

Ⓐ $\{0\}$ Ⓑ The empty set, $\emptyset$

Ⓒ $\{0, 1, 2, 3, 4\}$ Ⓓ $\{1, 2, 3, 4\}$

8. What is the range of the function?

$\{(0, 0), (1, 0), (2, 0), (3, 0), (4, 0)\}$

Ⓐ $\{0\}$ Ⓑ The empty set, $\emptyset$

Ⓒ $\{0, 1, 2, 3, 4\}$ Ⓓ $\{1, 2, 3, 4\}$

Use the graph below for Exercises 9 and 10.

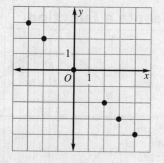

9. Which of the following numbers is *not* in the range of the function?

Ⓐ -4 Ⓑ -3 Ⓒ 2 Ⓓ 4

10. Which of the following numbers is *not* in the domain of the function?

Ⓐ -4 Ⓑ -3 Ⓒ 2 Ⓓ 4

11. Which of the following statements about the range of a function is false?

Ⓐ It contains the set of dependent variables.

Ⓑ It contains the set of all outputs.

Ⓒ It does not include every input.

Ⓓ It does not include every output.

12. Which of the following relations has a domain of $\{-8, -4, 0, 12\}$ when $y = -4, -2, 0,$ and 6?

Ⓐ $y = 2x$ Ⓑ $y = -\frac{1}{2}x$

Ⓒ $y = -2x$ Ⓓ $y = \frac{1}{2}x$

13. Which real number below is *not* in the domain of the function?

$\{(5, -8), (-8, 6), (-6, -8), (-8, 8), (-6, 4)\}$

Ⓐ -8 Ⓑ -6

Ⓒ 5 Ⓓ 4

14. Which real number below is *not* in the range of the function?

$\{(5, -8), (-8, -6), (-6, -8), (-8, 8), (-6, 4)\}$

Ⓐ -8 Ⓑ -6 Ⓒ 5 Ⓓ 4

15. Which of the following numbers is *not* in the range of $y = -x^2 + 2$?

Ⓐ -4 Ⓑ 0 Ⓒ 2 Ⓓ 4

16. Which of the following numbers is *not* in the range of $y = x^2 - 2$, regardless of the domain?

Ⓐ -4 Ⓑ -2 Ⓒ 0 Ⓓ 4

17. Which ordered pair(s) could be removed from the set below to create a function with a domain of $\{-2, 0, 2\}$?

$\{(-2, 2), (0, -1), (-2, 0), (-1, 2), (2, -2)\}$

Ⓐ $(0, -1)$

Ⓑ $(-1, 2)$ and $(-2, 2)$

Ⓒ $(0, -1)$ and $(-1, 2)$

Ⓓ $(0, -1)$ or $(-1, 2)$

Name _____ Date _____

California Standards
Algebra 18.0

Students determine whether a relation defined by a graph, a set of ordered pairs, or a symbolic expression is a function and justify the conclusion.

Functions

The **vertical line test** is used to determine whether a relation represented by a graph is a function. A relation is a function provided that no vertical line passes through more than one point on the graph.

Function
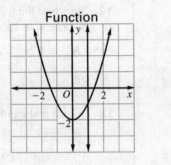

Not a Function
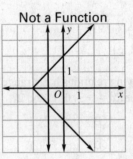

Example 1 ## Determine Whether a Rule is a Function

Let x be the independent variable. If the domain is the set of real numbers, determine whether the rule is a function.

    a. $y = \sqrt{x}$ **b.** $y = x^2$ **c.** $y = \dfrac{1}{x}$

Solution

a. Because every nonnegative number has exactly one square root, $y = \sqrt{x}$ is a function.

b. Because each input is paired with exactly one output, $y = x^2$ is a function.

c. Because every nonzero number is paired with exactly one output, $y = \dfrac{1}{x}$ is a function.

Example 2 ## Determine Whether a Graph Represents a Function

Determine whether the graph represents a function.

Solution

You can use the vertical line test to determine whether a relation represented by a graph is a function.

Answer The vertical line intersects the graph at approximately $(3, 2.6)$ and $(3, -2.6)$. Because a vertical line can intersect the graph at more than one point, the graph is not a function.

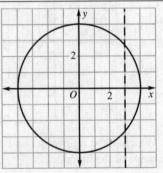

Name _____ **Date** _____

Exercises

1. Which of the following statements best defines a function?

(A) Any pairing of a set of inputs with a set of outputs where each input is paired with exactly one output.

(B) Any pairing of a set of inputs with a set of outputs where each output is paired with exactly one input.

(C) Any pairing of a set of inputs with a set of outputs.

(D) Any pairing of a set of independent variables with a set of dependent variables.

2. Which of the following graphs represents a function?

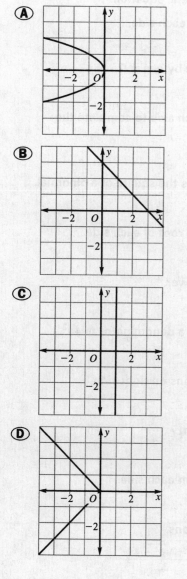

3. If a vertical line intersects a graph more than once, which of the following is true?

(A) The relation represented by the graph is a function.

(B) The relation represented by the graph is not a function.

(C) The graph does not represent a relation.

(D) None of the above.

4. Which of the following does *not* support the conclusion that the graph below is *not* a function?

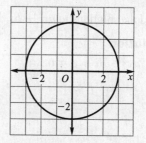

(A) The vertical line $x = -2$ intersects the graph twice.

(B) The vertical line $x = 2$ intersects the graph more than once.

(C) The vertical line $x = 3$ intersects the graph once.

(D) The vertical line $x = 0$ intersects the graph at $(0, 3)$ and $(0, -3)$.

5. The vertical line test is used to determine

(A) if a relation represented by a graph is a function.

(B) if the graph of a function is a relation.

(C) if the graph of a relation is a vertical line.

(D) if the graph of a function is a vertical line.

6. If x is the independent variable and the domain is the set of real numbers, which rule is a function?

(A) $x = y$ (B) $x = 1$
(C) $x = -y^2$ (D) $x = y^2$

7. If y is the dependent variable and the range is the set of real numbers, which rule is *not* a function?

(A) $y = -1$ (B) $|x| = y$
(C) $y = -x^2$ (D) $x = -1$

California Standards
Algebra 19.0

Students know the quadratic formula and are familiar with its proof by completing the square.

Quadratic Formula

The **quadratic formula** can be used to find the solutions of $ax^2 + bx + c = 0$ where $a \neq 0$ and $b^2 - 4ac \geq 0$. The quadratic formula is

$$x = \frac{-b \pm \sqrt{b^2 - 4ac}}{2a}.$$

Example

Derive the Quadratic Formula

Find the solutions to $ax^2 + bx + c = 0$.

Solution

$ax^2 + bx + c = 0$	Write the quadratic equation.
$ax^2 + bx = -c$	Subtract c from each side.
$x^2 + \frac{b}{a}x = -\frac{c}{a}$	Divide each side by a, $a \neq 0$.
$x^2 + \frac{b}{a}x + \left(\frac{b}{2a}\right)^2 = \left(\frac{b}{2a}\right)^2 - \frac{c}{a}$	Add $\left(\frac{b}{2a}\right)^2$ to each side to complete the square.
$\left(x + \frac{b}{2a}\right)^2 = \left(\frac{b}{2a}\right)^2 - \frac{c}{a}$	Write left side as the square of a binomial.
$x + \frac{b}{2a} = \pm \sqrt{\left(\frac{b}{2a}\right)^2 - \frac{c}{a}}$	Take the square root of each side.
$x + \frac{b}{2a} = \pm \sqrt{\frac{b^2}{4a^2} - \frac{c}{a}}$	Simplify the power.
$x + \frac{b}{2a} = \pm \sqrt{\frac{b^2}{4a^2} - \frac{4ac}{4a^2}}$	Rewrite $\frac{c}{a}$ with a denominator of $4a^2$.
$x + \frac{b}{2a} = \pm \sqrt{\frac{b^2 - 4ac}{4a^2}}$	Combine fractions on right side.
$x + \frac{b}{2a} = \pm \frac{\sqrt{b^2 - 4ac}}{2a}$	Quotient property
$x = \frac{-b}{2a} \pm \frac{\sqrt{b^2 - 4ac}}{2a}$	Subtract $\frac{b}{2a}$ from each side.
$x = \frac{-b \pm \sqrt{b^2 - 4ac}}{2a}$	Combine fractions.

Answer The solutions to $ax^2 + bx + c = 0$ are $x = \frac{-b \pm \sqrt{b^2 - 4ac}}{2a}$.

Exercises

1. Which is the correct formula for the quadratic formula?

(A) $x = \dfrac{b \pm \sqrt{b^2 - 4ac}}{2a}$

(B) $x = \dfrac{-b \pm \sqrt{b^2 - 4ac}}{2a}$

(C) $x = \dfrac{\pm b - \sqrt{b^2 - 4ac}}{2a}$

(D) $x = -\dfrac{b \pm \sqrt{b^2 + 4ac}}{2a}$

2. Which of the following is a solution of $x^2 - 14x = 21$?

(A) $7 + \sqrt{70}$ (B) $1 + \sqrt{70}$

(C) $-1 + \sqrt{30}$ (D) $7 + \sqrt{30}$

3. Four steps to derive the quadratic formula are shown below.

I: $x + \dfrac{b}{2a} = \pm\dfrac{\sqrt{b^2 - 4ac}}{2a}$

II: $x + \dfrac{b}{2a} = \pm\sqrt{\dfrac{b^2}{4a^2} - \dfrac{4ac}{4a^2}}$

III: $x + \dfrac{b}{2a} = \pm\sqrt{\dfrac{b^2}{4a^2} - \dfrac{c}{a}}$

IV: $x + \dfrac{b}{2a} = \pm\sqrt{\dfrac{b^2 - 4ac}{4a^2}}$

What is the correct order for these steps?

(A) II, I, III, IV

(B) III, II, IV, I

(C) IV, III, I, II

(D) I, II, III, IV

4. Which of the following is a solution of $0 = -x^2 - 3x + 6$?

(A) $\dfrac{1 - \sqrt{11}}{2}$ (B) $\dfrac{-1 - \sqrt{11}}{2}$

(C) $\dfrac{-3 - \sqrt{33}}{2}$ (D) $\dfrac{3 - \sqrt{33}}{2}$

5. Which step should be completed before determining the number required to complete the square of $4x^2 + 20x = -8$?

(A) Subtract 8 from both sides.

(B) Add 8 to both sides.

(C) Multiply both sides by 4.

(D) Divide both sides by 4.

6. Sal is solving the equation by completing the square.

$ax^2 + bx + c = 0$ (where $a \neq 0$)

Step 1: $ax^2 + bx = -c$

Step 2: $x^2 + \dfrac{b}{a}x = -\dfrac{c}{a}$

Step 3: $x^2 + \dfrac{b}{a}x + \left(\dfrac{b}{2a}\right)^2 = -\dfrac{c}{a} + \left(\dfrac{b}{2a}\right)^2$

Step 4: ?

Which should be Step 4 in the solution?

(A) $\left(x - \dfrac{b}{2a}\right)^2 = -\dfrac{c}{a} + \left(\dfrac{b}{2a}\right)^2$

(B) $x^2 + \dfrac{b}{a}x + \left(\dfrac{b}{2a}\right)^2 = \left(-\dfrac{c}{a} + \dfrac{b}{2a}\right)^2$

(C) $\left(x - \dfrac{b}{2a}\right)^2 = \left(-\dfrac{c}{a} + \dfrac{b}{2a}\right)^2$

(D) $\left(x + \dfrac{b}{2a}\right)^2 = -\dfrac{c}{a} + \left(\dfrac{b}{2a}\right)^2$

7. Which of the following expressions gives the correct solutions of $9x^2 - 18x - 36 = 0$?

(A) $\dfrac{-9 \pm \sqrt{9^2 - 4 \cdot 18 \cdot 36}}{2 \cdot 18}$

(B) $\dfrac{18 \pm \sqrt{9^2 - 4 \cdot 9 \cdot 36}}{2 \cdot 9}$

(C) $\dfrac{18 \pm \sqrt{(-18)^2 - 4 \cdot 9 \cdot (-36)}}{2 \cdot 9}$

(D) $\dfrac{9 \pm \sqrt{18^2 - 4 \cdot 18 \cdot (-36)}}{2 \cdot 18}$

8. Which of the following is the coefficient of x^2 in the equation $5x^2 - 20x + 15 = 0$?

(A) 5   (B) 2   (C) -2 (D) -5

9. Which of the following equations is equivalent to $9x^2 - 18x - 36 = 0$?

(A) $(x - 1)^2 = 5$ (B) $x^2 - 2x = -4$

(C) $(x - 2)^2 = 5$ (D) $9x^2 + 18x = 36$

10. Which statement best describes how to check solutions found by completing the square?

(A) Substitute the solutions into the last step of the completing the square process.

(B) Substitute the solutions after the first step of the completing the square process.

(C) Substitute the solutions into the original quadratic formula.

(D) Substitute the solutions into the original quadratic equation.

California Standards
Algebra 20.0

Students use the quadratic formula to find the roots of a second-degree polynomial and to solve quadratic equations.

Use the Quadratic Formula

You will learn how to use the quadratic formula to find the roots of a second-degree polynomial and to solve quadratic equations.

The quadratic formula can be used to find the solutions of $ax^2 + bx + c = 0$ where $a \neq 0$ and $b^2 - 4ac \geq 0$. The quadratic formula is $x = \dfrac{-b \pm \sqrt{b^2 - 4ac}}{2a}$.

Terms to Know	Example
A **monomial** is a number, variable or the product of a number and one or more variables with whole number exponents.	$3, \frac{1}{2}x, -0.2m^2n$
The **degree of a monomial** is the sum of the exponents of the variables in the monomial. The degree of a nonzero constant is zero.	3: Degree 0 $-0.2m^2n$: Degree 3
A **polynomial** is a monomial or a sum of monomials, each called a term of the polynomial.	$3 + \frac{1}{2}m - 0.2m^2n$
The **degree of a polynomial** is the greatest degree of the terms of the polynomial.	$3 + \frac{1}{2}m - 0.2m^2n$ has degree 3.
A **root** of a polynomial involving x is a value of x for which the corresponding value of the polynomial is 0.	The roots of $x^2 + x - 2$ are 1 and -2.

Example 1

Finding the Roots of a Second-Degree Polynomial

What are the roots of $3x^2 - 18x + 9$?

(A) 3, 9   (B) −3, 9

(C) $3 \pm \sqrt{6}$ (D) $-3 \pm \sqrt{6}$

Solution

STEP 1 Identify the values of *a*, *b*, and *c*.

Compare $3x^2 - 18x + 9$ to $ax^2 + bx + c$ to identify *a*, *b*, and *c*. Be careful to include the signs. So, $a = 3$, $b = -18$, and $c = 9$.

STEP 2 Substitute those values into the quadratic formula.

$$x = \frac{-(-18) \pm \sqrt{(-18)^2 - 4 \cdot 3 \cdot 9}}{2 \cdot 3}$$

STEP 3 Simplify to find the root of the second-degree polynomial.

$$x = \frac{-(-18) \pm \sqrt{(-18)^2 - 4 \cdot 3 \cdot 9}}{2 \cdot 3} = 3 \pm \sqrt{6}$$

Answer The roots of $3x^2 - 18x + 9$ are $3 \pm \sqrt{6}$. So, choice C is the correct answer.

Example 2   # Using the Quadratic Formula to Solve a Quadratic Equation

What are the solutions of $3x^2 - \dfrac{9}{4} = -3x$?

(A) $-1, \dfrac{1}{2}$ (B) $-\dfrac{3}{2}, \dfrac{1}{2}$ (C) $-\dfrac{1}{2}, 1$ (D) $-\dfrac{1}{2}, \dfrac{3}{2}$

Solution

STEP 1 Move all terms to one side of the equal sign.

Add $3x$ to both sides to get $3x^2 + 3x - \dfrac{9}{4} = 0$.

STEP 2 Identify the values of a, b, and c.

$a = 3$, $b = 3$, and $c = -\dfrac{9}{4}$.

STEP 3 Substitute and simplify.

$$x = \frac{-3 \pm \sqrt{3^2 - 4 \cdot 3 \cdot \left(-\frac{9}{4}\right)}}{2 \cdot 3} = -\frac{1}{2} \pm 1 = -\frac{3}{2}, \frac{1}{2}$$

Answer The solutions of $3x^2 - \dfrac{9}{4} = -3x$ are $-\dfrac{3}{2}$ and $\dfrac{1}{2}$. So, choice B is the correct answer.

Exercises

1. Which of the following is a root of $-2x^2 - 3x + 1$?

(A) $-\dfrac{1}{2}$ (B) $\dfrac{3}{4} - \dfrac{\sqrt{17}}{4}$

(C) $-\dfrac{3}{4} + \dfrac{\sqrt{17}}{4}$ (D) 1

2. If $3 - \sqrt{6}$ is a solution of a quadratic equation, is $3 + \sqrt{6}$ also a solution?

(A) Yes

(B) No

(C) No, but $-3 - \sqrt{6}$ is.

(D) No, but $-3 + \sqrt{6}$ is.

3. Which is one of the solutions to the equation $5x^2 - 10x = 5$?

(A) -1 (B) 1

(C) $-1 + \sqrt{2}$ (D) $1 + \sqrt{2}$

4. What are the roots of $12x^2 - 16x$?

(A) $-\dfrac{4}{3}$ (B) $-\dfrac{4}{3}, 0$ (C) $0, \dfrac{4}{3}$ (D) $\dfrac{4}{3}$

5. When a polynomial is evaluated using one of its roots, which of the following must be true?

(A) The polynomial is equal to zero.

(B) The polynomial is not equal to zero.

(C) The polynomial is equal to the root.

(D) The polynomial is not equal to the root.

6. This graph shows $y = ax^2 + bx + c$. What can you conclude about the roots of $ax^2 + bx + c$?

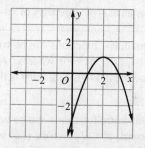

(A) One root is positive and one root is negative.

(B) They are both positive.

(C) They are both negative.

(D) There is only one and it is zero.

7. Which of the following equations has the same solutions as $-5n + 6 = 2n^2 - n$?

(A) $6n = 6$ (B) $2n^2 - 6n - 6 = 0$

(C) $n^2 + 2n - 3 = 0$ (D) $2n^2 - 3n + 3 = 0$

8. If a quadratic polynomial has 2 roots, what can you conclude about the expression $b^2 - 4ac$ under the radical sign in the quadratic formula?

(A) It equals zero.

(B) It equals 2.

(C) It must be positive.

(D) It must be negative.

California Standards
Algebra 21.0

Students graph quadratic functions and know that their roots are the x-intercepts.

Graphing Quadratic Functions

Terms to Know	Example
A **quadratic function** is a nonlinear function that can be written in the standard form $y = ax^2 + bx + c$ where $a \neq 0$.	The equation $y = 3x^2 - 12x + 13$ is a quadratic equation. The vertex of the graph of $y = 3x^2 - 12x + 13$ is $(2, 1)$. The axis of symmetry is the line $x = 2$.
The graph of a quadratic function is a U-shaped graph called a **parabola**. If $a > 0$, then the parabola opens up. If $a < 0$, then the parabola opens down.	
The lowest or highest point on a parabola is called the **vertex**.	
The vertical line that passes through the vertex and divides a parabola into two symmetric parts is called the **axis of symmetry**. The graph of $y = ax^2 + bx + c$ has an axis of symmetry of $x = -\dfrac{b}{2a}$.	
Quadratic functions can be written in **vertex form**, $y = a(x - h)^2 + k$ where $a \neq 0$, the vertex is (h, k), and the axis of symmetry is the line $x = h$.	The quadratic equation $y = 2(x + 4)^2 + 7$ is written in *vertex form*. The vertex is $(-4, 7)$ and the axis of symmetry is the line $x = -4$.
Quadratic functions can be written in **intercept form**, $y = a(x - p)(x - q)$ where $a \neq 0$. The values of p and q are the x-intercepts and the roots of the associated quadratic. The axis of symmetry is $x = \dfrac{p + q}{2}$.	The quadratic equation $y = 2(x - 3)(x + 2)$ is written in *intercept form*. The x-intercepts are 3 and -2. The axis of symmetry is the line $x = \dfrac{1}{2}$.

Example 1 ## Find the Axis of Symmetry and the Vertex

Consider the graph of $y = -3x^2 + 6x - 8$.

a. Find the axis of symmetry.   **b.** Find the vertex.

Solution

a. For the function $y = -3x^2 + 6x - 8$, $a = -3$ and $b = 6$.

Substitute -3 for a and 6 for b in the equation $x = -\dfrac{b}{2a}$. Then simplify.

The axis of symmetry is the vertical line $x = -\dfrac{b}{2a} = \dfrac{-6}{2(-3)} = 1$.

b. The x-coordinate of the vertex is 1.

To find the y-coordinate, substitute 1 for x in the function and simplify.

$$y = -3x^2 + 6x - 8 = -3(1)^2 + 6(1) - 8 = -5$$

The vertex is $(1, -5)$.

Example 2

Graph a Quadratic Function in Standard Form

Graph $y = 2x^2 - 8x + 2$.

Solution

STEP 1 Determine whether the parabola opens up or down. Because $a > 0$, the parabola opens up.

STEP 2 Find and draw the axis of symmetry.

$$x = -\frac{b}{2a} = -\frac{-8}{2(2)} = 2$$

STEP 3 Find and plot the vertex. Substitute 2 for x in the function to find the y-coordinate of the vertex.

$$y = 2x^2 - 8x + 2 = 2(2)^2 - 8(2) + 2 = -6$$

So, the vertex is $(2, -6)$.

STEP 4 Plot 2 points. Choose two x-values less than the x-coordinate of the vertex. Then find the corresponding y-values.

x	0	−1
y	2	12

STEP 5 Reflect the points plotted in Step 4 in the axis of symmetry.

STEP 6 Draw a parabola through the plotted points.

Example 3

Graph a Quadratic Function in Vertex Form

Graph $y = -2(x - 1)^2 + 3$.

Solution

STEP 1 Identify the values of a, h, and k: $a = -2$, $h = 1$, and $k = 3$. Because $a < 0$, the parabola opens down.

STEP 2 Draw the axis of symmetry, $x = h = 1$.

STEP 3 Plot the vertex $(h, k) = (1, 3)$.

STEP 4 Plot points. Evaluate the function for two x-values less than the x-coordinate of the vertex.

x	0	−1
y	1	−5

STEP 5 Reflect the points plotted in Step 4 in the axis of symmetry.

STEP 6 Draw a parabola through the plotted points.

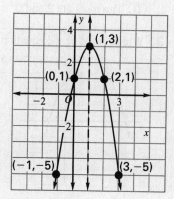

Name _____ Date _____

Example 4 **Graph a Quadratic Function in Intercept Form**

Graph $y = -(x - 2)(x + 4)$.

Solution

STEP 1 Find the x-intercepts.

The x-intercepts are $p = 2$ and $q = -4$. Plot $(2, 0)$ and $(-4, 0)$.

STEP 2 Find the axis of symmetry.

$$x = \frac{p + q}{2} = \frac{2 + (-4)}{2} = \frac{-2}{2} = -1$$

STEP 3 The x-coordinate of the vertex is -1. To find the y-coordinate, substitute -1 for x and simplify.

$$y = -(x - 2)(x + 1) = -(-1 - 2)(-1 + 4) = 9$$

So, the vertex is $(-1, 9)$.

STEP 4 Draw a parabola through the vertex and the points where the x-intercepts occur.

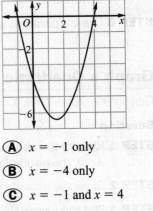

Exercises

1. If the vertex of $y = ax^2 + bx + c$ is $\left(\frac{1}{2}, -3\right)$, what is the axis of symmetry?

  A $y = -3$ **B** $y = \frac{1}{2}$

  C $x = \frac{1}{2}$ **D** $x = -3$

2. If the coordinates of one of the x-intercepts of $y = 2x^2 - 6x + 4$ are $(2, 0)$, what can you conclude about the roots?

  A One of the roots is 2.

  B One of the roots is 0.

  C One of the roots is -2.

  D The roots are 2 and 0.

3. Which could be the equation for the graph below?

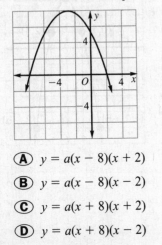

  A $y = a(x - 8)(x + 2)$

  B $y = a(x - 8)(x - 2)$

  C $y = a(x + 8)(x + 2)$

  D $y = a(x + 8)(x - 2)$

4. For what value or values of x is $y = 0$?

  A $x = -1$ only

  B $x = -4$ only

  C $x = -1$ and $x = 4$

  D $x = 1$ and $x = -4$

5. What are the x-intercepts of $y = -2(x + 3)(x - 5)$?

  A $-3, 5$ **B** $-5, 3$

  C $-6, 10$ **D** $-10, 6$

6. What are the x-intercepts of $y = 2x^2 + 5x - 12$?

  A $-12, 0$

  B $0, 12$

  C $-4, \frac{3}{2}$

  D $-\frac{3}{2}, 4$

California Standard Algebra 21.0

7. Which graph below has a vertex with a y-coordinate of -1 and an axis of symmetry of $x = 3$?

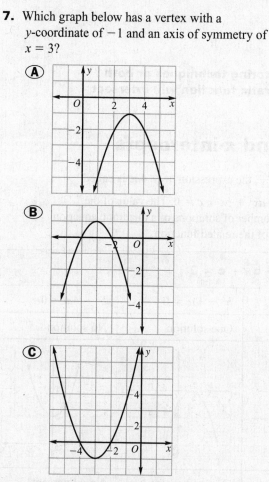

Ⓐ

Ⓑ

Ⓒ

Ⓓ

8. If one of the roots of $x^2 + 6x + 8$ is -4, what can conclude about the intercepts?

Ⓐ The x-intercepts are -2 and 2.

Ⓑ The y-intercepts are -4 and 4.

Ⓒ One of the y-intercepts is -4.

Ⓓ One of the x-intercepts is -4.

9. Which is the graph of $y = x^2 - 4x + 8$?

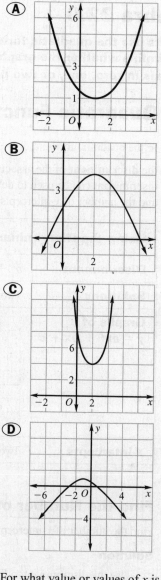

Ⓐ

Ⓑ

Ⓒ

Ⓓ

10. For what value or values of x is $y = 1$?

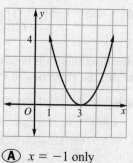

Ⓐ $x = -1$ only

Ⓑ $x = 2$ and $x = 4$

Ⓒ $x = 1$ and $x = -2$

Ⓓ $x = 1$ only

Name _____ Date _____

California Standards
Algebra 22.0

Students use the quadratic formula or factoring techniques or both to determine whether the graph of a quadratic function will intersect the x-axis in zero, one, or two points.

Quadratic Functions and *x*-intercepts

In the quadratic formula, $x = \dfrac{-b \pm \sqrt{b^2 - 4ac}}{2a}$, the expression $b^2 - 4ac$ is called the **discriminant** of the associated equation $ax^2 + bx + c = 0$. The value of the discriminant can be used to determine the number of solutions of a quadratic equation and the number of *x*-intercepts of the graph of the related function.

Using the Discriminant of $ax^2 + bx + c = 0$			
Discriminant	$b^2 - 4ac > 0$	$b^2 - 4ac = 0$	$b^2 - 4ac < 0$
Solutions	Two solutions	One solution	No solution
Graphs of $y = ax^2 + bx + c$			
***x*-intercepts**	Two *x*-intercepts	One *x*-intercept	No *x*-intercept

Example

Find the Number of Solutions

Find the number of *x*-intercepts of the graph of $y = x^2 - 8x + 16$.

Solution

Use the discriminant to find the number of solutions of $0 = x^2 - 8x + 16$.

$b^2 - 4ac = (-8)^2 - 4(1)(16)$ **Substitute 1 for *a*, −8 for *b*, and 16 for *c*.**

$\qquad\qquad = 0$ **Simplify.**

The discriminant is 0, so the equation has one solution. This means the graph of $y = x^2 - 8x + 16$ has one *x*-intercept.

Check You can graph the equation $y = x^2 - 8x + 16$ to check your answer.

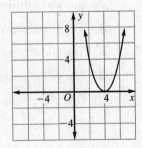

You can also use factoring to check the answer. Because $x^2 - 8x + 16 = (x - 4)^2$, the graph of $y = x^2 - 8x + 16$ intersects the *x*-axis at $x - 4 = 0$, or $x = 4$.

Exercises

1. If $ax^2 + bx = -c$ has no solution, how many times does the graph of $y = ax^2 + bx + c$ intersect the x-axis?

- **(A)** 0 times
- **(B)** 1 time
- **(C)** 2 times
- **(D)** 1 or 2 times

2. Which graph(s) below represent quadratic equation(s) with two real solutions?

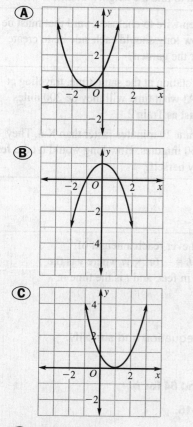

- **(D)** Both A and C

3. If $ax^2 + bx + c = 0$ has one solution, what can you conclude about the graph of $y = ax^2 + bx + c$?

- **(A)** The graph intersects the x-axis exactly once and does not intersect the y-axis.
- **(B)** The graph intersects the x-axis exactly once and the y-axis exactly once.
- **(C)** The graph intersects the x-axis when $x = 0$.
- **(D)** The graph intersects the y-axis when $y = 0$.

4. Because the discriminant of $-2x^2 - 3x - 5 = 0$ is less than 0, what can you conclude about the graph of $y = -2x^2 - 3x - 5$?

- **(A)** The x-intercepts are less than zero.
- **(B)** The x-intercepts are greater than zero.
- **(C)** The x-intercept is zero.
- **(D)** There are no x-intercepts.

5. Which graph(s) below represent quadratic equation(s) with no solution?

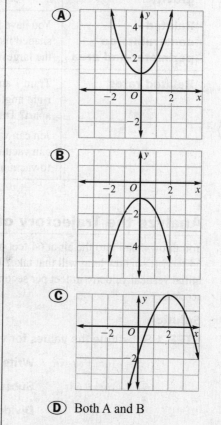

- **(D)** Both A and B

6. If the graph of $y = ax^2 + bx + c$ has two x-intercepts, what can you conclude?

- **(A)** The equation $ax^2 + bx = c$ has two solutions.
- **(B)** The equation $ax^2 + bx = -c$ has two solutions.
- **(C)** Zero is a solution of $ax^2 + bx = -c$.
- **(D)** The equation $ax^2 + bx + c = 0$ has no solution.

California Standards

Algebra 23.0

Students apply quadratic equations to physical problems, such as motion of an object under the force of gravity.

Using Quadratic Equations to Solve Problems

Problem Type	Example
Motion of objects under the force of gravity	A ball is thrown up into the air at a velocity of 160 feet per second. How many seconds later will it hit the ground? The equation $h = -16t^2 + 160t$ can be used to find the height h at time t.
Related constraints on perimeter and area	You have 900 feet of chicken wire to enclose a yard that must be shaped like a rectangle. How long should each side be to create the largest possible area for the garden?
Related rates	Train 1 and Train 2 leave a station at the same time, traveling at right angles to each other. At what time will they be 200 miles apart? Train 1 is twice as fast as Train 2.
	Jen can vacuum the restaurant 20 minutes faster than Kai. They can vacuum it together in 60 minutes. How long would it take Jen to vacuum the restaurant by herself?

Example

Analyze the Trajectory of an Object

You throw a ball into the air at 64 feet per second. Will it ever reach a height of 64 feet? If so, how long will that take? Use the equation $h = -16t^2 + vt$ where v is the initial vertical velocity in feet per second, h is the height in feet, and t is the time in seconds.

Solution

STEP 1 Substitute the values for v and h into the equation and simplify.

$$h = -16t^2 + vt$$ **Write equation.**

$$64 = -16t^2 + 64t$$ **Substitute 64 for v and 64 for h.**

$$-4 = t^2 - 4t$$ **Divide each side by −16.**

STEP 2 Solve this quadratic equation for t by factoring.

$$-4 = t^2 - 4t$$ **Write equation.**

$$0 = t^2 - 4t + 4$$ **Add 4 to each side.**

$$0 = (t - 2)(t - 2)$$ **Factor.**

The factored form of $t^2 - 4t + 4 = 0$ is $(t - 2)(t - 2) = 0$. So, $t = 2$.

STEP 3 Interpret the answer in the context of the problem.

After 2 seconds, the height of the ball is 64 feet.

Answer The ball does reach a height of 64 feet after two seconds.

Exercises

1. A rectangle has a perimeter of 38 inches and an area of 48 square inches. What are the dimensions of the rectangle?

  (A) 16 in. by 3 in.   (B) 8 in. by 6 in.

  (C) 12 in. by 4 in.   (D) 6 in. by 8 in.

2. The graph below gives the distance above the ground, in feet, of an object thrown upward. After how many seconds will the object reach its highest point above the ground?

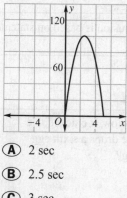

  (A) 2 sec

  (B) 2.5 sec

  (C) 3 sec

  (D) 2 sec and 3 sec

3. Trains 1 and 2 leave the same station at the same time. Train 1 is traveling due north and Train 2 is traveling due east. Train 2 travels $\frac{1}{3}$ faster than Train 1. After 2 hours, the two trains are 100 miles apart. What is the speed of Train 1?

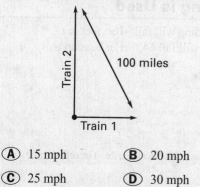

  (A) 15 mph   (B) 20 mph

  (C) 25 mph   (D) 30 mph

4. A rock is dropped from a bridge into a river. If the rock hits the water 5 seconds after it is dropped, what is the height h of the bridge above the water? Use the equation $h = -16t^2$ where t is the time in seconds.

  (A) 80 ft   (B) 160 ft

  (C) 400 ft   (D) 800 ft

5. A baseball is thrown upward with an initial velocity of 48 feet per second. The height (in feet) of the ball above the ground after t seconds is given by the formula $s = -16t^2 + 48t$. After how many seconds is the ball 20 feet above the ground?

  (A) 1 sec

  (B) $\frac{1}{2}$ sec and $2\frac{1}{2}$ sec

  (C) 1 sec and 2 sec

  (D) $1\frac{1}{2}$ sec and $3\frac{1}{2}$ sec

6. A 5-sided box (without a top) is to be folded from the diagram below. Note that squares with side lengths of 3 centimeters are removed from each corner. The resulting box has a volume of 243 cubic centimeters. What are the dimensions of the original square?

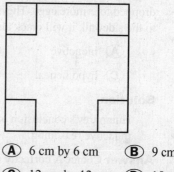

  (A) 6 cm by 6 cm   (B) 9 cm by 9 cm

  (C) 12 cm by 12 cm   (D) 15 cm by 15 cm

7. The sketch below shows the area enclosed along a river by 500 meters of fencing.

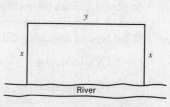

If there is no fencing along the river, for what values of x will the enclosed area be 20,000 square meters?

  (A) 50 and 200

  (B) 100 and 400

  (C) 150 and 250

  (D) 250 and 300

California Standards
Algebra 24.1

Students explain the difference between inductive and deductive reasoning and identify and provide examples of each.

Inductive and Deductive Reasoning

Terms to Know
Inductive reasoning is a form of reasoning in which a conclusion is based on several examples.
Deductive reasoning is a form of reasoning in which a conclusion is based on statements that are assumed or shown to be true.

Example 1

Identify When Inductive Reasoning is Used

When Humphrey dropped a raw egg off his porch to the sidewalk below, it cracked. He dropped four more eggs. They all cracked, too. He predicts that if he drops a sixth egg to the sidewalk it will crack also. What type of reasoning is he using?

(A) inductive   (B) deductive

(C) hypothetical   (D) theoretical

Solution

Humphrey's conclusion is based on several examples. Therefore, he is using inductive reasoning.

Answer Choice A correctly identifies the reasoning used as inductive.

Example 2

Identify When Deductive Reasoning is Used

In physics, Sarah learns that a ball dropped off a building will fall $-16t^2$ feet in t seconds until it hits the ground. She concludes a ball will fall 64 feet in 2 seconds. What type of reasoning did she use?

(A) inductive   (B) deductive

(C) hypothetical   (D) theoretical

Solution

Sarah's conclusion is based on a formula that is assumed to be true. Therefore, she used deductive reasoning.

Answer Choice B correctly identifies the reasoning used as deductive.

Name _____   Date _____

Exercises

1. Sylvia visits a downtown shopping area. The first four stores that she visits are open and having sales. Which conclusion is not valid using inductive reasoning?

   (A) The next store she visits will not be having a sale.

   (B) The next store she visits will be open.

   (C) The next store she visits will be having a sale.

   (D) The next store she visits will be open and having a sale.

2. The graph below predicts the trajectory of a ball thrown into the air at 96 feet per second. Which of the following is a valid conclusion using deductive reasoning based on the graph?

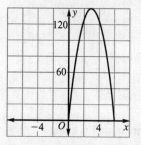

   (A) The ball hits the ground after six seconds.

   (B) The ball hits the ground after three seconds.

   (C) Any ball thrown into the air hits the ground after six seconds.

   (D) Any ball thrown into the air hits the ground after three seconds.

3. Which of the following is an example of inductive reasoning?

   (A) All of the teenagers in Kurt's neighborhood have cell phones, so they often talk on the phone.

   (B) It was warm all last week, so it is going to be cold next week.

   (C) Hawaii is part of the United States, so people who live in Hawaii live in the United States.

   (D) Angie got a B on her first three exams, so she will probably get a B on her next exam.

4. Which of the following is a correct description of deductive reasoning?

   (A) Its conclusions are based on statements that are assumed to be true.

   (B) Its assumptions are based on statements.

   (C) Its conclusions are based on examples.

   (D) Its assumptions are based on examples that are known to be true.

5. The graph below shows the trend in shoe sales for the past five years.

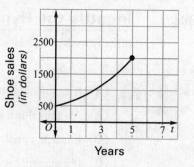

Years

Which of the following is a valid conclusion using the graph based upon inductive reasoning?

   (A) Shoe sales will increase next year.

   (B) Shoe sales will decrease next year.

   (C) Shoe sales will stay the same next year.

   (D) Shoe sales go up and down every year.

6. In biology class, Cindy learns that only female birds lay eggs. Which of the following is not a valid conclusion based on deductive reasoning?

   (A) If a bird lays an egg, it is female.

   (B) If a bird never lays an egg, it is male.

   (C) If a bird ever lays an egg, it cannot be male.

   (D) If a bird is male, it can never lay an egg.

California Standards
Algebra 24.2

Students identify the hypothesis and conclusion in logical deduction.

Hypothesis and Conclusion

Terms to Know

An **if-then statement** is a conditional statement with an *if* part and a *then* part. The *if* part contains the **hypothesis**, and the *then* part contains the **conclusion**.

Example   ## Identify the Hypothesis of an If-Then Statement

Identify the hypothesis in the statement below.

A dog is a mammal.

ⓐ If an animal is a dog, then it is a mammal.

ⓑ An animal is a dog.

ⓒ It is a mammal.

ⓓ If a mammal is a dog, then it is an animal.

Solution

The part following *if* is the hypothesis, so the hypothesis is "an animal is a dog."

Answer Choice B is the hypothesis.

Exercises

1. Identify the conclusion in the statement below.

If a triangle has an angle that measures 90°, then it is a right triangle.

ⓐ A triangle has an angle that measures 90°.

ⓑ It is a right triangle.

ⓒ If a triangle has an angle that measures 90°, then it is a right triangle.

ⓓ The sum of the measures of the remaining two angles is 90°.

2. Identify the hypothesis in the statement below.

If a bird lays an egg, then it is a female.

ⓐ If a bird lays an egg, then it is a female.

ⓑ A bird lays an egg.

ⓒ It is a female.

ⓓ If a bird is female, then it lays an egg.

3. Which of the following if-then statements is equivalent to the statement below?

All squares are rectangles.

ⓐ If a figure is a square, then it is a rectangle.

ⓑ If a figure is a rectangle, then it is a square.

ⓒ If a square is a rectangle, then it is a figure.

ⓓ If a rectangle is a square, then it is a figure.

4. Consider the if-then statement:

If an animal is a bat, then it has wings.

Which of the following statements is equivalent to the if-then statement above?

ⓐ All winged mammals are bats.

ⓑ All bats are winged mammals.

ⓒ All winged animals are bats.

ⓓ All bats are winged animals.

5. Which of the following statements is equivalent to the diagram below?

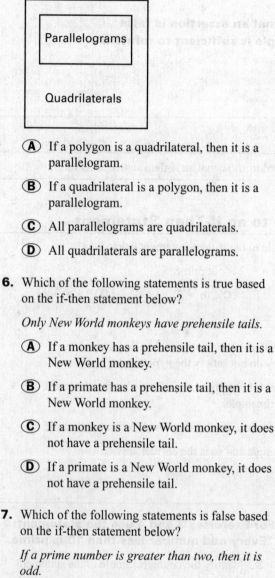

Ⓐ If a polygon is a quadrilateral, then it is a parallelogram.

Ⓑ If a quadrilateral is a polygon, then it is a parallelogram.

Ⓒ All parallelograms are quadrilaterals.

Ⓓ All quadrilaterals are parallelograms.

6. Which of the following statements is true based on the if-then statement below?

Only New World monkeys have prehensile tails.

Ⓐ If a monkey has a prehensile tail, then it is a New World monkey.

Ⓑ If a primate has a prehensile tail, then it is a New World monkey.

Ⓒ If a monkey is a New World monkey, it does not have a prehensile tail.

Ⓓ If a primate is a New World monkey, it does not have a prehensile tail.

7. Which of the following statements is false based on the if-then statement below?

If a prime number is greater than two, then it is odd.

Ⓐ The conclusion is true.

Ⓑ The number 2 satisfies the hypothesis.

Ⓒ The hypothesis is "a prime number greater than 2."

Ⓓ The conclusion is "it is odd."

8. Which of the following statements is *not* valid based on the diagram below?

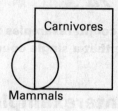

Ⓐ Some mammals are carnivores.

Ⓑ Some mammals are not carnivores.

Ⓒ There are no mammals that are not carnivores.

Ⓓ There are mammals that are not carnivores.

9. Which of the following statements is valid based on the statement below?

If a book is nonfiction, it is not a novel.

Ⓐ If a book is not nonfiction, it is a novel.

Ⓑ If a book is not a novel, it is nonfiction.

Ⓒ All fictional books are novels.

Ⓓ All novels are fictional.

10. Identify the hypothesis in the statement below.

All triangles are polygons.

Ⓐ A geometric object is a polygon.

Ⓑ A geometric object is a triangle.

Ⓒ A triangle is a polygon.

Ⓓ A polygon is a triangle.

11. Identify the conclusion in the statement below.

Every polygon with exactly three sides is a triangle.

Ⓐ A geometric object is a polygon.

Ⓑ A geometric object is a triangle.

Ⓒ A triangle has exactly three sides.

Ⓓ A polygon has exactly three sides.

California Standards
Algebra 24.3

Students use counterexamples to show that an assertion is false and recognize that a single counterexample is sufficient to refute an assertion.

Counterexamples

Terms to Know

A **counterexample** is an example used to show that an if-then statement is false.

Example | ### Identify a Counterexample to an If-Then Statement

Which value of n provides a counterexample to the if-then statement below?

$$\text{If } n \text{ is prime, then } n + 2 \text{ is not prime.}$$

(A) $n = 0$ **(B)** $n = 1$ **(C)** $n = 2$ **(D)** $n = 3$

Solution

Test each answer choice. The numbers 0 and 1 are not prime, so they cannot provide a counterexample because they do not satisfy the hypothesis.

When $n = 2$, then $n + 2 = 4$. Because 4 is not prime, $n = 2$ satisfies the statement and therefore cannot provide a counterexample.

When $n = 3$, then $n + 2 = 5$, which is prime. So 3 does provide a counterexample.

Answer Choice D provides a counterexample and so is the correct answer.

Exercises

For Exercises 1 and 2, refer to this statement: "The square of a number is always greater than the number."

1. Which of the following is a valid counterexample to the statement above?

   (A) $\left(-\frac{1}{2}\right)^2 = \frac{1}{4}$

   (B) $2 \cdot 2 = 4$

   (C) $(3x)^2 = 9x^2$

   (D) $1 \cdot 1 = 1$

2. Which of the following is *not* a valid counterexample to the statement above?

   (A) $0 \cdot 0 = 0$ **(B)** $(0.5)^2 = 0.25$

   (C) $(-0.5)^2 = 0.25$ **(D)** $(0.15)^2 = 0.0225$

For Exercises 3 and 4 use the statement: "Every odd number less than 18 is prime."

3. Identify the counterexample to the statement above.

   (A) $15 = 3 \cdot 5$

   (B) 19 is a prime number.

   (C) 2 is not a prime number.

   (D) 2 is a prime number.

4. Which of the following is *not* a valid counterexample to the statement above?

   (A) 1 is not a prime number.

   (B) 1 is a prime number.

   (C) 3 and 5 are factors of 15.

   (D) 7 divides 14.

Name _____ Date _____

5. If a statement is true, is it possible to provide a valid counterexample to it?

(A) No   (B) Yes

(C) Sometimes   (D) It depends.

6. If a statement is false, is it possible to provide a valid counterexample to it?

(A) No   (B) Yes

(C) Sometimes   (D) It depends.

For Exercises 7 and 8 use the statement:
"The only factors of 2 are 1 and 2."

7. For which of the following is the above statement not a valid counterexample?

(A) All prime numbers are odd.

(B) All odd numbers are prime.

(C) There are no prime numbers less than 3.

(D) 3 is the smallest prime number.

8. For which of the following is the above statement a valid counterexample?

(A) All odd numbers between 0 and 10 are prime.

(B) Some odd numbers between 0 and 10 are prime.

(C) No even numbers between 0 and 10 are prime.

(D) Some even numbers between 0 and 10 are prime.

9. Which of the following types of quadrilaterals is a counterexample to the statement below?

If a quadrilateral has one pair of parallel sides, it must have two pairs of parallel sides.

(A) Trapezoid   (B) Rectangle

(C) Rhombus   (D) Parallelogram

10. How many valid counterexamples are there to the statement below?

The absolute value of a number is never equal to the number.

(A) None   (B) 1

(C) Infinitely many   (D) 3

11. Which of the following is true about the statement below?

All squares are rectangles.

(A) There is only one valid counterexample to the statement.

(B) There is no valid counterexample to the statement.

(C) There are many valid counterexamples to the statement.

(D) The statement is false.

12. Which of the following is not a valid statement-counterexample pair?

(A) Statement: *The absolute value of a negative number is never equal to the number.*

Counterexample: $1 = |1|$

(B) Statement: *The absolute value of a positive number is never equal to the number.*

Counterexample: $|1| = 1$

(C) Statement: *The absolute value of the multiple of a negative number is always equal to the multiple of the absolute value of the number.*

Counterexample:
$|(-2)(-1)| = 2 \neq -2|-1|$

(D) Statement: *The absolute value of the multiple of a positive number is always equal to the multiple of the absolute value of the number.*

Counterexample:
$|(-2)(1)| = 2 \neq -2|1|$

13. Which of the following is a valid means of creating a counterexample to the statement below?

All triangles have right angles.

(A) Draw a right triangle.

(B) State that all triangles have angles whose measures sum to 180°.

(C) Draw an isosceles right triangle.

(D) Draw an equilateral triangle.

California Standards
Algebra 25.1

Students use properties of numbers to construct simple, valid arguments (direct and indirect) for, or formulate counterexamples to, claimed assertions.

Analyze Claimed Assertions

Example 1   ### Prove a Statement is True

Which of the following statements proves that the assertion is true?

The square of a number may equal the number.

Ⓐ $(-1)^2 = 1$

Ⓑ Any number plus zero is itself.

Ⓒ $2 \cdot 1 = 2$

Ⓓ Any number times zero is zero.

Solution

Test the choices. Choices B and C do not involve the square of a number, so they are not applicable. In Choice A, the square of the number does not equal the number. Choice D implies $0 \cdot 0 = 0$, so $0^2 = 0$, which is an example of the square of a number being equal to the number.

Answer Choice D proves the statement is true and so is the correct answer.

Example 2   ### Prove a Statement is False

Which of the following proves the statement below is false?

All five angles of a pentagon may be right angles.

Ⓐ A pentagon can never be a square.

Ⓑ A pentagon can never be a rectangle.

Ⓒ The sum of the measures of the angles of a pentagon is 540°.

Ⓓ The sum of the measures of the angles of a pentagon is 450°.

Solution

Test the choices. Only choices C and D address the measures of angles. Choice D is false. Choice C is true; the sum of the measures of angles of a pentagon are 540°. If all 5 angles were right angles, they would sum to $90° \cdot 5 = 450°$, which is impossible.

Answer Choice C proves the statement is false and is the correct answer.

Exercises

**For Exercises 1 and 2 use the statement:
"All odd numbers are prime."**

1. Which of the following does *not* prove that the statement above is false?

(A) 2 is a prime number.

(B) 1 is not a prime number.

(C) $15 = 3 \cdot 5$

(D) 81 is divisible by 3.

2. Which of the following proves that the statement above is false?

(A) 11 and 13 are both odd numbers and prime numbers.

(B) The number 6 is divisible by both 2 and 3, which are both prime.

(C) Every two-digit number that ends in 5 is always divisible by 5.

(D) $10 = 2 \cdot 5$

For Exercises 3 and 4 use the equation:

$$\frac{1}{3} = 0.\overline{3}$$

3. Which of the following statements is *not* supported by the equation above?

(A) $0.\overline{3}$ is a rational number.

(B) All rational numbers can be expressed as terminating decimals.

(C) Some rational numbers can be expressed as repeating decimals.

(D) Repeating decimals are rational numbers.

4. The equation above provides a counterexample to which of the following statements?

(A) The decimal form of any rational number must be terminating.

(B) The decimal form of any rational number must be repeating.

(C) Every terminating decimal must be a rational number.

(D) Every repeating decimal must be a rational number.

5. Josh wants to prove $\sqrt{d^3} = d\sqrt{d}$, but one step is missing from his argument. Which of the following is the best choice for the missing step?

$$\sqrt{d^3} = \sqrt{d^2 \cdot d} = \underline{\quad ? \quad} = d\sqrt{d}$$

(A) $\sqrt{d^2} \cdot \sqrt{d}$

(B) $\sqrt{d^3}$

(C) $d^2\sqrt{d}$

(D) $\sqrt{d^2} \cdot d$

6. Which of the following is the best counterexample to $(a + b)^2 = a^2 + b^2$?

(A) $(3 + 2)^2 \neq 3^2 + 2^2$

(B) $6^2 + 4^2 \neq 100$

(C) $3^2 + 4^2 \neq 5^2$

(D) $36 + 64 \neq 14^2$

**For Exercises 7 and 8 use the statement:
"The reciprocal of an integer is always less than the integer."**

7. Which of the following does *not* prove that the statement above is false?

(A) $\frac{1}{1} = 1$

(B) $\frac{1}{(-2)} = -\frac{1}{2}$

(C) $\frac{1}{2}$ is the reciprocal of 2.

(D) $-\frac{1}{2}$ is the reciprocal of -2.

8. Which of the following proves the statement above is false?

(A) 0 does not have a reciprocal.

(B) $1 \cdot 1 = 1$

(C) $\frac{1}{2}$ is the reciprocal of 2.

(D) 2 is the reciprocal of $\frac{1}{2}$.

9. Which of the following is *not* a valid means of proving a statement is false?

(A) Providing a counterexample

(B) Disproving the hypothesis

(C) Proving the hypothesis does not lead the conclusion

(D) Disproving the conclusion

California Standards
Algebra 25.2

Students judge the validity of an argument according to whether the properties of the real number system and the order of operations have been applied correctly at each step.

Judge the Validity of an Argument

Example   ## Determine Whether an Argument is Valid

Determine if the argument below is valid.

$$x^2 = -x \text{ implies } x = -1$$

Ⓐ Valid.

Ⓑ Invalid; replace "-1" with "1" to create a valid argument.

Ⓒ Invalid; replace "-1" with "-1" and "1" to create a valid argument.

Ⓓ Invalid; replace "-1" with "-1" and "0" to create a valid argument.

Solution

Solve by factoring: $x^2 + x = 0$ implies $x(x + 1) = 0$.

So, $x = 0$ or $x = -1$.

Answer Choice D is the correct answer.

Exercises

1. Which statement best describes the error (if any) between Steps 2 and 3?

Step 1: $64 \div 4^2 \cdot 3 + 3^2 - 8$

Step 2: $64 \div 16 \cdot 3 + 9 - 8$

Step 3: $4 \cdot 3 \cdot 1$

Ⓐ The power was performed after division.

Ⓑ The power was interpreted incorrectly.

Ⓒ Addition was performed before multiplication.

Ⓓ There was no error made.

2. Choose the best next step to take when solving the equation below.

$$5x = -10$$

Ⓐ Divide only the right hand side by 5.

Ⓑ Divide each side by 5.

Ⓒ Divide only the right hand side by -10.

Ⓓ Divide the left hand side by 5 and the right hand side by -10.

3. Which statement best describes the error (if any) between Steps 2 and 3?

Step 1: $4 - 2 \cdot 3^2 \div 9$

Step 2: $4 - 2 \cdot 9 \div 9$

Step 3: $4 - 18 \div 9$

Ⓐ The multiplication property of equality was used incorrectly.

Ⓑ The division property of equality was used incorrectly.

Ⓒ The subtraction property of equality was used incorrectly.

Ⓓ There was no error made.

4. What is the next step in solving $18 \div 2^3 - 3 \cdot 0.2$?

Ⓐ $18 \div 1 \cdot 0.2$

Ⓑ $18 \div 6 - 0.6$

Ⓒ $18 \div 8 \cdot 0.2$

Ⓓ $18 \div 8 - 3 \cdot 0.2$

5. What is the next step in solving
$5 - 4x \div 2 + 2$?

   Ⓐ $5 - x$ Ⓑ $5 - 4x \div 4$

   Ⓒ $5 - 2x + 2$ Ⓓ $x \div 2 + 2$

In Exercises 6 and 7, determine whether the argument is valid. If it is invalid, identify the reason it is invalid.

6. $\frac{x^2}{x} > \frac{0}{x}$ implies $x > 0$.

   Ⓐ Valid

   Ⓑ Invalid because $\frac{x^2}{x} = \frac{1}{x}$

   Ⓒ Invalid because $\frac{x^2}{x} = -\frac{1}{x}$

   Ⓓ Invalid because x may be less than zero

7. $\frac{x^3}{x^2} < \frac{0}{x^2}$ implies $x < 0$.

   Ⓐ Valid

   Ⓑ Invalid because it violates the order of operations

   Ⓒ Invalid because x may be less than zero

   Ⓓ Invalid because x may be zero

8. Which statement best describes the error in Step 3 below?

Step 1: $42 \div (5 - 3) + 16$

Step 2: $42 \div 2 + 16$

Step 3: $42 \div 18$

   Ⓐ The power was performed before division.

   Ⓑ Multiplication was performed before division.

   Ⓒ Subtraction was performed before multiplication.

   Ⓓ Addition was performed before division.

In Exercises 9 through 12, identify the error (if any) between Steps 2 and 3.

9. Step 1: $9x \div 3 - 2 = 4 - 3x$

   Step 2: $3x - 2 = 4 - 3x$

   Step 3: $3x - 2 = x$

   Ⓐ There was no error made.

   Ⓑ Division was performed before subtraction.

   Ⓒ Unlike terms were combined.

   Ⓓ The associative property was violated.

10. Step 1: $x^2 - 1 = 0$

   Step 2: $(x + 1)(x - 1) = 0$

   Ⓐ There was no error made.

   Ⓑ Unlike terms were combined.

   Ⓒ The additive property of equality was violated.

   Ⓓ Both sides were divided by zero.

11. Step 1: $x^2 = -x$

   Step 2: $x = -1$

   Ⓐ There was no error made.

   Ⓑ Unlike terms were combined.

   Ⓒ The additive property of equality was violated.

   Ⓓ Both sides may have been divided by zero.

12. Step 1: $(2x - 3)^2 = 4x^2$

   Step 2: $4x^2 - 12x + 9 = 4x^2$

   Step 3: $9 - 12x = 0$

   Ⓐ There was no error made.

   Ⓑ Unlike terms were combined.

   Ⓒ The additive property of equality was violated.

   Ⓓ Both sides may have been divided by zero.

13. Which statement best describes the error below?

$$(3 - 2)^2 = 3^2 - 2^2$$

   Ⓐ Subtraction in parentheses was performed before division.

   Ⓑ Subtraction in parentheses was performed before exponent was applied.

   Ⓒ The power was performed after subtraction in parentheses.

   Ⓓ The power was performed before subtraction in parentheses.

California Standards
Algebra 25.3

Given a specific algebraic statement involving linear, quadratic, or absolute value expressions or equations or inequalities, students determine whether the statement is true sometimes, always, or never.

Determine When a Statement is True

Example   **Sometimes True, Always True, or Never True?**

When is the following statement true? $x^2 < x$

   (A) Always   (B) Never

   (C) When $x < 1$ (D) When $0 < x < 1$

Solution

The inequality should be solved by graphing $y = x^2 - x$ or factoring $x^2 - x < 0$.

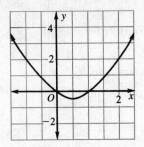

The graph shows that $x^2 - x$ is below the x-axis (that is, < 0) when $x > 0$ and $x < 1$.

Factoring $x^2 - x < 0$ leads to $(x - 1)(x) < 0$. $(x - 1)(x) < 0$ when $x - 1 < 0$ and $x > 0$ or when $x - 1 > 0$ and $x < 0$ (but that is impossible). Notice $x - 1 < 0$ and $x > 0$ imply $x > 0$ and $x < 1$.

Answer Choice D correctly identifies when $x^2 < x$ and so it is the correct answer.

Exercises

In Exercises 1 through 4, determine when the given statement is true.

1. $|x| = x$

   (A) Always   (B) Only when $x \geq 0$

   (C) Never   (D) Only when $x = 0$

2. $x > -x$

   (A) Always   (B) Only when $x < 0$

   (C) Never   (D) Only when $x > 0$

3. $2x \cdot 0.5 = x$

   (A) Always

   (B) When $x = -2$ or $x = 2$

   (C) Never

   (D) Only when $x \neq 0$

4. $x = x + 1$

   (A) Always   (B) Only when $x = 1$

   (C) Never   (D) Only when $x = -1$

In Exercises 5 through 8, determine when the given statement is true.

5. $|x| = \sqrt{x^2}$

   (A) Always   (B) Only when $x < 0$

   (C) Never   (D) Only when $x > 0$

6. $\frac{1}{2}(2x + 8) = \frac{3x + 12}{3}$

   (A) Always

   (B) Never

   (C) Only when $x \geq 0$

   (D) When $x = -2$ or $x = 2$

7. $\sqrt{x^2 + y^2} = |x + y|$

   (A) Always

   (B) When $y = 0$

   (C) Never

   (D) Only when $x = y = 0$

8. $\sqrt{x^2 - y^2} = |x - y|$

   (A) Always

   (B) Only when $x = y = 0$

   (C) Never

   (D) Only when $y = 0$

9. Which of the following statements is never true?

   (A) $(x + y)^2 = x^2 + y^2$

   (B) $(x - y)^2 = x^2 - y^2$

   (C) $2(x - y) = 2(x + y)$

   (D) $\frac{x - y}{x - y} = 2 + \frac{x + y}{x + y}$

10. Which of the following statements is always true?

    (A) $|x| \geq x$ (B) $|x| > x$

    (C) $x^2 \geq x$ (D) $x^2 > x$

11. Which of the following statements is sometimes true?

    (A) $x = x + 1$

    (B) $x^2 - 1 = x - 1$

    (C) $\frac{2x}{3x} = 1.5$

    (D) $\sqrt{x^2} - |x| \neq 0$

12. Which of the following statements is not always true?

    (A) $x^2 - y^2 = (x + y)(x - y)$

    (B) $x^2 + y^2 = (x + y)^2 - 2xy$

    (C) $2x \geq x$

    (D) $x + 1 \geq x$

In Exercises 13 through 16, determine when the given statement is true.

13. $-x \geq x^2$

    (A) When $x \leq 0$

    (B) When $x \leq -1$

    (C) When $-1 \leq x \leq 0$

    (D) When $x \leq -1$ or $x \geq 0$

14. $x^2 - y^2 = (x - y)^2$

    (A) When $x = -y$

    (B) When $x = 0$ or $y = 0$

    (C) When $y = 0$

    (D) When $x = 0$

15. $-x > |x^2|$

    (A) Never

    (B) When $x < 0$

    (C) When $-1 < x < 0$

    (D) When $-1 > x > 0$

16. $1 + x^2 = -2x$

    (A) Never

    (B) When $x < -1$

    (C) When $x = -1$ or $x = 1$

    (D) Only when $x = -1$

17. When is $-\frac{1}{2}x + 3 > 2x - 3$ true?

    (A) Always

    (B) Never

    (C) When $x \geq 2.4$

    (D) When $x < 2.4$

California Standards Review and Practice

Intensive Review

California Standards
Pretest

DIRECTIONS

Read each question. Then, on your answer sheet, fill in the bubble for the correct answer.

1. What is the factored form of $36a^2 - 9b^2$? *(Alg. 11.0)*

   Ⓐ $(6a - 3b)(6a + 3b)$

   Ⓑ $(6a - 9b)(6a + b)$

   Ⓒ $9(2a + b)(2a - b)$

   Ⓓ $(36a - 9b)(a + b)$

2. Let $a < 0$ and $b < 0$. Which statement is *true* for *all* values of a and b? *(Alg. 1.1)*

   Ⓐ $(ab)^2 < 0$

   Ⓑ $a^2 b < 0$

   Ⓒ $a^2 b^3 > 0$

   Ⓓ $ab^3 < 0$

3. What is the reciprocal of -4? *(Alg. 2.0)*

   Ⓐ $\frac{1}{4}$

   Ⓑ 4

   Ⓒ $-\frac{1}{4}$

   Ⓓ $\frac{1}{2}$

4. The graph of $y = x^2 - 4x + 4$ is shown below. For what value(s) of x is $x^2 - 4x + 4 = 0$? *(Alg. 21.0)*

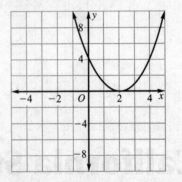

   Ⓐ $x = 4$

   Ⓑ $x = 4$ and $x = 2$

   Ⓒ $x = -2$

   Ⓓ $x = 2$

5. Which inequality is shown in the graph below? *(Alg. 6.0)*

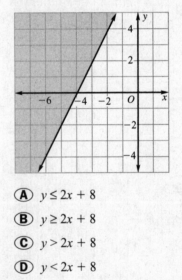

   Ⓐ $y \leq 2x + 8$

   Ⓑ $y \geq 2x + 8$

   Ⓒ $y > 2x + 8$

   Ⓓ $y < 2x + 8$

California Standards
Pretest *continued*

6. Which equation represents a line that is perpendicular to the line defined by $y - 3x = 6$? *(Alg. 8.0)*

(A) $x - \frac{1}{3}y = -10$

(B) $x + \frac{1}{3}y = 10$

(C) $x + 3y = 12$

(D) $-x + 3y = 12$

7. What is the solution to the system $y = 2x - 9$ and $y = 4 + 3x$? *(Alg. 9.0)*

(A) $(5, 19)$

(B) $(-5, -11)$

(C) $(-13, -35)$

(D) $(13, 42)$

8. What is the equation of the line that has a slope of 0 and passes through the point $(1, 6)$? *(Alg. 7.0)*

(A) $y = x + 6$

(B) $y = x - 6$

(C) $y = 6$

(D) $y = -6$

9. Which equation represents a line that is parallel to the line represented by $x - y = 1$? *(Alg. 8.0)*

(A) $4x + 4y = 3$

(B) $2x - 2y = 5$

(C) $7x + 7y = 13$

(D) $-6x - 6y = 2$

10. Identify the property being illustrated. *(Alg. 1.0)*

$$6 \cdot (-7r) = -7r \cdot 6$$

(A) Distributive property

(B) Associative property

(C) Commutative property

(D) Multiplication property

11. Which is the first *incorrect* step in the solution shown below? *(Alg. 5.0)*

Solve: $2(x - 7) = -12 + 4x$

Step 1: $2x - 14 = -12 + 4x$

Step 2: $-14 = -12 - 2x$

Step 3: $-2 = -2x$

Step 4: $1 = x$

(A) Step 1

(B) Step 2

(C) Step 3

(D) Step 4

12. $\sqrt{64} + 3 =$ *(Alg. 2.0)*

(A) 5

(B) 19

(C) 11

(D) 27

13. What is the solution of $|2x + 4| = -10$? *(Alg. 3.0)*

(A) $\{2, -4\}$

(B) $\{7, -3\}$

(C) $\{4, -2\}$

(D) No solution

14. Solve $2x + 4 = -10 + 8x$. *(Alg. 5.0)*

(A) $x = \frac{7}{3}$

(B) $x = \frac{3}{7}$

(C) $x = -\frac{3}{7}$

(D) $x = -\frac{7}{3}$

California Standards
Pretest *continued*

15. Which equation is equivalent to
$9x - 3 = 4(x - 5)$? *(Alg. 4.0)*

  (A) $9x - 15 = -20$

  (B) $5x - 12 = 6x + 8$

  (C) $4x - 20 = 9x - 3$

  (D) $13x + 15 = 4x - 8$

16. What is the x-intercept of the graph of
$5x - 2 = 8y + 3$? *(Alg. 6.0)*

  (A) -1

  (B) $-\dfrac{1}{5}$

  (C) 1

  (D) $\dfrac{1}{5}$

17. What is the equation of the line that has a slope of
-3 and passes through the point $(-2, 0)$?
(Alg. 7.0)

  (A) $3x + y = -3$

  (B) $3x + y = 6$

  (C) $3x + y = 3$

  (D) $3x + y = -6$

18. Tim's work is shown below.

Simplify: $(3 + 2) - 12 \div 2^2$

Step 1: $(3 + 2) - 12 \div 4$

Step 2: $5 - 12 \div 4$

Step 3: $5 - 3$

Step 4: 2

Which is the first incorrect step? *(Alg. 25.2)*

  (A) Step 1

  (B) Step 2

  (C) Step 3

  (D) Step 4

19. Simplify $(-1)(-x + y)$. *(Alg. 1.0)*

  (A) $y - x$

  (B) $x + y$

  (C) $-y - x$

  (D) $x - y$

20. Line A has a slope of $\dfrac{1}{4}$. Which equation
represents a line perpendicular to line A?
(Alg. 8.0)

  (A) $-4x + y = -2$

  (B) $-4x - y = 2$

  (C) $-4x + 2y = 1$

  (D) $-4x - 2y = -1$

21. Which point lies on the line defined by
$x - 3y = 7$? *(Alg. 7.0)*

  (A) $(-13, -2)$

  (B) $(-13, 2)$

  (C) $(13, -2)$

  (D) $(13, 2)$

22. $\dfrac{16x^2}{56x^7} =$

(Alg. 10.0)

  (A) $\dfrac{x^4}{7}$

  (B) $6x^3$

  (C) $\dfrac{2}{7x^5}$

  (D) $\dfrac{4x^5}{7}$

23. Which of the following points lies in the solution
set of the system $y > 4x - 2$ and $y < -2x + 1$?
(Alg. 9.0)

  (A) $(-1, 2)$

  (B) $(-1, 6)$

  (C) $(2, 1)$

  (D) $(2, -7)$

California Standards
Pretest *continued*

24. Which is an example of the associative property of addition? *(Alg. 1.0)*

   (A) $3 - (x + 7) = 3 - x - 7$

   (B) $3 + (-x + 7) = 3 - x + 7$

   (C) $(3 - x) + 7 = (-x + 3) + 7$

   (D) $(3 - x) + 7 = 3 + (-x + 7)$

25. $(5x^2 - 3x + 7) - (x^2 - 6x + 2) =$ *(Alg. 10.0)*

   (A) $4x^2 + 3x + 5$

   (B) $6x^2 + 3x + 5$

   (C) $4x^2 - 3x + 5$

   (D) $6x^2 - 3x + 5$

26. Which number should be added to both sides of the equation $x^2 - 10x = -6$ to complete the square? *(Alg. 14.0)*

   (A) 10

   (B) 25

   (C) 8

   (D) 6

27. Which of the following relations is a function? *(Alg. 16.0)*

   (A) $\{(1, -5), (7, 1), (-5, -5), (0, -3)\}$

   (B) $\{(-3, 0), (7, 1), (-3, -5), (0, -3)\}$

   (C) $\{(0, -2), (7, 1), (-3, 7), (0, -3)\}$

   (D) $\{(1, -2), (-3, 0), (-3, -3), (1, -4)\}$

28. Which relation is *not* a function? *(Alg. 16.0)*

   (A) $\{(0, 0), (1, 1)\}$

   (B) $\{(1, -2), (-2, 0), (0, 1), (-3, -3)\}$

   (C) $\{(1, -2), (7, 1), (-5, -2), (0, -3)\}$

   (D) $\{(1, -2), (-5, 0), (0, -3), (-5, 8)\}$

29. What is the range of $y = x^2$ when the domain is $\{-5, -4, 0, 3, 4\}$? *(Alg. 17.0)*

   (A) $\{0, 9, 16, 25\}$

   (B) $\{2, 3\}$

   (C) $\{-25, -16, 0, 9, 16\}$

   (D) $\{-5, -4, 0, 2, 3\}$

30. Which is a factor of $x^2 - 9$? *(Alg. 11.0)*

   (A) $x + 6$

   (B) $x - 3$

   (C) $x - 9$

   (D) $x^2 + 3$

31. What is the domain of the following function? *(Alg. 17.0)*

   $\{(0, 0), (1, 0), (2, 0), (3, 0), (4, 0)\}$

   (A) $\{0\}$

   (B) The empty set, Ø

   (C) $\{0, 1, 2, 3, 4\}$

   (D) $\{1, 2, 3, 4\}$

32. What is the range of the following function? *(Alg. 17.0)*

   $\{(0, 0), (1, 0), (2, 0), (3, 0), (4, 0)\}$

   (A) $\{0\}$

   (B) The empty set, Ø

   (C) $\{0, 1, 2, 3, 4\}$

   (D) $\{1, 2, 3, 4\}$

33. Which of the following is *always* a function? *(Alg. 18.0)*

   (A) A line through the origin

   (B) A line with negative slope

   (C) A vertical line

   (D) A line that passes through the point (1, 2)

Name _____ Date _____

34. Simplify the expression below to lowest terms. *(Alg. 12.0)*

$$\frac{3x^2 - 7x - 6}{x^2 - 2x - 3}$$

(A) $\frac{3x - 2}{x + 1}$

(B) $\frac{x + 3}{x + 1}$

(C) $\frac{3x - 2}{x - 3}$

(D) $\frac{3x + 2}{x + 1}$

35. $\frac{6x + 18}{2x + 8} \div \frac{3x - 3}{x^2 + 3x - 4} =$

(Alg. 13.0)

(A) $\frac{x + 3}{x - 1}$

(B) $x + 3$

(C) $\frac{x + 3}{x + 4}$

(D) $x + 4$

36. Jen's average speed jogging was 146 yards per minute for 30 minutes. During the first 10 minutes she jogged 176 yards per minute. What was her average speed for the remaining 20 minutes? *(Alg. 15.0)*

(A) 131 yards per minute

(B) 136 yards per minute

(C) 141 yards per minute

(D) 146 yards per minute

37. Which relation is a function? *(Alg. 18.0)*

(A) $\{(-1, 1), (2, 1), (-1, -1), (3, 1)\}$

(B) $\{(2, 2), (3, 3), (4, 4), (5, 5)\}$

(C) $\{(-3, 4), (4, -3), (-3, 5), (5, -3)\}$

(D) $\{(0, 0), (1, -4), (6, 2), (0, 4)\}$

38. Four steps to derive the quadratic formula are shown below.

I $x + \frac{b}{2a} = \pm\sqrt{\frac{b^2 - 4ac}{4a^2}}$

II $x = -\frac{b}{2a} \pm \frac{\sqrt{b^2 - 4ac}}{2a}$

III $x = \frac{-b \pm \sqrt{b^2 - 4ac}}{2a}$

IV $x + \frac{b}{2a} = \pm\frac{\sqrt{b^2 - 4ac}}{2a}$

What is the correct order for these steps? *(Alg. 19.0)*

(A) II, I, III, IV

(B) I, II, III, IV

(C) IV, III, I, II

(D) I, IV, II, III

39. Which of the following is *not* correct? *(Alg. 24.1)*

(A) Pat found five pennies. They all had the Lincoln Memorial on them. The next penny Pat finds will have the Lincoln Memorial on it. This is an example of inductive reasoning.

(B) Objects weigh less on the moon than they do on earth. You conclude you will weigh less on the moon than you do on earth. This is an example of deductive reasoning.

(C) Every quadrilateral has four sides. A five-sided polygon is not a quadrilateral. This is an example of inductive reasoning.

(D) The sum of any two odd numbers is an even number. The sum of 13 and 5 is even. This is an example of deductive reasoning.

California Standards
Pretest *continued*

40. Which statement best explains why there are no solutions to the equation $-3x^2 + 2x - 1 = 0$? *(Alg. 20.0)*

- Ⓐ The value of $2^2 + 4(-3)(-1)$ is positive.
- Ⓑ The value of $2^2 - 4(-3)(-1)$ is negative.
- Ⓒ The value of $(-2)^2 - 4(3)(1)$ is negative.
- Ⓓ The value of $(-2)^2 + 4(-3)(-1)$ is positive.

41. The graph of which quadratic function opens upward? *(Alg. 21.0)*

- Ⓐ $y = x^2 - 7x$
- Ⓑ $y = -6x^2 - 7x + 14$
- Ⓒ $y = -x^2 - 9x + 4$
- Ⓓ $y = -2x^2 - 4x$

42. What is the conclusion of the statement "If x is a negative integer, then x cannot be a whole number"? *(Alg. 24.2)*

- Ⓐ x is a whole number
- Ⓑ x is a negative integer
- Ⓒ x is a positive integer
- Ⓓ x cannot be a whole number

43. Tell whether the statement is true or false. If it is false, select the choice that gives a valid counterexample. "If x is a positive number, then x is an integer." *(Alg. 24.3)*

- Ⓐ false; $x = 1.5$
- Ⓑ false; $x = 0$
- Ⓒ true
- Ⓓ false; $x = 12$

44. $\sqrt[3]{8} - \sqrt{64} \cdot \sqrt[3]{125} =$

(Alg. 2.0)

- Ⓐ -38
- Ⓑ -30
- Ⓒ 12
- Ⓓ -5

45. Solve $|3x - 3| \geq 6$. *(Alg. 3.0)*

- Ⓐ $x \leq -1$ or $x \geq 3$
- Ⓑ $x \leq -3$ or $x \geq 1$
- Ⓒ $-1 \leq x \leq 3$
- Ⓓ $-3 \leq x \leq 1$

46. How many times does the graph of $y = 3x^2 + x - 4$ intersect the x-axis? *(Alg. 22.0)*

- Ⓐ none
- Ⓑ one
- Ⓒ two
- Ⓓ three

47. What is the hypothesis of the statement "If school is in session, then it must be a weekday"? *(Alg. 24.2)*

- Ⓐ it must be a weekend
- Ⓑ it must be a weekday
- Ⓒ school is in session
- Ⓓ school is not in session

48. A cliff diver dives off a cliff that is 64 feet above the water. The diver's height h above the water after t seconds is given by $h = -16t^2 + 64$. How many seconds is the diver in the air? *(Alg. 23.0)*

- Ⓐ 1
- Ⓑ 2
- Ⓒ 3
- Ⓓ 4

49. Which inequality is equivalent to $3x - 8 \geq 5x + 3$? *(Alg. 4.0)*

- Ⓐ $8x \leq -11$
- Ⓑ $8x \leq -5$
- Ⓒ $2x \leq -11$
- Ⓓ $2x \leq -5$

California Standards
Pretest *continued*

50. Sara claims that the quotient of an irrational number and another irrational number is always irrational. Which is the best counterexample to Sara's claim? *(Alg. 25.1)*

(A) $\dfrac{\sqrt{4}}{\sqrt{4}} = 1$

(B) $\dfrac{\sqrt{3}}{\sqrt{3}} = 1$

(C) $\dfrac{1.\overline{33}}{1.\overline{33}} = 1$

(D) $\dfrac{5}{5} = 1$

51. Which of the following correctly completes the statement "If x^2 is a perfect square, then x is __?__ " *(Alg. 25.3)*

(A) never a natural number.

(B) never a negative integer.

(C) always an integer.

(D) never a positive number.

52. Which shows $x^4 + 3x^3 - 10x^2$ factored completely? *(Alg. 11.0)*

(A) $x^2(x - 2)(x + 5)$

(B) $x^2(x + 2)(x - 5)$

(C) $x(x - 2)(x + 5)$

(D) $x(x + 2)(x - 5)$

53. Solve for n. *(Alg. 5.0)*

$$\frac{n}{1-n} \le 3$$

(A) $n \le \dfrac{3}{4}$

(B) $n \le \dfrac{4}{3}$

(C) $n \le -\dfrac{3}{4}$

(D) $n \le -\dfrac{4}{3}$

54. What are the coordinates of the y-intercept of the line $5x - 4y = 20$? *(Alg. 6.0)*

(A) $(0, -5)$

(B) $(0, 4)$

(C) $(10, 0)$

(D) $(-5, 0)$

55. Solve $3 + 5x - 2x^2 = 0$ by factoring. *(Alg. 14.0)*

(A) $x = -\dfrac{1}{2}$ or 3

(B) $x = \dfrac{1}{2}$ or 3

(C) $x = -\dfrac{1}{2}$ or -3

(D) $x = \dfrac{1}{2}$ or -3

56. The temperature outside an airplane flying 5 miles above Earth's surface is twice the opposite of the temperature on the ground which is 15°C. What is the temperature outside the airplane? *(Alg. 2.0)*

(A) $-30°C$

(B) $-15°C$

(C) $15°C$

(D) $30°C$

57. Which of the following best explains why the graph below is *not* a function? *(Alg. 18.0)*

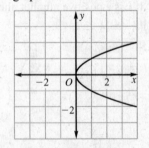

(A) The vertical line $x = -1$ does not intersect the graph.

(B) The vertical line $x = 0$ intersects the graph only once.

(C) The horizontal line $y = 1$ passes through the graph only once.

(D) The vertical line $x = 1$ intersects the graph twice.

Name _____ Date _____

California Standards
Algebra 1.0, 1.1

Properties of Numbers

Example   ### Identify Properties of Numbers

Identify the property being illustrated.

$5(x + 3) = 5x + 15$

   Ⓐ Distributive property

   Ⓑ Identity property

   Ⓒ Commutative property

   Ⓓ Transitive property

Solution

$5(x + 3) = (5 \cdot x) + (5 \cdot 3)$ **Multiply each term by 5.**

$= 5x + 15$ **Simplify.**

Each term within the parentheses is multiplied by the number on the outside of the parentheses. This is an example of the distributive property. So, choice A is the correct answer.

Exercises

1. If $2(m - 6n) = -78$, which of the following is equal to $2(m - 6n) + 38$?

   Ⓐ -48 Ⓑ -40 Ⓒ 40 Ⓓ -30

2. If $x - 29 = m + n$, then which of the following is equal to $m + n + 29$?

   Ⓐ 29 Ⓑ -29 Ⓒ x Ⓓ $-x$

3. If $(a + 32b) = -32$ and $(m + 23n) = 32$, then what is $(a + 32b) - (m + 23n)$ equal to?

   Ⓐ -24 Ⓑ 0 Ⓒ 24 Ⓓ -64

4. If $M = 3x + (2y - 5x)$, then which equality is true?

   Ⓐ $M = 3(x + y)$ Ⓑ $M = 2(x - y)$

   Ⓒ $M = -2(x - y)$ Ⓓ $M = -2(y - x)$

5. Which equation demonstrates the distributive property?

   Ⓐ $3x(-5 - 11y) = 3x(-5) + 3x(11y)$

   Ⓑ $-3x(-5 - 11y) = 3x(-5) + 3x(-11y)$

   Ⓒ $3x(5 - 11y) = 3x(5) + 3x(-11y)$

   Ⓓ $3x(-5 - 11y) = 3x(5) + 3x(11y)$

6. Which set is closed under division?

   Ⓐ Set of whole numbers

   Ⓑ Set of rational numbers excluding 1

   Ⓒ Set of irrational numbers

   Ⓓ Set of real numbers excluding zero

7. Let $a < 0$ and $b < 0$. Which statement is true for all values of a and b?

   Ⓐ $\frac{a}{b} < 0$

   Ⓑ $ab > 0$

   Ⓒ $a + b = 0$

   Ⓓ $b - a > 0$

8. Which of the following is an example of the identity property of addition?

   Ⓐ $n \cdot \frac{1}{n} = 1$

   Ⓑ $n + 0 = n$

   Ⓒ $n + 1 = n + 1$

   Ⓓ $n + (-n) = 0$

California Standards
Intensive Review

California Standards
Algebra 2.0

Opposites, Reciprocals, Roots, and Exponents

Example   **Simplify an Expression**

a. Simplify $(ab)^{-11}(abc)^8 b^4 c^3$.

b. Simplify $3\sqrt{4} + 6\sqrt{25} - 8\sqrt{121}$.

Solution

a. $(ab)^{-11}(abc)^8 b^4 c^3$

$= a^{-11} \cdot b^{-11} \cdot a^8 \cdot b^8 \cdot c^8 \cdot b^4 \cdot c^3$ **Power of a product property**

$= (a^8 \cdot a^{-11}) \cdot (b^8 \cdot b^{-11} \cdot b^4) \cdot (c^8 \cdot c^3)$ **Associative and commutative properties**

$= a^{-3} b c^{11}$ **Product of powers property**

b. $3\sqrt{4} + 6\sqrt{25} - 8\sqrt{121}$

$= 3\sqrt{2^2} + 6\sqrt{5^2} - 8\sqrt{11^2}$ **Rewrite 4, 25, and 121 as powers.**

$= 3 \cdot 2 + 6 \cdot 5 - 8 \cdot 11$ **Use definition of square root.**

$= -52$ **Simplify.**

Exercises

1. If $A = a^6 b^{-6}$ and $P = a^{-11} b^6$, then which is equivalent to $A \cdot P$?

  (A) a^{-5} **(B)** $a^5 b$

  (C) ab^{11} **(D)** $a^{11} b$

2. Simplify $x \cdot y^3 \cdot (2xy)^2 \cdot (4xy)$.

  (A) $24x^4 y^6$

  (B) $8x^4 y^6$

  (C) $16x^4 y^6$

  (D) $32x^5$

3. $9\sqrt{81} - 81\sqrt{9} =$

  (A) 0 **(B)** $72\sqrt{72}$

  (C) $-72\sqrt{72}$ **(D)** -162

4. $(3\sqrt{21})^2 - 3\sqrt{16} =$

  (A) 168 **(B)** 177

  (C) 189 **(D)** 207

5. What is the reciprocal of $-\dfrac{4}{3a}$?

  (A) $\dfrac{4}{3a}$ **(B)** $-\dfrac{4}{3}$

  (C) $-\dfrac{3a}{4}$ **(D)** $-\dfrac{4}{3a}$

6. Simplify $2x \cdot 3y^2 \cdot (xy)^3 \cdot 4y^4$.

  (A) $24x^4 y^9$ **(B)** $9x^3 y^5$

  (C) $16x^2 y^5$ **(D)** $32x^2$

7. $3\sqrt{64} - 16\sqrt{4} =$

  (A) 56 **(B)** $8\sqrt{64}$

  (C) -8 **(D)** $-72\sqrt{72}$

California Standards
Algebra 3.0

Absolute Value Equations and Inequalities

Example   **Solve an Absolute Value Equation**

Solve $|4x - 12| = 24$.

Solution

To solve $|4x - 12| = 24$, rewrite the equation as two simple linear equations.

$$4x - 12 = 24 \text{ and } 4x - 12 = -24$$

First equation:

$4x - 12 = 24$	**Write equation.**
$4x - 12 + 12 = 24 + 12$	**Add 12 to each side.**
$4x = 36$	**Simplify.**
$x = 9$	**Divide each side by 4.**

Second equation:

$4x - 12 = -24$	**Write equation.**
$4x - 12 + 12 = -24 + 12$	**Add 12 to each side.**
$4x = -12$	**Simplify.**
$x = -3$	**Divide each side by 4.**

Answer $x = -3$ or $x = 9$

Exercises

1. What is the solution set of $|12 - x| = 29$?

   Ⓐ $\{17, 31\}$ Ⓑ $\{-17, 41\}$

   Ⓒ $\{27, 31\}$ Ⓓ $\{-17, -34\}$

2. What is the solution set of $|5x + 3| = -12$?

   Ⓐ no solution   Ⓑ $\{3, -3\}$

   Ⓒ $\{5, 2\}$ Ⓓ $\{4, 3\}$

3. Solve $|-2x + 1| - 3 = 18$.

   Ⓐ $x = -3$ or $x = 13$

   Ⓑ $x = -10$ or $x = 11$

   Ⓒ $x = 5$ or $x = 13$

   Ⓓ $x = 2$ or $x = 12$

4. Which is a solution of $|7y + 33| - 11 = 29$?

   Ⓐ 2   Ⓑ 1   Ⓒ 4   Ⓓ 11

5. What is the solution of $|2y - 31| \geq 7$?

   Ⓐ $y \geq 8$ or $y \leq 1$ Ⓑ $y \geq 19$ or $y \leq 13$

   Ⓒ $y \geq 19$ or $y \leq 14$ Ⓓ $y \geq 19$ or $y \leq 12$

6. What is the solution of $|9x - 25| < 18$?

   Ⓐ $\dfrac{7}{9} < x < \dfrac{43}{9}$

   Ⓑ $\dfrac{7}{9} < x < 5$

   Ⓒ $-2 < x < \dfrac{43}{9}$

   Ⓓ $-2 < x < 5$

7. Solve $|4y + 4| - 11 \leq 53$.

   Ⓐ $y \leq -17$ or $y \geq 15$

   Ⓑ $y \geq 17$ or $y \leq 15$

   Ⓒ $-17 \leq y \leq 15$

   Ⓓ $-15 \leq y \leq 17$

California Standards
Intensive Review

California Standards
Algebra 1.0, 1.1, 2.0, 3.0

Mixed Review

1. Simplify $-(19 + 15 - 16) + 3$.

   (A) -24 (B) 21

   (C) 20 (D) -15

2. Which equation demonstrates the associative property of multiplication?

   (A) $5(3^4 + 6) = (5 \cdot 3^4) + (5 \cdot 6)$

   (B) $5 \cdot (-6) = -6 \cdot 5$

   (C) $5 \cdot (3^4 \cdot 6) = (5 \cdot 3^4) \cdot 6$

   (D) $(3^4)^2 \cdot 8 = 3^8 \cdot 8$

3. Which expression is equivalent to a positive number?

   (A) $-(-11)^4$ (B) $-[-(-11)^5]$

   (C) $(-11)^4$ (D) $-[(11)^5]$

4. Simplify $3x^2y^3 \cdot 6x^{-4}y^8$.

   (A) $18x^6y^{-5}$

   (B) $18x^2y^{11}$

   (C) $18x^{-5}y^{-4}$

   (D) $18x^{-2}y^{11}$

5. Which expression is equivalent to a negative number?

   (A) $[-(2)^3] + 7$

   (B) $[(-3)^2] + 11$

   (C) $-[-(-4)^4] + 36$

   (D) $[(2)^5] - 27$

6. Simplify $34 - [-(-19 + 2) + (16 - 15)]$.

   (A) -18 (B) 16

   (C) 22 (D) 28

7. Simplify $\sqrt[3]{27} - \sqrt{121} + 5$.

   (A) -6 (B) 17

   (C) -11 (D) -3

8. Which expression is equivalent to $5(x - 3y) - 9a + 2n(12)$?

   (A) $5x - 15y - 9a + 24n$

   (B) $5x + 15y - 9a + 12n$

   (C) $5x - 5y - 9a + 24n$

   (D) $5x + 15y - 9a + 24n$

9. Solve for x. $\dfrac{13x}{2} = 52$

   (A) 14 (B) 8

   (C) 4 (D) 2

10. Which equation demonstrates the associative property?

   (A) $2 \cdot 9 = 18$

   (B) $12a - 3 = 3 - 12a$

   (C) $(6x + 3) + 15 = 6x + (3 + 15)$

   (D) $3a(5 \cdot 4y) = 3a(4y \cdot 5)$

11. What is the opposite of $-3m$?

   (A) 3 (B) -3 (C) $3m$ (D) $-3m$

12. If $P = 9x^2y^3$ and $Q = 3y^5z^2$, then $P \div Q =$

   (A) $27x^7y^{-2}z^2$

   (B) $3y^3z^{-2}$

   (C) $3x^2y^{-2}z^{-2}$

   (D) $6x^{-3}y$

13. If $m + n = 12$ and $2p = 24$, then which of the following is true?

   (A) $m - n = 12$

   (B) $m + n = p$

   (C) $m - n = 24$

   (D) $m + n = 2p$

14. What is the reciprocal of $\dfrac{13}{4}$?

   (A) $-\dfrac{4}{13}$ (B) $13 \cdot 4$

   (C) $\dfrac{4}{13}$ (D) $13 \cdot (-4)$

15. $\dfrac{16x^3y^4}{2x^4y^2} =$

   Ⓐ $8x^{-1}y^2$

   Ⓑ $8x^7y^6$

   Ⓒ $8xy^{-2}$

   Ⓓ $8x^{-7}y^{-6}$

16. Simplify $-(-3^{-2})^{-1} \cdot [(-6)^{-1}]^{-1}$.

   Ⓐ -112 Ⓑ 112

   Ⓒ 54 Ⓓ -54

17. If $A = a^{-2}b^{-3}c^4$ and $B = a^{-7}b^{-6}c^{-4}$, then $A \cdot B =$

   Ⓐ $(ab)^4$

   Ⓑ $(ab)^9$

   Ⓒ $(ab)^{-9}$

   Ⓓ $(ab)^{-18}$

18. Which equation demonstrates the commutative property?

   Ⓐ $4x + 16y = -(4x - 16y)$

   Ⓑ $2(x + y) = 2x + 2y$

   Ⓒ $(2a + 6b) - 3c = 2a + (6b - 3c)$

   Ⓓ $3x + 12y = 12y + 3x$

19. What is the solution of $|3a + 6| \geq 4$?

   Ⓐ $a \geq -\dfrac{2}{3}$

   Ⓑ $\dfrac{10}{3} \geq a$ or $a \leq \dfrac{2}{3}$

   Ⓒ $a \geq -\dfrac{2}{3}$ or $a \leq -\dfrac{10}{3}$

   Ⓓ $a \leq -\dfrac{10}{3}$

20. Identify the property being illustrated.

$$13y \cdot (6x \cdot 4) = (13y \cdot 6x) \cdot 4$$

   Ⓐ Associative property

   Ⓑ Symmetric property

   Ⓒ Reflexive property

   Ⓓ Distributive property

21. Which of the following is incorrect?

   Ⓐ $-3x + 5(-3y) = -3x - 15y$

   Ⓑ $(6 - 2m) \cdot 3 = 6 - 6m$

   Ⓒ $(3 + y^2)5 + 6y^2 = 11y^2 + 15$

   Ⓓ $8^2 - 5 \cdot (12 \div 2) + 3 = 37$

22. What is the solution of the inequality $|2y - 9| \geq 7$?

   Ⓐ $y \geq 8$ or $y \leq 1$

   Ⓑ $14 \leq y \leq 19$

   Ⓒ $y \geq 19$ or $y \leq 14$

   Ⓓ $1 \leq y \leq 8$

23. Solve $|y - 12| = 6$.

   Ⓐ $\{-6, -12\}$ Ⓑ $\{12, -18\}$

   Ⓒ $\{6, -6\}$ Ⓓ $\{6, 18\}$

24. Which inequality is equivalent to the compound inequality $-19x + 44 < -11$ or $-19x + 44 > 11$?

   Ⓐ $|-19x + 44| > 11$

   Ⓑ $|19x + 44| < 11$

   Ⓒ $|-19x + 44| > -11$

   Ⓓ $-|-19x + 44| < 11$

25. Which inequality does not have a solution?

   Ⓐ $-|12x + 32| + 32 > -22$

   Ⓑ $|12x + 32| - 42 > -42$

   Ⓒ $-|12x + 32| + 42 > 42$

   Ⓓ $|-12x + 32| + 22 > 32$

26. What is the solution set of $|11 - 3x| = 2$?

   Ⓐ $\left\{\dfrac{13}{3}, 3\right\}$

   Ⓑ $\left\{\dfrac{3}{13}\right\}$

   Ⓒ The empty set, Ø

   Ⓓ $\left\{-3, \dfrac{13}{3}\right\}$

California Standards
Algebra 4.0

Expressions, Equations, and Inequalities

Example   ### Solve an Inequality

Solve the inequality $8 - 2x \leq 3(x + 5)$.

Solution

$8 - 2x \leq 3(x + 5)$	Write original inequality.
$8 - 2x \leq 3x + 15$	Distributive property
$8 \leq 5x + 15$	Add 2*x* to each side.
$-7 \leq 5x$	Subtract 15 from each side.
$-\frac{7}{5} \leq x$	Divide each side by 5.

Exercises

1. Which equation is equivalent to
$-6 = 9m - 12 - 6m$?

   A $15m = 18$ **B** $15m = 6$

   C $3m = 18$ **D** $3m = 6$

2. Solve the equation $-29 = -7h + 1 + h$ for *h*.

   A $h = -36$ **B** $h = 5$

   C $h = 6$ **D** $h = -30$

3. Which equation could be Step 2 of the solution?

Given: $4(3t - 2) - 7t = 7$

Step 1: $12t - 8 - 7t = 7$

Step 2: ?

   A $12t + 7t = 15$ **B** $12t - 7t = -1$

   C $12t - 7t = 1$ **D** $12t - 7t = 15$

4. Which is equivalent to $7 + 3(y + 6) = 49$?

   A $10y + 6 = 49$

   B $7 + 3y + 12 = 49$

   C $7 + 3y + 18 = 49$

   D $10y + 60 = 49$

5. Solve $3(3p - 4) + 3(3p + 8) = 12$.

   A $p = 27$ **B** $p = 3$

   C $p = 0$ **D** $p = 12$

6. Which equation is equivalent to
$6x + 5(x + 4) = 53$?

   A $6x + 5x + 20 = 53$

   B $6x + 5x + 4 = 53$

   C $6x + 5 + x + 4 = 53$

   D $6x + 9 + x = 53$

7. Solve $t - 3 \geq 5$.

   A $t \geq 2$ **B** $t \geq 5$ **C** $t \geq 8$ **D** $t \geq \frac{8}{5}$

8. Which inequality is equivalent to
$6m + 3(11 - m) > 48$?

   A $6m + 33 - m < 48$

   B $5m + 33 > 48$

   C $6m + 33 - 3m > 48$

   D $6m + 33 + 3m < 48$

9. Solve $\frac{5}{6}(b + 9) = 10$.

   A $b = 3$ **B** $b = \frac{45}{6}$

   C $b = -6$ **D** $b = \frac{51}{6}$

10. What is the solution of this inequality?

$$2x - 3 > 7$$

   A $x > 2$ **B** $x < 2$

   C $x > 5$ **D** $x < 5$

California Standards
Algebra 5.0

Problem Solving with Linear Equations

Example   **Solve a Linear Equation**

Solve $4(y + 1) = 7(y - 1) + 6$. Justify each step.

Solution

$4(y + 1) = 7(y - 1) + 6$	**Write original equation.**
$4y + 4 = 7y - 7 + 6$	**Distributive property**
$4y + 4 = 7y - 1$	**Simplify.**
$4 = 3y - 1$	**Subtract 4y from each side.**
$5 = 3y$	**Add 1 to each side.**
$\frac{5}{3} = y$	**Divide each side by 3.**

Exercises

1. Solve $6x - 2 = x + 13$.

   A $x = 3$ **B** $x = 5$

   C $x = 15$ **D** $x = \frac{12}{5}$

2. Solve $2n - 5 = 8n + 7$.

   A $n = -4$ **B** $n = -2$

   C $n = 2$ **D** $n = 4$

3. Solve $8 + 4m = 8(m - 7)$.

   A $m = -12$ **B** $m = 12$

   C $m = 16$ **D** $m = -16$

4. Solve $2(2p - 5) = p + 3p - 2p$ for p.

   A -5 **B** -2

   C 5 **D** 2

5. Solve $3 + 4x = 3(x + 2)$.

   A $x = 3$ **B** $x = 0$

   C $x = \frac{5}{7}$ **D** $x = 1$

6. Brenda bought x CDs at \$15 each and received a \$10 discount. Willis bought x CDs for \$12.50 each. If they each spent the same amount of money, how many CDs did Brenda buy?

   A 2   **B** 10   **C** 4   **D** 8

7. Solve $18x - 5 = 3(6x - 2)$.

   A $x = 3$

   B $x = 5$

   C $x = 8$

   D no solution

8. Solve $6(6g - 2) + 8(1 - 5g) = 0$.

   A $g = -1$

   B $g = -3$

   C $g = 2$

   D $g = 8$

9. What is the solution set of $2w - 3 \geq 8w + 69$?

   A $\{w : w \geq 12\}$

   B $\{w : w \geq -12\}$

   C $\{w : w \leq -12\}$

   D $\{w : w \leq 12\}$

10. A grocery store sells a quart of orange juice for \$1.25 and 12 muffins for \$5. You have a coupon for \$0.15 off each quart of juice if you buy a dozen muffins. How many quarts of orange juice can you buy if you also buy a dozen muffins without spending more than \$10?

   A 4   **B** 3   **C** 0   **D** 10

California Standards
Intensive Review

California Standards
Algebra 4.0, 5.0

Mixed Review

1. Solve $9d - 2d + 4 = 32$.

    (A) $d = -2$ (B) $d = 8$

    (C) $d = -4$ (D) $d = 4$

2. Which equation is equivalent to $6c - 8 - 2c = -16$?

    (A) $4c = -8$ (B) $-8c = 24$

    (C) $8c = 12$ (D) $4c = 16$

3. Solve $4 = \frac{2}{9}(4y - 2)$.

    (A) $y = 5$ (B) $y = -5$

    (C) $y = \frac{4}{9}$ (D) $y = -\frac{4}{9}$

4. Tara needs to buy paint for a home improvement project. The hardware store sells the paint she needs for $13 a gallon. If Tara has $41, which inequality can she use to determine how many gallons of paint she can buy?

    (A) $41 \div x \geq 13$ (B) $41x \geq 13$

    (C) $13x \leq 41$ (D) $x - 13 \leq 41$

5. Which is the first *incorrect* step in the solution shown below?

    Given: $5x - 3(x - 6) = 2$

    Step 1: $5x - 3x - 18 = 2$

    Step 2: $2x - 18 = 2$

    Step 3: $2x = 20$

    Step 4: $x = 10$

    (A) Step 1   (B) Step 2

    (C) Step 3   (D) Step 4

6. Solve $2a - 18 \leq 5a + 3$.

    (A) $\{a : a \leq -7\}$ (B) $\{a : a \geq 7\}$

    (C) $\{a : a \leq 7\}$ (D) $\{a : a \geq -7\}$

7. Solve $\frac{1}{4}z - 1 \geq 3$.

    (A) $\{z : z \leq 16\}$ (B) $\{z : z \geq 16\}$

    (C) $\{z : z \leq -16\}$ (D) $\{z : z \geq -16\}$

8. Which is the first *incorrect* step in the solution shown below?

    Given: $\frac{1}{2}(2x - 10) = 4$

    Step 1: $2x - 10 = 2$

    Step 2: $2x = 12$

    Step 3: $x = 6$

    (A) Step 1   (B) Step 2

    (C) Step 3   (D) No errors

9. Solve $5a - 14 = -5 + 8a$.

    (A) $a = 6$ (B) $a = -6$

    (C) $a = 3$ (D) $a = -3$

10. Which equation is equivalent to $5(n + 2) = 5(1 + 2n)$?

    (A) $5n + 10 = 5 + 10n$

    (B) $5n + 10 = 3 + 6n$

    (C) $5n + 10 = 5$

    (D) $-5n + 10 = -3 + 6n$

11. Solve $-3f - 7 \geq -f + 9$.

    (A) $\{f : f \leq 8\}$ (B) $\{f : f \geq -8\}$

    (C) $\{f : f \geq 8\}$ (D) $\{f : f \leq -8\}$

12. Solve $5c + 12 = 2c - 9$.

    (A) $c = 6$ (B) $c = -7$

    (C) $c = 3$ (D) $c = -5$

13. Dantrell needs two bicycle tires, but he only has $50 to spend. Tires are on sale at the bike shop for $6 less than the regular price. Which inequality can Dantrell use to determine the most expensive pair of tires he can purchase?

    (A) $2x - 6 \leq 50$

    (B) $2x - 12 \geq 48$

    (C) $2x - 12 \leq 50$

    (D) $2x + 6 \leq 62$

California Standards
Intensive Review

14. Which is the first *incorrect* step in the solution shown below?

Given: $4(2x - 3) < 28$

Step 1: $8x - 12 < 28$

Step 2: $8x < 16$

Step 3: $x < 2$

(A) Step 1   **(B)** Step 2

(C) Step 3   **(D)** No errors

15. Solve $2m + 3 > 11$.

(A) $\{m : m < 4\}$

(B) $\{m : m < -4\}$

(C) $\{m : m > 4\}$

(D) $\{m : m > -4\}$

16. A gym is offering a 6-month trial membership by discounting the regular monthly rate by \$20. Mina will only join if the total cost of the trial membership is less than \$500. Which inequality can Mina use to determine the range of possible regular monthly rates?

(A) $6x - 20 < 500$

(B) $6x - 20 > 500$

(C) $6(x - 20) < 500$

(D) $6(x - 20) > 500$

17. Solve for q.

$$5q - 4 \geq 12 - 3q$$

(A) $\{q : q \leq 2\}$ **(B)** $\{q : q \leq -2\}$

(C) $\{q : q \geq -2\}$ **(D)** $\{q : q \geq 2\}$

18. Solve $8 + v \geq 2v - 1$.

(A) $\{v : v \leq 9\}$ **(B)** $\{v : v \leq -9\}$

(C) $\{v : v \geq -9\}$ **(D)** $\{v : v \geq 9\}$

19. Solve $3(2 - c) = 4(c + 2)$.

(A) $c = -\dfrac{9}{2}$ **(B)** $c = -4$

(C) $c = -14$ **(D)** $c = -\dfrac{2}{7}$

20. Which inequality is equivalent to $5x - 8 \leq 15$?

(A) $x < \dfrac{7}{5}$ **(B)** $x > -\dfrac{5}{7}$

(C) $5x \leq 23$ **(D)** $5x \geq 7$

21. Solve $4 = \dfrac{5}{8}(k + 8)$.

(A) $k = -\dfrac{8}{3}$ **(B)** $k = \dfrac{3}{8}$

(C) $k = -\dfrac{8}{5}$ **(D)** $k = -\dfrac{5}{8}$

22. Which is the first *incorrect* step in the solution shown below?

Given: $5(x - 2) = -4(3 - 2x)$

Step 1: $5x - 10 = -12 + 8x$

Step 2: $-10 = -12 + 13x$

Step 3: $2 = 13x$

Step 4: $\dfrac{13}{2} = x$

(A) Step 1

(B) Step 2

(C) Step 3

(D) Step 4

23. Solve $2w - 3 \leq 8w + 69$.

(A) $\{w : w \leq 12\}$ **(B)** $\{w : w \leq -12\}$

(C) $\{w : w \geq -12\}$ **(D)** $\{w : w \geq 12\}$

24. Solve for y.

$$6 = \dfrac{3}{4}(8y - 1)$$

(A) $y = \dfrac{6}{7}$ **(B)** $y = -\dfrac{6}{7}$

(C) $y = \dfrac{9}{8}$ **(D)** $y = -\dfrac{9}{8}$

25. Solve for x.

$$3x - 5 \leq 16$$

(A) $x \leq 3$ **(B)** $x \leq 7$

(C) $x \leq -3$ **(D)** $x \leq -7$

26. Solve $4 - 6d + 8d = 36$.

(A) $d = 16$ **(B)** $d = 8$

(C) $d = -16$ **(D)** $d = -8$

27. Solve for y.

$$\dfrac{5}{9}(3y + 6) = 3$$

(A) $y = 5$ **(B)** $y = -5$

(C) $y = \dfrac{1}{5}$ **(D)** $y = -\dfrac{1}{5}$

California Standards
Algebra 24.1, 24.2, 24.3

Logical Arguments

Example   ### Analyze an Argument

During basketball practice, Wilona takes 10 shots and makes all of them. Sue takes 10 shots and makes 1 of them. Coach Jones predicts that the team will win their next game, if Wilona takes more shots than Sue. What is the hypothesis and conclusion of Coach Jones' prediction? Is the coach using inductive or deductive reasoning?

Solution

The hypothesis is Wilona takes more shots than Sue. The conclusion is the team will win. Coach Jones is basing his prediction on several examples, so he is using inductive reasoning.

Exercises

1. Tell whether the statement below is true or false. If it is false, select the choice that gives a valid counterexample.

"If a number is to the left of the number 1 on the number line, it is a negative number."

(A) false; $x = 0$

(B) true

(C) false; $x = -10$

(D) false; $x = 14$

2. Determine whether inductive reasoning or deductive reasoning is used: Your friend walks the same route to school four days in a row. You conclude that your friend will walk the same route on the fifth day.

(A) inductive

(B) deductive

(C) neither

(D) cannot be determined

3. What is the hypothesis of the statement "If a parabola opens upward, then the coefficient of the x^2 term is positive"?

(A) the coefficient of the x^2 term is positive

(B) the parabola looks like a "U"

(C) a parabola opens upward

(D) the parabola has a maximum point

4. Determine whether inductive reasoning or deductive reasoning is used: The length and width of your kitchen are 15 feet and 12 feet, respectively. You conclude that the area of the kitchen is 180 square feet.

(A) inductive

(B) deductive

(C) neither

(D) cannot be determined

5. What is the conclusion of the statement "If x is less than zero, then x is a negative number"?

(A) x is greater than zero

(B) x is less than zero

(C) x is a negative number

(D) x is a positive number

6. What is the hypothesis of the statement "If x is a negative integer, then x cannot be a natural number"?

(A) x cannot be a natural number

(B) x is a negative integer

(C) x is greater than or equal to zero

(D) x is less than zero

California Standards
Algebra 25.1, 25.2, 25.3

Analyze Results, Procedures, and Statements

Example   **Judge the Validity of an Argument**

Julie argues that $x = 12$ is the solution of $2(x - 7) = 10$. Her work is shown below. Determine whether her argument is valid.

Solve: $2(x - 7) = 10$

STEP 1: $2x - 14 = 10$		**Distributive property**
STEP 2: $2x = 24$		**Addition property of equality**
STEP 3: $x = 12$		**Multiplication property of equality**

Solution

The first step in solving $2(x - 7) = 10$ is to multiply $(x - 7)$ by 2 using the distributive property. Julie's first step is correct. The second step is to add 14 to each side of the equation. Julie's second step is correct. The last step is to multiply each side by $\frac{1}{2}$. Julie's third step is correct. Julie's argument is valid.

Exercises

1. The table shows the population of several states in 2000. Which states serve as a counterexample to the statement "No state has a population smaller than 15 million"?

State Population (in millions)			
Arizona	5.13	Utah	2.23
California	33.87	New York	18.98
New Jersey	8.41		

  Ⓐ New York

  Ⓑ California

  Ⓒ New York and California

  Ⓓ Arizona, New Jersey, and Utah

2. Which of the following correctly completes the statement "If $y = 2x + b$, then the graph __?__ "

  Ⓐ always intersects the y-axis below the origin.

  Ⓑ sometimes has a negative slope.

  Ⓒ always intersects the y-axis at $(0, b)$.

  Ⓓ never intersects the y-axis.

3. Which of the following correctly completes the statement "If $y = x^2 + 12x + 36$, then the graph is __?__ "

  Ⓐ always a parabola.

  Ⓑ sometimes a circle.

  Ⓒ never a parabola.

  Ⓓ always a line.

4. Tim's solution to an equation is shown below.

Given: $|2x - 1| = 1$

Step 1: $2x - 1 = 1$ or $2x - 1 = -1$

Step 2: $2x = 2$ or $2x = 0$

Step 3: $x = 1$ or $x = 0$

Which property of real numbers did Tim use for Step 2?

  Ⓐ Multiplication property of equality

  Ⓑ Addition property of equality

  Ⓒ Associative property of multiplication

  Ⓓ Associative property of addition

California Standards
Algebra 24.1, 24.2, 24.3, 25.1, 25.2, 25.3

Mixed Review

1. Determine whether inductive reasoning or deductive reasoning is used: The length and width of a playground are 25 feet and 20 feet. You conclude that the perimeter of the playground is 90 feet.

   Ⓐ inductive

   Ⓑ deductive

   Ⓒ neither

   Ⓓ cannot be determined

2. Tell whether the statement is true or false. If it is false, select the choice that gives a valid counterexample. "If the area of a square is s^2, then the side length of the square is s."

   Ⓐ false; If $A = 1000 = 10^3$, then $s = 100 = s^2$

   Ⓑ true

   Ⓒ false; If $A = 25 = 5^2$, then $s = 5 = s^1$

   Ⓓ false; If $A = 125 = 5^3$, then $s = 25 = s^2$

3. Which property of equality is illustrated by the statement "$3(x - 2) = 3x - 6$"?

   Ⓐ Reflexive property

   Ⓑ Distributive property

   Ⓒ Transitive property

   Ⓓ Addition property

4. Which of the following is an example of inductive reasoning?

   Ⓐ If the first term of a sequence is 8, then the last term is 16.

   Ⓑ If the plane took off at 6:00 on Tuesday and Wednesday, then the plane will take off at 6:00 on Thursday.

   Ⓒ If the first term of a sequence is 2 and the last term is 37, then the fifth term is 9.

   Ⓓ If the side of a square is 10 inches, then the area is 100 square inches.

5. What is the conclusion of the statement "If x is an irrational number, then its decimal part continues without repeating"?

   Ⓐ x is an irrational number

   Ⓑ x is a decimal

   Ⓒ its decimal part continues without repeating

   Ⓓ x is not an irrational number

6. Which of the following is an example of inductive reasoning?

   Ⓐ If the first term of a sequence is 18 and the last term is 18, then the fourth term is 12.

   Ⓑ If the first term of a sequence is 7, then the last term is 10.

   Ⓒ If the area of a square is 144 square inches, then the side is 12 inches.

   Ⓓ If the first three terms of a sequence are 8, 10, and 12, then the fourth term is 14.

7. What is the conclusion of the statement "If x is 1, 3, 5, or 7, then x is an odd number"?

   Ⓐ x is 1, 3, 5, or 7

   Ⓑ x is an odd number

   Ⓒ x is an even number

   Ⓓ x is 2, 4, 6, or 8

8. Tell whether the statement is true or false. If it is false, select the choice that gives a valid counterexample. "If $|x| \geq 0$, then $x > 0$ or $x < 0$."

   Ⓐ true   Ⓑ false; $x = 0$

   Ⓒ false; $x = 9$ Ⓓ false; $x = -8$

9. Determine whether inductive reasoning or deductive reasoning is used: Saria wears jeans the first day of school. You guess that she will wear a dress on the second day of school.

   Ⓐ inductive

   Ⓑ deductive

   Ⓒ neither

   Ⓓ cannot be determined

10. The table shows the population of several metropolitan areas in 2000. Which areas serve as a counterexample to the statement "No metropolitan area on the table has a population less than 8 million"?

Metropolitan Area	Population (in millions)
Cleveland, OH	2.94
Chicago, IL	9.16
Detroit, MI	5.46
Los Angeles, CA	16.37
New York, NY	21.20

(A) Cleveland, Detroit, and Chicago

(B) Cleveland and Detroit

(C) New York and Los Angeles

(D) Los Angeles, Chicago, and Cleveland

11. Which property is illustrated by the statement "$x + (3 \cdot 9y) = (3 \cdot 9y) + x$"?

(A) Addition property

(B) Symmetric property

(C) Commutative property

(D) Transitive property

12. Which property is illustrated by the statement "$8x + 4 = 4 + 8x$"?

(A) Addition property

(B) Symmetric property

(C) Commutative property

(D) Transitive property

13. Determine whether inductive reasoning or deductive reasoning is used: Your friend leaves for school at 8:00 on Monday, Tuesday, and Wednesday. You conclude that your friend will leave for school at 8:00 on Thursday.

(A) inductive

(B) deductive

(C) neither

(D) cannot be determined

14. Which of the following is *not* an example of deductive reasoning?

(A) If the volumes of two cubes are each 64 cubic inches, their sides are the same length.

(B) If the length and width of a rectangle are 8 inches and 2 inches, then the perimeter is 20 inches.

(C) If the first three sides of a quadrilateral are 12, 14, and 16 inches, then the fourth side is 18 inches.

(D) If the length of a rectangle is 9 inches and the area is 27 square inches, then the width is 3 inches.

15. What is the hypothesis of the statement "If x is an irrational number, then x could be the square root of a prime number"?

(A) x is an irrational number

(B) x is a square root

(C) x could be the square root of a prime number

(D) x is not the square root of a prime number

16. Tell whether the statement is true or false. If it is false, select the choice that gives a valid counterexample. "If two lines are in the same plane, then they can only intersect at 1 point."

(A) false; they cannot intersect

(B) false; they can intersect at only 2 points

(C) true

(D) false; they can intersect at an infinite number of points

17. Tell whether the statement below is true or false. If it is false, select the choice that gives a valid counterexample.

"Because x^2 is a perfect square, x must be a positive number."

(A) false; $(-9)^2 = 81$, which is a perfect square

(B) false; $-(9)^2 = -81$, which is a perfect square

(C) false; $x = y$

(D) true

California Standards

Algebra 6.0

Graph Linear Equations and Inequalities

Example | **Graph a Linear Equation**

Graph $x - 2y = 4$.

Solution

STEP 1 Find the coordinates of the x- and y-intercepts.

y-intercept:	x-intercept:
$x - 2y = 4$	$x - 2y = 4$
$0 - 2y = 4$	$x - 2(0) = 4$
$-2y = 4$	$x - 0 = 4$
$y = -2$	$x = 4$

The coordinates of the y-intercept are $(0, -2)$. The coordinates of the x-intercept are $(4, 0)$.

STEP 2 Plot the points $(0, -2)$ and $(4, 0)$. Then draw a straight line through both points.

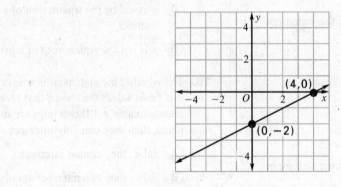

Exercises

1. Which inequality is shown on the graph below?

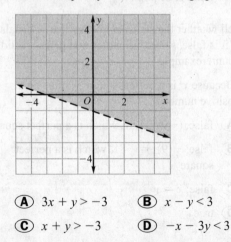

    A $3x + y > -3$ **B** $x - y < 3$

    C $x + y > -3$ **D** $-x - 3y < 3$

2. The graph of which function has an x-intercept of 3 and a y-intercept of -17?

    A $x - 8y = 1$ **B** $3x - y = 32$

    C $17x - 3y = 51$ **D** $6x - 5y = 44$

3. The graph of which function has x- and y-intercepts at the origin?

    A $y = 2x + 3$ **B** $y = -3x - 4$

    C $y = x + 1$ **D** $y = 3x$

4. What are the coordinates of the x-intercept of the line $4x - 2y = 16$?

    A $(0, 4)$ **B** $(-8, 0)$

    C $(0, -8)$ **D** $(4, 0)$

California Standards
Algebra 7.0

Points, Lines, and Linear Equations

Example   **Write an Equation of a Line**

Find an equation for the line that passes through (3, 2) and has a slope of -4. Does the point (1, 10) lie on the line?

Solution

$(y - y_1) = m(x - x_1)$	**Write the point-slope formula.**
$(y - 2) = -4(x - 3)$	**Substitute 3 for x and 2 for y.**
$y = -4x + 14$	**Simplify.**
$10 = (-4)(1) + 14$	**Substitute 1 for x and 10 for y.**
$10 = 10$ ✓	

Answer The points (3, 2) and (1, 10) lie on the line $y = -4x + 14$.

Exercises

1. What is the equation of the line that has a slope of 6 and passes through the point (3, 5)?

Ⓐ $y = -6x - 19$ Ⓑ $y = 6x - 19$

Ⓒ $y = -6x - 12$ Ⓓ $y = 6x - 13$

2. Which pair of points is on the line $y = 7x - 3$?

Ⓐ (2, 11), (1, −10)

Ⓑ (3, 2), (−1, −10)

Ⓒ (3, 18), (−4, −31)

Ⓓ (5, 28), (−1, −10)

3. Which line passes through the origin?

Ⓐ $y = 3x + 4$ Ⓑ $y = 9x - 1$

Ⓒ $y = -6x$ Ⓓ $y = -6x - 6$

4. What is the slope of $y = -6x + 3$?

Ⓐ 6   Ⓑ −6   Ⓒ 3   Ⓓ −3

5. Which line passes through (1, 2) and $\left(4, \frac{16}{11}\right)$?

Ⓐ $2x + 11y = 24$

Ⓑ $3x + y = 11$

Ⓒ $-x + 9y = 22$

Ⓓ $2x - 7y = 24$

6. Which line has the greatest slope?

Ⓐ $3x - y = 11$ Ⓑ $7x + 9y = 22$

Ⓒ $6x + 2y = 22$ Ⓓ $7x - 11y = 9$

7. What is the equation of the line that has a slope of 9 and passes through the point (9, 9)?

Ⓐ $9x + y + 90 = 0$

Ⓑ $9x - y + 72 = 0$

Ⓒ $9x - y - 72 = 0$

Ⓓ $9x + y - 90 = 0$

8. Which pair of points lies on the line $7x + 4y = -12$?

Ⓐ (0, −3), (−2, 0)

Ⓑ $\left(1, -\frac{19}{4}\right)$, (1, 4)

Ⓒ (0, −3), $\left(1, -\frac{19}{4}\right)$

Ⓓ (1, −3), (2, 0)

9. Which point does *not* lie on the line $3x + 9y = 12$?

Ⓐ (3, 3)   Ⓑ $\left(-1, \frac{5}{3}\right)$

Ⓒ (−2, 2)   Ⓓ (−5, 3)

California Standards
Algebra 6.0, 7.0

Mixed Review

1. Which pair of points lies on the graph of
   $y = 3x - 8$?

   Ⓐ $(-1, -11), (3, 1)$

   Ⓑ $(-1, -11), (1, 3)$

   Ⓒ $(2, 4), (3, -3)$

   Ⓓ $(-2, -14), (3, 17)$

2. Which function has the same graph as the graph
   of $12x - 4y + 4 = 0$?

   Ⓐ $y = 3x + 4$ Ⓑ $y = 3x - 1$

   Ⓒ $y = 3x + 1$ Ⓓ $y = 3x - 4$

3. Which pair of lines has the same x-intercept?

   Ⓐ $y = 3x - 4$ and $2x + 6y - 8 = 0$

   Ⓑ $y = 2x - 8$ and $3x + 7y - 12 = 0$

   Ⓒ $y = x - 8$ and $x + y - 1 = 0$

   Ⓓ $y = -x - 2$ and $x - 2y + 3 = 0$

4. Which inequality is shown on the graph below?

   Ⓐ $3x - 2y \geq 4$

   Ⓑ $5x + y < 3$

   Ⓒ $-5x + y > -3$

   Ⓓ $3x + 2y \leq -4$

5. Which pair of lines has the same y-intercept?

   Ⓐ $y = x - 5$ and $3x + y - 6 = 0$

   Ⓑ $y = -2x - 2$ and $6x + y - 21 = 0$

   Ⓒ $y = x - 7$ and $x - 3y - 21 = 0$

   Ⓓ $y = 5x - 12$ and $x - y + 7 = 0$

6. Which line does *not* have a negative y-intercept?

   Ⓐ $y = 3x - 11$

   Ⓑ $y = -x - 9$

   Ⓒ $y = -x + 5$

   Ⓓ $y = 2x - 6$

7. Which point lies on the line defined by
   $4x - 3y = 15$?

   Ⓐ $(-6, -13)$ Ⓑ $(3, 2)$

   Ⓒ $(-5, -10)$ Ⓓ $(6, 7)$

8. Which point lies on the line $y = 3$?

   Ⓐ $\left(\frac{5}{6}, -3\right)$ Ⓑ $\left(\frac{2}{3}, 6\right)$

   Ⓒ $\left(\frac{6}{7}, 3\right)$ Ⓓ $\left(\frac{1}{4}, -6\right)$

9. Which pair of points lies on the line defined by
   $x - 2y = 8$?

   Ⓐ $(5, -2)$ and $(2, -8)$

   Ⓑ $(6, -1)$ and $(2, -3)$

   Ⓒ $(8, 1)$ and $(-3, 5)$

   Ⓓ $(4, 2)$ and $(-4, 4)$

10. What is the equation of the line that has a slope
    of 0 and passes through the point $(6, 1)$?

    Ⓐ $y = x + 1$ Ⓑ $y = x - 1$

    Ⓒ $y = -1$ Ⓓ $y = 1$

11. Which set represents all values of x such that
    $(x, 0)$ is a solution of $x < \frac{3}{4}y - \frac{9}{4}$?

    Ⓐ $\left\{x : x < \frac{9}{4}\right\}$

    Ⓑ $\left\{x : x < -\frac{4}{9}\right\}$

    Ⓒ $\left\{x : x < -\frac{9}{4}\right\}$

    Ⓓ $\left\{x : x < \frac{4}{9}\right\}$

Name _____ Date _____

12. Which equation is shown on the graph below?

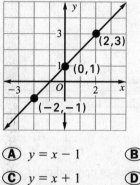

  Ⓐ $y = x - 1$ Ⓑ $y = \frac{1}{2}x + 2$

  Ⓒ $y = x + 1$ Ⓓ $y = 2x - 3$

13. Which of the following is *not* an equation of a line with a slope of 3?

  Ⓐ $-3x + y = 2$ Ⓑ $3x + y = 6$

  Ⓒ $3x - y = -8$ Ⓓ $-3x + y = 2$

14. What are the coordinates of the y-intercept of the graph of $2x - 5y = -10$?

  Ⓐ $(0, 2)$ Ⓑ $(0, -2)$

  Ⓒ $\left(\frac{2}{5}, 0\right)$ Ⓓ $\left(0, \frac{2}{5}\right)$

15. What are the coordinates of the x-intercept of the graph of $9x + 3y = 4$?

  Ⓐ $\left(\frac{4}{9}, 0\right)$ Ⓑ $\left(-\frac{4}{9}, 0\right)$

  Ⓒ $\left(0, -\frac{4}{3}\right)$ Ⓓ $\left(0, \frac{3}{4}\right)$

16. What are the coordinates of the x-intercept of the graph of $y = \frac{3}{5}x$?

  Ⓐ $(0, 0)$ Ⓑ $(3, 0)$

  Ⓒ $(5, 0)$ Ⓓ $(0, 5)$

17. Which inequality is shown on the graph below?

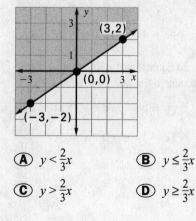

  Ⓐ $y < \frac{2}{3}x$ Ⓑ $y \leq \frac{2}{3}x$

  Ⓒ $y > \frac{2}{3}x$ Ⓓ $y \geq \frac{2}{3}x$

18. What are the coordinates of the y-intercept of the graph of $6 - x = 2y - 3$?

  Ⓐ $\left(0, \frac{9}{2}\right)$ Ⓑ $\left(-\frac{9}{2}, 0\right)$

  Ⓒ $\left(0, -\frac{2}{9}\right)$ Ⓓ $\left(0, \frac{2}{9}\right)$

19. Which set represents all values of y such that $(0, y)$ is a solution of $-4x + 7y \geq -2$?

  Ⓐ $\left\{y : y \leq -\frac{7}{2}\right\}$ Ⓑ $\left\{y : y \leq \frac{7}{2}\right\}$

  Ⓒ $\left\{y : y \geq -\frac{2}{7}\right\}$ Ⓓ $\left\{y : y \geq \frac{2}{7}\right\}$

20. Which function has the same graph as the graph of $2x - 4y + 8 = 0$?

  Ⓐ $y = \frac{1}{2}x + 2$ Ⓑ $y = \frac{1}{2}x - 4$

  Ⓒ $y = -2x - 4$ Ⓓ $y = 2x + 2$

21. Which inequality is shown on the graph below?

  Ⓐ $x + y \leq -2$ Ⓑ $x > -2$

  Ⓒ $x - y < -2$ Ⓓ $x \leq 2$

22. Which of the following equations represents a line with a slope of $\frac{1}{3}$ and y-intercept $(0, 2)$?

  Ⓐ $x + 3y = 6$ Ⓑ $-x + 3y = -6$

  Ⓒ $x + 3y = -6$ Ⓓ $x - 3y = -6$

23. Which point lies on the line defined by $-x - 3y = 3$?

  Ⓐ $(3, 2)$ Ⓑ $(-1, -3)$

  Ⓒ $(3, -2)$ Ⓓ $(-1, 0)$

24. Which of the following points lies on the line defined by $4y = 7x$?

  Ⓐ $\left(-2, \frac{7}{2}\right)$ Ⓑ $\left(-\frac{7}{2}, 1\right)$

  Ⓒ $\left(-1, -\frac{7}{4}\right)$ Ⓓ $\left(\frac{7}{2}, 2\right)$

Name _____ Date _____

Parallel and Perpendicular Lines

Example   ## Write an Equation of a Perpendicular Line

Write an equation of a line that passes through $(3, 5)$ and is perpendicular to $y = 3x + 1$.

Solution

STEP 1 Identify the slope.

The graph of $y = 3x + 1$ has a slope of 3. Because the slopes of perpendicular lines are negative reciprocals, the slope of a line perpendicular to $y = 3x + 1$ is $-\frac{1}{3}$.

STEP 2 Find the y-intercept by using the slope $-\frac{1}{3}$ and the point $(3, 5)$.

$y = mx + b$ **Write the slope-intercept form.**

$5 = -\frac{1}{3}(3) + b$ **Substitute 5 for y, $-\frac{1}{3}$ for m, and 3 for x.**

$6 = b$ **Solve for b.**

STEP 3 Write the equation using slope-intercept form.

$y = -\frac{1}{3}x + 6$

Exercises

1. Which of the following lines is perpendicular to $2x - 4y = 2$?

   (A) $y = -4x + 2$ (B) $y = \frac{1}{2}x + 2$

   (C) $y = -\frac{1}{2}x + 4$ (D) $y = -2x + 2$

2. Which equation represents a line parallel to the line $y = 2x + 3$?

   (A) $y = 2x - 1$ (B) $y = -2x + 1$

   (C) $y = \frac{1}{2}x - 1$ (D) $y = -\frac{1}{2}x - 1$

3. Which is an equation of a line that passes through $(1, 3)$ and is parallel to the line $y = -2x + 2$?

   (A) $y = 2x + 2$ (B) $y = -2x + 5$

   (C) $y = 2x - 5$ (D) $y = -2x - 2$

4. What is the slope of a line perpendicular to the line below?

   $y = \frac{2}{3}x - 4$

   (A) $-\frac{2}{3}$ (B) $\frac{2}{3}$ (C) $-\frac{3}{2}$ (D) $\frac{3}{2}$

5. The equation of Line A is $4x - 2y = 8$ and the equation of Line B is $8x - 4y = 20$. Which statement about the two lines is true?

   (A) Lines A and B are perpendicular.

   (B) Lines A and B are parallel.

   (C) Lines A and B have the same x-intercept.

   (D) Lines A and B have the same y-intercept.

6. Which equation represents a line perpendicular to the line $y = 3x + 6$?

   (A) $y = \frac{1}{3}x + 4$ (B) $y = -3x - 4$

   (C) $y = -\frac{1}{3}x + 4$ (D) $y = 3x - 4$

7. Which is an equation of a line that is perpendicular to the line $y = 5x + 4$?

   (A) $y = -\frac{1}{5}x + 5$ (B) $y = \frac{1}{5}x + 5$

   (C) $y = -5x - \frac{1}{5}$ (D) $y = 5x - \frac{1}{5}$

California Standards
Algebra 9.0

Solve Linear Systems

Example 1 **Solve a System of Equations**

Solve the linear system: $-9x + y = 29$ **Equation 1**

$4x - 3y = -18$ **Equation 2**

Solution

STEP 1 Multiply Equation 1 by 3.

$$-9x + y = 29 \quad \times 3 \quad -27x + 3y = 87$$
$$4x - 3y = -18 \qquad\qquad \underline{4x - 3y = -18}$$

STEP 2 Add the equations. $-23x = 69$

STEP 2 Solve for x. $x = -3$

STEP 3 Substitute -3 for x in either equation and solve for y.

$4x - 3y = -18$ **Write Equation 2.**

$4(-3) - 3y = -18$ **Substitute -3 for x.**

$y = 2$ **Solve for y.**

Answer The solution is $(-3, 2)$.

Exercises

1. What is the solution of the system $-3x + 5y = 14$ and $-x + 3y = 18$?

  (A) $(12, 10)$ (B) $(12, -10)$

  (C) $(-10, 12)$ (D) $(16, 10)$

2. The length of a rectangle is 12 feet longer than its width. If the perimeter of the rectangle is 56 feet, what is the area of the rectangle?

  (A) 240 ft^2 (B) 180 ft^2

  (C) 140 ft^2 (D) 160 ft^2

3. Which of the following points is in the solution set of the system shown below?

$$x + y < 5$$
$$2x - y \geq 3$$

  (A) $(-3, -2)$ (B) $(-1, 4)$

  (C) $(2, 6)$ (D) $(3, -6)$

4. If $x - y = 18$ and $\frac{1}{5}x - \frac{1}{3}y = 4$, what is $\frac{x}{y}$?

  (A) 2 (B) -5 (C) 4 (D) -3

5. What is the solution of the system shown below?

$$2x - 11y = 45$$
$$-x + 15y = -70$$

  (A) $(-5, -5)$ (B) $(-5, -4)$

  (C) $(-5, 5)$ (D) $(6, -6)$

6. What is the solution of the system shown below?

$$x = -3y$$
$$x - 9y = 36$$

  (A) $(-9, 9)$ (B) $(-9, 3)$

  (C) $(9, -3)$ (D) $(-1, -9)$

7. Which of the following points is in the solution set of the system shown below?

$$4x - 2y \geq 2$$
$$x - y < 6$$

  (A) $(-3, 3)$ (B) $(4, 4)$

  (C) $(-2, -4)$ (D) $(1, -6)$

Example 2   ## Solve a System of Inequalities

Graph the system of inequalities: $y - 3x < 5$ **Inequality 1**

$y + 3x \geq -7$ **Inequality 2**

Solution

Graph both inequalities in the same coordinate plane. The graph of the intersection of the two half-planes is the darker shaded region.

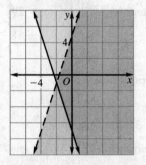

Answer The solution to the system of equations $y - 3x < 5$ and $y + 3x \geq -7$ is the intersection of the two half-planes shown above.

Check Choose a point in the darker shaded region, such as $(2, 0)$. To check the solution, substitute 2 for x and 0 for y in each inequality.

$$y - 3x < 5$$
$$0 - 3(2) \overset{?}{<} 5$$
$$-6 < 5 \checkmark$$

$$y + 3x \geq -7$$
$$0 + 3(2) \overset{?}{\geq} -7$$
$$6 \geq -7 \checkmark$$

Exercises

1. The solution set of which system of inequalities contains the point $(5, -4)$?

Ⓐ $-x + y \leq -5$
  $x < 5$

Ⓑ $-x + y < -5$
  $x \leq 5$

Ⓒ $-x + y > -5$
  $x \geq 5$

Ⓓ $-x + y \geq -5$
  $x > 5$

2. Which system of inequalities does *not* have a solution?

Ⓐ $x + 8y < 32$
  $\frac{3}{4}x + 6y > -12$

Ⓑ $x + 8y \geq 32$
  $\frac{3}{4}x + 6y > -12$

Ⓒ $x + 8y > 32$
  $\frac{3}{4}x + 6y < -12$

Ⓓ $x + 8y \leq 32$
  $\frac{3}{4}x + 6y \leq -12$

3. What is the area of the figure that shows the solution of the system $-x + y \geq 0$, $y \geq -2$, and $x \leq 4$ when graphed on a coordinate plane?

Ⓐ 4 square units

Ⓑ 12 square units

Ⓒ 18 square units

Ⓓ 36 square units

4. Which point is in the solution set of the system shown below?

$$-x + 2y \geq -2$$
$$x + 4y \leq 4$$

Ⓐ $(0, 1)$

Ⓑ $(1, -2)$

Ⓒ $(1, 1)$

Ⓓ $(1, -1)$

California Standards
Algebra 8.0, 9.0

Mixed Review

1. What is the slope of $y = \frac{3}{5}x + 5$?

  Ⓐ $\frac{5}{3}$ Ⓑ 3   Ⓒ $\frac{3}{5}$ Ⓓ 5

2. Which of the following equations represents a line that is parallel to $y = \frac{1}{5}x - 3$?

  Ⓐ $y = 5x - 2$ Ⓑ $y = -\frac{1}{5}x - 2$

  Ⓒ $y = \frac{1}{5}x + 3$ Ⓓ $y = -5x - 2$

3. Which of the following equations represents a line that is parallel to $y = 2x - 3$?

  Ⓐ $y = 2x - 1$

  Ⓑ $y = \frac{1}{2} - 1$

  Ⓒ $y = -2x + 1$

  Ⓓ $y = -\frac{1}{2}x - 1$

4. The graph of which system of inequalities is shown below?

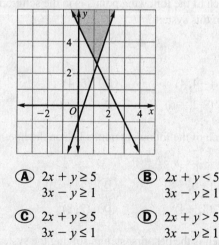

  Ⓐ $2x + y \geq 5$ Ⓑ $2x + y < 5$
     $3x - y \geq 1$ $3x - y \geq 1$

  Ⓒ $2x + y \geq 5$ Ⓓ $2x + y > 5$
     $3x - y \leq 1$ $3x - y \geq 1$

5. Which equation represents the line that passes through $(4, -5)$ and is perpendicular to the line $y = 2x + 3$?

  Ⓐ $y = -\frac{1}{2}x + 3$ Ⓑ $y = \frac{1}{2}x - 3$

  Ⓒ $2y = \frac{1}{2}x + 3$ Ⓓ $y = -\frac{1}{2}x - 3$

6. What is the negative reciprocal of -8?

  Ⓐ 8   Ⓑ $\frac{1}{8}$ Ⓒ -0.8 Ⓓ $-\frac{1}{8}$

7. The solution set of which system of inequalities contains the point $(-3, 1)$?

  Ⓐ $4y - 2x > -2$ Ⓑ $4y - 2x \leq -2$
     $-y + 5x \leq -4$ $-y + 5x < -4$

  Ⓒ $4y - 2x \leq -2$ Ⓓ $4y - 2x \geq -2$
     $-y + 5x > -4$ $-y + 5x \geq -4$

8. Which equation represents a line that passes through $(2, 8)$?

  Ⓐ $y = -6x - 2$ Ⓑ $y = 6x - 4$

  Ⓒ $y = 4x + 6$ Ⓓ $y = -6x - 4$

9. Which equation can be obtained from the following system?

$$3x + 11y = -2$$
$$-11x + y = 1$$

  Ⓐ $124x = -13$ Ⓑ $124x = 9$

  Ⓒ $124x = 13$ Ⓓ $124x = 13$

10. Which of the following lines is perpendicular to $y = -\frac{1}{5}x + \frac{1}{2}$?

  Ⓐ $y = -5x + 2$ Ⓑ $y = -2x + 5$

  Ⓒ $y = x - 5$ Ⓓ $y = 5x - 3$

11. Which line is *not* perpendicular to the line $y = -\frac{1}{7}x + 7$?

  Ⓐ $y = 7(x + 7)$ Ⓑ $y = -7(3 - x)$

  Ⓒ $y = -7(3 + x)$ Ⓓ $y = 7(x - 7)$

12. What is the solution of the system shown below?

$$x - 11y = -123$$
$$11x - y = -33$$

  Ⓐ $(-11, 1)$ Ⓑ $(11, -1)$

  Ⓒ $(-12, -1)$ Ⓓ $(-2, 11)$

13. What is the negative reciprocal of 6?

   (A) $-\frac{1}{6}$ (B) $\frac{1}{6}$

   (C) -6 (D) -0.6

14. The length of a rectangle is 8 feet longer than its width. If the perimeter of the rectangle is 64 feet, what is the area of the rectangle?

   (A) 240 ft^2 (B) 260 ft^2

   (C) 120 ft^2 (D) 140 ft^2

15. Which equation represents the line that passes through $(-3, -5)$ and is perpendicular to the line $y = \frac{2}{3}x + 3$?

   (A) $y = \frac{2}{3}x + \frac{9}{10}$ (B) $y = -\frac{3}{2}x + \frac{9}{10}$

   (C) $y = \frac{2}{3}x - \frac{19}{2}$ (D) $y = -\frac{3}{2}x - \frac{19}{2}$

16. Which step could eliminate a variable in the system shown below?

$$-x + 5y = 23$$
$$-23x - 5y = 7$$

   (A) Multiply the first equation by -1 and add the equations.

   (B) Subtract the second equation from the first equation.

   (C) Add the equations.

   (D) Multiply the second equation by -1 and add the equations.

17. Which equation is a proper combination of the system?

$$-3m - n = 21$$
$$-11m - 9n = 5$$

   (A) $27m - 11m = -189 + 5$

   (B) $27m - m = 189 + 5$

   (C) $-3m - 11m = 189 + 5$

   (D) $27m - 11m = -189 - 5$

18. Which of the following points is in the solution set of this system?

$$2x + y < 8$$
$$6x - 3y \geq 6$$

   (A) $(4, -6)$ (B) $(3, 5)$

   (C) $(-1, 2)$ (D) $(10, 3)$

19. The difference of two angles in a triangle is $40°$ and their sum is $130°$. Which is the measure of the largest angle?

   (A) $45°$ (B) $55°$ (C) $50°$ (D) $85°$

20. Which is the solution to the system below?

$$-3x + 5y = 90$$
$$-x + 3y = 46$$

   (A) $(12, 10)$ (B) $(12, -10)$

   (C) $(-10, 12)$ (D) $(16, 10)$

21. Which of the following points is in the solution set of this system?

$$x + 3y > 0$$
$$x - 9y > 12$$

   (A) $(-3, 1)$ (B) $(-9, 3)$

   (C) $(5, -1)$ (D) $(-9, -3)$

22. Which of the following systems has the solution $(-11, 1)$?

   (A) $x - y = 12$ (B) $x - 5y = -13$
        $4x + 2y = 4$ $2x - 5y = -27$

   (C) $x - 2y = -13$ (D) $x + y = -10$
        $x - 3y = 9$ $x - y = -12$

23. Which of the following points is in the solution set of this system?

$$3x - 3y > 12$$
$$6x + 2y < 10$$

   (A) $(-4, 4)$ (B) $(5, 4)$

   (C) $(-2, -6)$ (D) $(1, -6)$

24. Which of the following points lies on the line $-\frac{1}{4}y = \frac{2}{5}x + 3$?

   (A) $(-6, -8)$ (B) $(5, -20)$

   (C) $(3, -4)$ (D) $(2, 8)$

25. Which is the best first step in solving the system of equations shown below?

$$-9x + 11y = 15$$
$$21x - y = 19$$

   (A) Multiply the first equation by 21.

   (B) Multiply the second equation by 11.

   (C) Multiply the second equation by -9.

   (D) Multiply the first equation by 9.

Name _____ Date _____

California Standards
Algebra 10.0

Operations on Monomials and Polynomials

Example 1 **Subtract and Multiply Polynomials**

Simplify.

a. $(4x^2y + y^3 - 7) - (14y^3 - 8)$

b. $(7a^2b)(3a - 6b)$

c. $(5x^3y - 4y^2)(3x^2y^3 - xy^2 + 2)$

Solution

a. $(4x^2y + y^3 - 7) - (14y^3 - 8)$

$\quad = 4x^2y + y^3 - 7 - 14y^3 + 8$ **Distributive property**

$\quad = 4x^2y + (y^3 - 14y^3) + (-7 + 8)$ **Combine like terms.**

$\quad = 4x^2y - 13y^3 + 1$ **Simplify.**

b. $7a^2b(3a - 6b) = (7a^2b)(3a) - (7a^2b)(6b)$ **Distributive property**

$\quad\quad\quad\quad\quad\quad\quad = 21a^3b - 42a^2b^2$ **Product of powers property.**

c. $(5x^3y - 4y^2)(3x^2y^3 - xy^2 + 2)$

$\quad = (5x^3y)(3x^2y^3 - xy^2 + 2) - (4y^2)(3x^2y^3 - xy^2 + 2)$ **Distributive property**

$\quad = 15x^5y^4 - 5x^4y^3 + 10x^3y - 12x^2y^5 + 4xy^4 - 8y^2$ **Distributive property**

Exercises

1. $3m + 5m =$

(A) $15m$ (B) $-2m$ (C) $8m$ (D) $8m^2$

2. $(8x^2y - 2xy)(3x^2 - 6x - 1) =$

(A) $-24x^{15}y^6$

(B) $24x^4y + 12x^2y - 1$

(C) $24x^4y + 42x^3y - 20x^2y - 2xy$

(D) $24x^4y - 54x^3y + 4x^2y + 2xy$

3. The length of a rectangular garden is $10x$ feet and the width is $4x$ feet. Andy walks around the perimeter of the garden. Which expression represents the distance Andy walks, in feet?

(A) $28x$

(B) $28x^2$

(C) $14x$

(D) $14x^2$

4. $3x^2 \cdot (-4x) =$

(A) $-x^3$ (B) $-12x^3$

(C) $4x$ (D) $-12x^2$

5. $6x^2(2x^3 - 4x^2 + 5x - 1) =$

(A) $6x^5 + 2x^4 + 11x^3 - 6x^2$

(B) $7x^5 + 2x^4 + 11x^3 - 6x^2$

(C) $7x^5 - 24x^4 + 30x^3$

(D) $12x^5 - 24x^4 + 30x^3 - 6x^2$

6. A rectangular sports field has a length of $5x + 9$ feet and a width of $3x - 3$ feet. Which polynomial gives the area of the field?

(A) $8x^2 - 42x + 27$

(B) $15x^2 + 42x - 27$

(C) $8x^2 + 12x - 27$

(D) $15x^2 + 12x - 27$

Example 2

Divide Polynomials

Simplify.

a. $(4a^3b - 6a^2b^2 + ab^2) \div 2ab$

b. $(-6x^2 - xy + 15y^2) \div (3x + 5y)$

Solution

a. $(4a^3b - 6a^2b^2 + ab^2) \div 2ab$

$$= \frac{4a^3b - 6a^2b^2 + ab^2}{2ab} \qquad \text{Write as fraction.}$$

$$= \frac{4a^3b}{2ab} - \frac{6a^2b^2}{2ab} + \frac{ab^2}{2ab} \qquad \text{Rewrite as sum of fractions.}$$

$$= \frac{2a^2 - 3ab + b}{2} \qquad \text{Write as fraction.}$$

b. To divide a polynomial by a binomial, use long division.

$$
\begin{array}{r}
-2x + 3y \\
3x + 5y \overline{\smash{\big)}\, -6x^2 - xy + 15y^2} \\
\underline{-6x^2 - 10xy} \\
9xy + 15y^2 \\
\underline{9xy + 15y^2} \\
0
\end{array}
$$

Multiply $3x + 5y$ by $-2x$.

Subtract $-6x^2 - 10xy$. Bring down $15x^2$.

Multiply $3x + 5y$ by $3y$.

Subtract $9xy + 15y^2$.

Exercises

1. $\dfrac{12y}{6y} =$

(A) $18y$ (B) 2 (C) $2y$ (D) $2y^2$

2. $\dfrac{-24x^4y^3z}{6x^2y^2z} =$

(A) $4x^2y$

(B) $-4x^2yz$

(C) $-4x^2y$

(D) $18x^2y$

3. $\dfrac{20x^3}{5x^2} =$

(A) $15x$ (B) 4 (C) $4x$ (D) $4x^2$

4. A rectangle has an area of $2x^2 + x - 3$ square inches. Its width is $2x + 3$ inches. What is its length?

(A) $x - 7$

(B) $x - 1$

(C) $2x^2 + x - 6$

(D) $10x^3 + 10x^2 - 2x - 12$

5. $\dfrac{3a^4 - a^2b - 10b^2}{a^2 - 2b} =$

(A) $3a^2 - 5b$

(B) $3b^2 - 5a$

(C) $3a^2 + 5b$

(D) $3b^2 + 5a$

6. $(2x^2 - 8x + 8) \div (x - 2) =$

(A) $x - 4$

(B) $4x + 4$

(C) $2x - 4$

(D) $x^2 + 4$

7. $\dfrac{3m^4 + 7m^2 - 6}{m^2 + 3} =$

(A) $2m^2 - 3$

(B) $3m^2 - 2$

(C) $3m^2 + 2$

(D) $2m^2 + 3$

Name _____ Date _____

Factor Polynomials and Solve Quadratic Equations

Example   **Solve a Quadratic Equation**

Solve $36x^2 - 48x + 16 = 0$ by factoring.

Solution

$36x^2 - 48x + 16 = 0$	Write original equation.
$4(9x^2 - 12x + 4) = 0$	Factor out 4.
$9x^2 - 12x + 4 = 0$	Divide each side by 4.
$(3x - 2)(3x - 2) = 0$	Factor left side.
$3x - 2 = 0 \; or \; 3x - 2 = 0$	Zero-product property
$x = \frac{2}{3}$	Because both factors are the same, solve one of them for x.

Exercises

1. What is the greatest common factor of $6x^2 + 2x - 20$?

  Ⓐ 2   Ⓑ −3   Ⓒ 6   Ⓓ −20

2. What is the greatest common factor of $-16x^3 + 8x^2 - 36x$?

  Ⓐ $3x$ Ⓑ $4x$ Ⓒ $6x$ Ⓓ $8x$

3. Solve $6x^2 + 24x = 12$ by completing the square.

  Ⓐ $2 \pm \sqrt{6}$ Ⓑ -2

  Ⓒ $-\sqrt{6}$ Ⓓ $-2 \pm \sqrt{6}$

4. What is the factored form of $x^2 + 6x + 9$?

  Ⓐ $(x + 9)^2$

  Ⓑ $(x + 3)^2$

  Ⓒ $(x + 6)^2$

  Ⓓ $(x + 3)(x - 3)$

5. What is the factored form of $x^3 - 9x$?

  Ⓐ $x^2(x - 3)(x + 3)$

  Ⓑ $x(x + 3)^2$

  Ⓒ $x(x + 3)(x - 3)$

  Ⓓ $(x - 9)^2$

6. What is the factored form of $x^4 - 81x^2$?

  Ⓐ $x^2(x - 9)(x + 9)$

  Ⓑ $x(x + 9)^2$

  Ⓒ $x(x + 9)(x - 9)$

  Ⓓ $(x - 9)^2$

7. Solve $7x^2 + 15x - 2 = 6x^2 + 13x$ by completing the square.

  Ⓐ -4 Ⓑ $1 \pm \sqrt{3}$

  Ⓒ $-1 \pm \sqrt{3}$ Ⓓ 4

8. Solve $7x^2 + 28x - 35 = 0$ by completing the square.

  Ⓐ -5 Ⓑ $-5, 1$

  Ⓒ $35 \pm \sqrt{7}$ Ⓓ $7 \pm \sqrt{35}$

9. What is the factored form of $x^3 - 11x^2 + 28x$?

  Ⓐ $x^2(x - 14)(x - 2)$

  Ⓑ $x(x - 4)^2$

  Ⓒ $x(x - 7)(x - 4)$

  Ⓓ $(x - 4)^2$

Name _____   Date _____

Mixed Review

1. What number must be added to both sides of $x^2 + 18x = 2$ in order to complete the square?

    (A) 36   (B) 9   (C) 81   (D) 144

2. Solve $x^2 + 8x = 15$ by completing the square.

    (A) 16   (B) 4, 3
    (C) $-4 \pm \sqrt{31}$ (D) $3 \pm \sqrt{21}$

3. Solve $x^2 + 4x = 21$ by factoring.

    (A) $-7, 3$ (B) $-7, -3$
    (C) $7, -3$ (D) $7, 3$

4. $(-8x^2 + 3x + 8) + (2x^2 - 5x + 12) =$

    (A) $-6x^2 + 8x + 20$
    (B) $10x^2 - 2x + 20$
    (C) $-6x^2 - 2x + 20$
    (D) $-10x^2 + 8x + 20$

5. Solve $7x^2 - 7x = 140$ by factoring.

    (A) $4, -5$ (B) $4, 5$
    (C) $-4, -5$ (D) $-4, 5$

6. $-9m + 5m =$

    (A) $-4m$ (B) $-14m$
    (C) $4m$ (D) $4m^2$

7. What number must be added to each side of $x^2 + 14x = -3$ in order to complete the square?

    (A) 28   (B) 7   (C) 49   (D) 56

8. Solve $4x^2 - 20x + 24 = 0$ by factoring.

    (A) $3, 2$ (B) $-4, 3$
    (C) $-3, -2$ (D) $-3, 4$

9. $3x \cdot (-6x) =$

    (A) $-3x^2$ (B) $-3x$ (C) $18x$ (D) $-18x^2$

10. $\dfrac{14z^2}{7z} =$

    (A) $21z$ (B) $2z$ (C) z (D) $2z^2$

11. What is the factored form of $x^2 - 144$?

    (A) $(x - 12)(x + 12)$
    (B) $(x + 12)^2$
    (C) $(x - 16)^2$
    (D) $(x + 16)(x - 9)$

12. The width of a rectangular golf course is $100x$ yards and the length is $150x$ yards. Rich walks around the perimeter of the course. Which expression represents the distance Rich walks, in yards?

    (A) $500x$ (B) $500x^2$ (C) $250x$ (D) $250x^2$

13. Solve $3x^2 - 24x = 6$ by completing the square.

    (A) $6, 3$ (B) $4 \pm 3\sqrt{2}$
    (C) $2 \pm \sqrt{3}$ (D) $3, -6$

14. $(8x^2 - 6x - 10) - (-7x^2 + 7x + 12) =$

    (A) $x^2 - 13x - 22$
    (B) $x^2 - 13x - 2$
    (C) $15x^2 - 13x - 22$
    (D) $15x^2 - x - 22$

15. Solve $4x^2 = 16x + 84$ by factoring.

    (A) $7, -3$ (B) $-3, 4$
    (C) $-7, 3$ (D) $-3, -4$

16. Monika measures the length of a raft and finds it to be $8x$ inches. She measures the width and it is $7x$ inches. What is the area of Monika's raft?

    (A) $30x$ in.^{2} (B) $56x^2$ in.^{2}
    (C) $56x$ in.^{2} (D) $15x^2$ in.^{2}

17. $13x - (-5x) =$

    (A) $8x$ (B) $-8x$ (C) $18x$ (D) $18x^2$

18. What is the greatest common factor of $9x^2 + 12x - 27$?

    (A) 3   (B) -9 (C) 9   (D) -3

19. $(4x - 2)(5x - 7) =$

    Ⓐ $9x^2 - 18x - 9$

    Ⓑ $20x^2 - 18x - 14$

    Ⓒ $20x^2 - 38x + 14$

    Ⓓ $9x - 9$

20. $-5x^2(3x^3 - 6x^2 + 2x - 4) =$

    Ⓐ $2x^5 + 30x^4 + 10x^3 + 20x^2$

    Ⓑ $15x^5 + 30x^4 + 10x^3 - 20x^2$

    Ⓒ $-2x^5 - 11x^4 - 3x^3 - 9x^2$

    Ⓓ $-15x^5 + 30x^4 - 10x^3 + 20x^2$

21. $\dfrac{a^4 b^6 c^7}{a^2 b^4 c^4} =$

    Ⓐ $a^2 b c^3$ Ⓑ $a^2 b^2 c^3$

    Ⓒ $a^6 b^{10} c^{11}$ Ⓓ $a^2 b^{10} c^3$

22. Solve $2x^2 - 24x = -8$ by completing the square.

    Ⓐ $4, -2$ Ⓑ $2, 8$

    Ⓒ $6 \pm 4\sqrt{2}$ Ⓓ $-2 \pm \sqrt{6}$

23. What is the greatest common factor of $21x^4 + 14x^3 - 35x^2$?

    Ⓐ $21x$ Ⓑ $-35x$

    Ⓒ $7x^2$ Ⓓ $14x^2$

24. $(x + 6)(x - 6) =$

    Ⓐ $x^2 + 6x - 6$ Ⓑ $x^2 - 36$

    Ⓒ $x^2 - x - 6$ Ⓓ $x^2 - 7x - 6$

25. What is the greatest common factor of $-12x^2y - 9x - 15y$?

    Ⓐ 4 Ⓑ -3 Ⓒ 5 Ⓓ -5

26. A rectangular airport has a length of $7x + 8$ yards and a width of $5x - 3$ yards. Which polynomial gives the area of the airport?

    Ⓐ $24x^2 + 10$ Ⓑ $12x^2 + 19x - 24$

    Ⓒ $35x^2 - 19x + 5$ Ⓓ $35x^2 + 19x - 24$

27. Solve $4x^2 + 32x + 12 = 0$ by completing the square.

    Ⓐ $-4 \pm \sqrt{13}$ Ⓑ $-2, 4$

    Ⓒ $4 \pm \sqrt{26}$ Ⓓ $3, -4$

28. What is the factored form of $x^3 - 4x$?

    Ⓐ $(x - 3)(x + 3)$ Ⓑ $x(x + 2)^2$

    Ⓒ $x(x + 2)(x - 2)$ Ⓓ $(x - 9)^2$

29. $-8m^2 + 7m^2 + 5m - (-3m) =$

    Ⓐ $-15m^2 + 2m$ Ⓑ $-m^2 + 2m$

    Ⓒ $-m^2 + 8m$ Ⓓ $15m^2 + 5m$

30. What is the greatest common factor of $14x^3 + 140x^2 - 28x$?

    Ⓐ $7x$ Ⓑ $-7x$ Ⓒ $14x$ Ⓓ $7x^2$

31. What is the factored form of $x^2 + 10x + 25$?

    Ⓐ $(x + 10)^2$ Ⓑ $(x + 5)^2$

    Ⓒ $(x - 5)^2$ Ⓓ $(x + 5)(x - 5)$

32. What is the greatest common factor of $-12x^4 + 24x^3 - 36x^2$?

    Ⓐ $3x^2$ Ⓑ $-4x$ Ⓒ $6x$ Ⓓ $12x^2$

33. What is the factored form of $x^3 - 10x^2 + 25x$?

    Ⓐ $(x - 5)(x + 25)$ Ⓑ $x(x - 5)^2$

    Ⓒ $x(x + 4)(x - 6)$ Ⓓ $(x - 5)^2$

34. What is the greatest common factor of $-4x^2 - 24x - 32x$?

    Ⓐ $-2x$ Ⓑ 2 Ⓒ $-4x$ Ⓓ $-8x$

35. What is the factored form of $x^2 - 6x - 16$?

    Ⓐ $(x - 16)^2$ Ⓑ $(x + 4)(x - 4)$

    Ⓒ $(x - 4)^2$ Ⓓ $(x + 2)(x - 8)$

36. What is the greatest common factor of $14x^3 + 56x^2$?

    Ⓐ $14x$ Ⓑ $7x^2$ Ⓒ $14x^2$ Ⓓ $7x$

37. Solve by completing the square.

$$6x^2 - 28x - 20 = 2x^2 + 4x$$

    Ⓐ $-4, 7$ Ⓑ $4 \pm \sqrt{21}$

    Ⓒ $6 \pm \sqrt{3}$ Ⓓ $3, -2$

38. Solve $5x^2 - 18x - 88 = 3x^2 - 4x$ by factoring.

    Ⓐ $11, -2$ Ⓑ $-4, 11$

    Ⓒ -4 Ⓓ $5, -9$

California Standards
Algebra 19.0, 20.0

Quadratic Formula

Example **Find the Roots of a Polynomial**

Find the roots of $x^2 - 12x + 27$.

Solution

$$x = \frac{-b \pm \sqrt{b^2 - 4ac}}{2a}$$ Quadratic formula

$$= \frac{-(-12) \pm \sqrt{(-12^2) - 4(1)(27)}}{2(1)}$$ Substitute values in the quadratic formula: $a = 1$, $b = -12$, and $c = 27$.

$$= \frac{12 \pm \sqrt{36}}{2}$$ Simplify.

$$= \frac{12 \pm 6}{2}$$ Simplify the square root.

Answer The roots of $x^2 - 12x + 27$ are $x = 9$ and $x = 3$.

Exercises

1. Which of the following polynomials has two roots that are opposites of each other?

   (A) $3x^2 - 4x + 1$

   (B) $-x^2 + 9x - 7$

   (C) $16x^2 - 25$

   (D) $16x^2 + 4$

2. Which of the following polynomials has only one root?

   (A) $x^2 + 4x + 1$

   (B) $4x^2 + 16x + 16$

   (C) $14x^2 + 3x + 1$

   (D) $4x^2 + 48x + 24$

3. Which of the following equations has two real solutions?

   (A) $3x^2 - 2x + 1 = 0$

   (B) $6x^2 + x - 11 = 0$

   (C) $5x^2 + 2x + 31 = 0$

   (D) $x^2 + 11x + 39 = 0$

4. Solve $30x^2 - 47x + 7 = 0$.

   (A) $\left\{-\dfrac{1}{6}, -\dfrac{7}{5}\right\}$

   (B) $\left\{\dfrac{1}{6}, \dfrac{9}{5}\right\}$

   (C) $\left\{\dfrac{5}{6}, \dfrac{7}{5}\right\}$

   (D) $\left\{\dfrac{1}{6}, \dfrac{7}{5}\right\}$

5. Which of the following polynomials has only one root?

   (A) $9y^2 - 24y + 16$

   (B) $6y^2 - 24y + 16$

   (C) $6y^2 - 48y + 4$

   (D) $y^2 - 4y + 16$

6. What is the solution set of $x^2 - 12x + 27 = 0$?

   (A) $\{3, 9\}$ (B) $\{3, -9\}$

   (C) $\{-3, 9\}$ (D) $\{12, 27\}$

7. What is the solution set of $3x^2 + 18x + 27 = 0$?

   (A) $\{4, -18\}$ (B) $\{-3, 9\}$

   (C) $\{18, 27\}$ (D) $\{-3\}$

California Standards Intensive Review

California Standards
Algebra 21.0, 22.0

Graphs of Quadratic Functions

Example   **Find the *x*-intercepts of a Function**

Find the x-intercepts of $y = x^2 + 6x - 2$.

Solution

STEP 1 Identify the values of a, b, and c.

Compare $x^2 + 6x - 2$ to $ax^2 + bx + c$ to identify a, b, and c.
So, $a = 1$, $b = 6$, and $c = -2$.

STEP 2 Substitute those values into the quadratic formula.

$$x = \frac{-6 \pm \sqrt{6^2 - (4)(1)(-2)}}{2(1)}$$

$$= \frac{-6 \pm \sqrt{44}}{2}$$

$$= \frac{-6 \pm 2\sqrt{11}}{2}$$

Answer The x-intercepts of the graph of $y = x^2 + 6x - 2$ are $\frac{-6 \pm 2\sqrt{11}}{2}$.

Exercises

1. How many times does the graph of
   $y = 3x^2 + 10x + 10$ intersect the x-axis?

   (A) none   (B) one

   (C) two   (D) three

2. What is the vertex of the graph of the function
   $y = \frac{1}{4}x^2 - 5x + 25$?

   (A) $(0, 10)$ (B) $(10, 0)$

   (C) $(0, -10)$ (D) $(-10, 0)$

3. Which value of a gives the graph of
   $y = 3x^2 + 5x - a$ two x-intercepts?

   (A) $a = -3$ (B) $a = -9$

   (C) $a = -4$ (D) $a = -1$

4. The graph of which function has two positive
   x-intercepts?

   (A) $y = x^2 - 11x + 21$

   (B) $y = x^2 + 3x + 2$

   (C) $y = 7x^2 + 5x - 9$

   (D) $y = 2x^2 + 5x - 9$

5. Which of the following functions has a graph that
   opens upward?

   (A) $y = x^2 - 7x$

   (B) $y = -6x^2 - 7x - 14$

   (C) $y = -x^2 - 9x + 4$

   (D) $y = -2x^2 - 4x$

6. The graph of which function has an axis of
   symmetry of $x = 0$?

   (A) $y = x^2 - 7x + 11$

   (B) $y = -5x^2 - 9x$

   (C) $y = x^2 - 7$

   (D) $y = 3x^2 - x + 1$

7. If one of the x-intercepts of the graph of
   $y = x^2 + 6x - p$ is $x = -2$, then what is the value
   of p?

   (A) -8 (B) 8

   (C) -2 (D) -3

California Standards
Algebra 23.0

Applications of Quadratic Equations

Example   ## Solve a Problem

During a track and field competition, an athlete throws a shot put. The height h of the shot put is given by $h = -16t^2 + 35t + 5$, where t is the time (in seconds) after it is thrown. Find the time that the shot put is in the air.

Solution

The shot put lands when $h = 0$. So, to find the time t when $h = 0$, solve the equation $0 = -16t^2 + 35t + 5$ using the quadratic formula.

$$x = \frac{-b \pm \sqrt{b^2 - 4ac}}{2a}$$ **Quadratic formula**

$$= \frac{-35 \pm \sqrt{35^2 - 4(-16)(5)}}{2(-16)}$$ **Substitute values in the quadratic formula: $a = -16$, $b = 35$, and $c = 5$.**

$$= \frac{-35 \pm \sqrt{1545}}{2(-16)}$$ **Simplify.**

$$= \frac{-35 \pm \sqrt{1545}}{-32}$$ **Simplify the denominator.**

The solutions of the equation are $\dfrac{-35 + \sqrt{1545}}{-32} \approx -0.135$ and $\dfrac{-35 - \sqrt{1545}}{-32} \approx 2.3$.

Because t cannot be negative, the answer -0.135 can be discarded.

Answer The shot put was in the air for about 2.3 seconds.

Exercises

1. The velocity V (in meters per second) of a projectile after its launch is given by

$$V(t) = 7t^2 - 420t$$

where t is the time in seconds. After how many seconds would the velocity of the projectile be zero?

(A) 30 seconds

(B) 60 seconds

(C) 42 seconds

(D) 70 seconds

2. The cost C (in dollars) for a manufacturer to produce m radios per day is given by

$$C(m) = m^2 - 160m + 8400.$$

How many radios can be produced to keep the daily production cost at $2000?

(A) 70   (B) 80

(C) 85   (D) 92

3. The area of an ellipse is given by

$$A(x) = x^2 - 14x + 67,$$

where x denotes the length (in meters) of its major axis. What is the value of x when the area of the ellipse is 18 square meters?

(A) 12

(B) 14

(C) 7

(D) 5

Name _____   Date _____

California Standards
Algebra 19.0, 20.0, 21.0, 22.0, 23.0

Mixed Review

1. Which value of m allows the expression $\dfrac{x-m}{x^2-49}$ to be further simplified?

   Ⓐ 49   Ⓑ 7   Ⓒ -14 Ⓓ 2

2. What is the discriminant of $11x^2+9x+1=0$?

   Ⓐ 44   Ⓑ 81   Ⓒ 37   Ⓓ -44

3. What are the roots of $(x-4)(x^2-16x+15)$?

   Ⓐ $x=1, x=4,$ and $x=15$

   Ⓑ $x=1, x=16,$ and $x=15$

   Ⓒ $x=-1, x=4,$ and $x=15$

   Ⓓ $x=1, x=-4,$ and $x=15$

4. Solve the equation $-2=2y^2-5y$.

   Ⓐ $y=1$ or $y=-\dfrac{1}{2}$

   Ⓑ $y=-1$ or $y=\dfrac{1}{2}$

   Ⓒ $y=2$ or $y=\dfrac{1}{2}$

   Ⓓ $y=2$ or $y=-\dfrac{1}{2}$

5. Which of the following polynomials has two roots that are both rational numbers?

   Ⓐ $x^2-35x+66$

   Ⓑ x^2+5x+1

   Ⓒ x^2+9x+2

   Ⓓ $x^2+11x+1$

6. To complete the square, what number must be added to each side of the equation $x^2-12x=-5$?

   Ⓐ 5   Ⓑ 6   Ⓒ 12   Ⓓ 36

7. If the discriminant of $ax^2+bx+c=0$ is negative, what can you conclude about the graph of $y=ax^2+bx+c$?

   Ⓐ It opens downward.

   Ⓑ It does not intersect the y-axis.

   Ⓒ It intersects the x-axis.

   Ⓓ It does not intersect the x-axis.

8. If s is a root of ax^2+bx+c, what can you conclude?

   Ⓐ $ax^2+bx+c=s$

   Ⓑ $s^2-4ac=0$

   Ⓒ $as^2+bs+c=0$

   Ⓓ $as^2+bs=c$

9. The graph of which function has x-intercepts of $\dfrac{1}{2}$ and -7?

   Ⓐ $y=2x^2-7x-2$

   Ⓑ $y=5x^2-13x+7$

   Ⓒ $y=2x^2+13x-7$

   Ⓓ $y=x^2-7x-13$

10. What is the axis of symmetry of the graph of $y=3x^2-42x-7$?

   Ⓐ $x=7$ Ⓑ $x=6$

   Ⓒ $x=-7$ Ⓓ $x=3$

11. What are the x-intercepts of the graph of $y=x^2-11x+28$?

   Ⓐ $x=4$ and $x=7$

   Ⓑ $x=-4$ and $x=7$

   Ⓒ $x=3$ and $y=7$

   Ⓓ $x=-4$ and $y=3$

12. The area of the following figure is 217 square inches. What is the value of x?

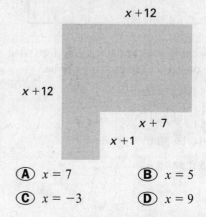

   Ⓐ $x=7$ Ⓑ $x=5$

   Ⓒ $x=-3$ Ⓓ $x=9$

13. The graph of which function does not have an
   x-intercept of -3?

   (A) $y = -2(x + 3)(x - 1)$

   (B) $y = (x - 3)(x - 2)$

   (C) $y = (x + 3)(x - 2)$

   (D) $y = (x + 3)(x - 1)$

14. If the discriminant of $2x^2 + 3x + 10 = 0$ is zero,
   what can you conclude about the polynomial
   $2x^2 + 3x + 10$?

   (A) The polynomial has no real roots.

   (B) The polynomial has one real root.

   (C) The polynomial has two real roots.

   (D) The polynomial has at least two real roots.

15. If $ax^2 + bx + c = 0$ has one real solution, what
   can you conclude?

   (A) The graph of $y = ax^2 + bx + c$ has one
      x-intercept.

   (B) The graph of $y = ax^2 + bx + c$ has one
      y-intercept.

   (C) The graph of $y = ax^2 + bx - c$ has no
      x-intercepts.

   (D) The graph of $y = ax^2 + bx - c$ has no
      y-intercepts.

16. Mathilda needs to create six pigpens for her
   farm. The pens will be arranged as shown in the
   diagram below.

   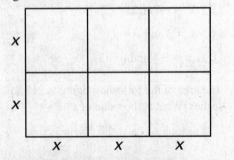

   If she wants to enclose 5400 square feet, what
   will the dimensions of each pig pen be?

   (A) 15 ft by 15 ft

   (B) $21\frac{1}{4}$ ft by $21\frac{1}{4}$ ft

   (C) 30 ft by 30 ft

   (D) 45 ft by 45 ft

17. Which graph below represents a quadratic
   equation with two real solutions?

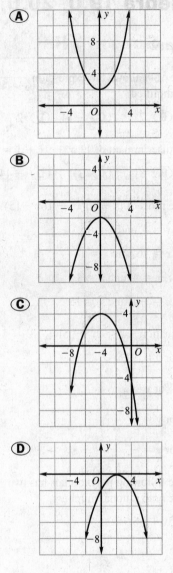

California Standards
Intensive Review

California Standards
Algebra 12.0

Simplify Rational Expressions

Example   **Simplify an Expression**

Simplify $\dfrac{2x^2 - 4x - 6}{x^2 - 9}$ to lowest terms.

Solution

$$\frac{2x^2 - 4x - 6}{x^2 - 9} = \frac{2(x + 1)(x - 3)}{(x + 3)(x - 3)}$$ **Factor numerator and denominator.**

$$= \frac{2(x + 1)(\cancel{x - 3})}{(x + 3)(\cancel{x - 3})}$$ **Divide out common factor.**

$$= \frac{2(x + 1)}{x + 3}$$ **Simplify.**

Exercises

1. Simplify $\dfrac{x^2 - x}{x^2 - 3x + 2}$ to lowest terms.

Ⓐ $\dfrac{1}{x - 2}$ Ⓑ $\dfrac{x}{x + 1}$

Ⓒ $\dfrac{1}{x(x + 1)}$ Ⓓ $\dfrac{x}{x - 2}$

2. What is $\dfrac{9m^2 - 16n^2}{3m - 4n}$ reduced to lowest terms?

Ⓐ $3m - 4n$ Ⓑ $3m + 4n$

Ⓒ 1   Ⓓ 0

3. Simplify $\dfrac{x - 6}{x^2 - 4x - 12}$ to lowest terms.

Ⓐ $\dfrac{1}{x - 2}$ Ⓑ $\dfrac{1}{x + 4}$

Ⓒ $\dfrac{1}{x + 2}$ Ⓓ 0

4. Which of the following expressions is in lowest terms?

Ⓐ $\dfrac{x + 1}{x^2 - 1}$

Ⓑ $\dfrac{x^2 - 1}{x - 1}$

Ⓒ $\dfrac{x^2 + 1}{x^3 + x}$

Ⓓ $\dfrac{x^2 + 1}{x^2 - 1}$

5. Simplify $\dfrac{9m^2 + 6m + 1}{3m + 1}$ to lowest terms.

Ⓐ $2m$ Ⓑ $3m + 1$

Ⓒ $3m^2 + 1$ Ⓓ $6m + 1$

6. Which of the following expressions is equivalent to $\dfrac{x^3 - 2x^2}{x^2 - 4x + 4}$?

Ⓐ $\dfrac{x^2}{x - 2}$

Ⓑ $\dfrac{x}{x - 2}$

Ⓒ $\dfrac{x^2}{x + 2}$

Ⓓ $\dfrac{x^2}{x - 4}$

7. Which of the following expressions is equivalent to $\dfrac{x^2 y^6 (a^3 b^{-2} c^5)^3}{a^6 b^4 c^4 (xy^2)^3}$?

Ⓐ $\dfrac{a^3 b^{10}}{c^{10} x}$

Ⓑ $\dfrac{a^3 c^{-11}}{b^{10} x}$

Ⓒ $\dfrac{a^3 c^{10}}{b^{11} x}$

Ⓓ $\dfrac{a^3 c^{11}}{b^{10} x}$

8. What is the common factor of the denominator and numerator in the expression $\dfrac{xy^2 - xy}{2y - 2}$?

Ⓐ 2   Ⓑ $y - 1$

Ⓒ y Ⓓ xy

California Standards
Algebra 13.0

Operations With Rational Expressions

Example   **Divide Rational Expressions**

Simplify. $\dfrac{y^2 + y - 42}{y^2 + 2y} \div \dfrac{y^2 - 36}{y + 2}$

Solution

$\dfrac{y^2 + y - 42}{y^2 + 2y} \div \dfrac{y^2 - 36}{y + 2}$

$= \dfrac{y^2 + y - 42}{y^2 + 2y} \cdot \dfrac{y + 2}{y^2 - 36}$ **Multiply by the multiplicative inverse.**

$= \dfrac{(y + 7)(y - 6)}{y(y + 2)} \cdot \dfrac{(y + 2)}{(y + 6)(y - 6)}$ **Factor numerators and denominators.**

$= \dfrac{(y + 2)(y + 7)(y - 6)}{y(y + 2)(y + 6)(y - 6)}$ **Multiply expressions and divide out.**

$= \dfrac{(y + 7)}{y(y + 6)}$ **Simplify.**

Exercises

1. Which of the following expressions is equivalent to $\dfrac{m^4 n^6 dx}{m^{-2} n^{-2} d^2 x^3}$?

A $\dfrac{m^6 n^8}{dx^2}$

B $\dfrac{m^6 n^6}{dx^2}$

C $\dfrac{m^7 n^8}{dx^2}$

D $\dfrac{m^{-6} n^{-8}}{dx^2}$

2. Which is a common denominator of the fractions in $\dfrac{1}{4(x + 3)} - \dfrac{1}{6(x^2 - 9)}$?

A $24(x^2 + 9)$

B $12(x^2 - 3)$

C $12(x^2 - 9)$

D $12x^2 - 3$

3. $\dfrac{12am^3}{2m(x + 11)} \div \dfrac{4m^2}{2(x + 11)} =$

A $8am^4$ **B** $8am$

C $4m$ **D** $3a$

4. To eliminate the denominators in $\dfrac{1}{2x} - \dfrac{1}{x - 5} = \dfrac{1}{x + 5}$, each fraction must be multiplied by

A $2x(x^2 + 5)$

B $2x(x^2 - 25)$

C $x^2 - 25$

D $x^2 + 25$

5. $\dfrac{3xy}{2} \cdot \left(\dfrac{2y}{x} + \dfrac{4x}{y} \right) =$

A $3y^2 + x^2$

B $3y^2 + 6x^2$

C $3y^2 + 12x^2$

D $3y^2 + 2x^2$

6. $\left(\dfrac{1}{x} + \dfrac{1}{y} \right) \div \left(\dfrac{1}{x} - \dfrac{1}{y} \right) =$

A $\dfrac{y - x}{(x + y)}$

B $\dfrac{(x + y)}{y - x}$

C $(x - y)(x + y)$

D $xy - x - y$

California Standards
Algebra 15.0

Rate, Work, and Percent Mixture Problems

Example   **Solve a Work Problem**

Carolyn can clear all the snow from the sidewalk in 40 minutes. It takes Judy 60 minutes to do the same job. How long would it take them to shovel the sidewalk together?

Solution

STEP 1 Find the work rates for Carolyn and Judy.

Because Carolyn can do the entire job in 40 minutes, her rate is $\frac{1}{40}$ per minute. Judy's work rate is $\frac{1}{60}$ job per minute.

STEP 2 Find the part of the job done by each person.

Let t be the time (in minutes) they take to complete the job together.

Carolyn's work done: $\frac{1}{40} \cdot t = \frac{t}{40}$

Judy's work done: $\frac{1}{60} \cdot t = \frac{t}{60}$

STEP 3 Write an equation for the total work done. Then solve the equation.

The parts of the job found in Step 2 must add up to 1 whole job.

$\frac{t}{40} + \frac{t}{60} = 1$ **Write equation.**

$3t + 2t = 120$ **Multiply each side by LCD, 120.**

$t = 24$ **Solve for t.**

Answer Together, Carolyn and Judy can clear all the snow from the sidewalk in 24 minutes.

Exercises

1. How much pure water must be added to 5 liters of 42% solution of acid in order to obtain a 24% solution of acid?

   (A) 4.5 L   (B) 3.75 L

   (C) 2.75 L   (D) 3.25 L

2. A car's radiator contains 2 liters of 24% antifreeze. Approximately how many liters of 80% antifreeze must be added to the radiator in order to obtain a 50% antifreeze mixture?

   (A) 1.73 L

   (B) 2.18 L

   (C) 4.19 L

   (D) 3.24 L

3. A train travels 92 miles in 40 minutes. What is the train's average speed per hour?

   (A) 114 miles per hour

   (B) 141 miles per hour

   (C) 144 miles per hour

   (D) 138 miles per hour

4. Radmann can type 48 words per minute and Glenda can type 72 words per minute. If they type together, how long does it take them to type a text that contains 36,000 words?

   (A) 5 hours   (B) 4 hours

   (C) 3 hours   (D) 2 hours

California Standards
Algebra 12.0, 13.0, 15.0

Mixed Review

1. Which value of m allows the expression $\dfrac{x - m}{x^2 - 25}$ to be further simplified?

   (A) 25   (B) 5

   (C) -10 (D) 15

2. Equal volumes of two acid solutions with 24% and 38% concentrations are mixed. Which is the concentration of the mixed solution?

   (A) 28%   (B) 31%

   (C) 62%   (D) 54%

3. Which value of q allows the expression below to be further simplified?

$$\frac{x - q}{x^2 - 81}$$

   (A) -27 (B) 9

   (C) -9 (D) 81

4. What is the common factor of the denominator and numerator in the expression

$$\frac{x^2 y - x^4 y^2}{x^2 - x^3}?$$

   (A) x^2

   (B) $1 - x^2$

   (C) y

   (D) $x^2 y$

5. Which of the following expressions is equivalent to $\dfrac{x^5 y^3 (m^4 n^2 p^2)^3}{m^3 n^3 p^5 (xy^2)^2}$?

   (A) $x^3 m^9 n^3$

   (B) $\dfrac{m^3 n^3 p}{xy^3}$

   (C) $x^2 y^4 m n^3 p$

   (D) $\dfrac{x^3 m^9 n^3 p}{y}$

6. Simplify $\dfrac{12n^2 + 4n - 1}{2n + 1}$ to lowest terms.

   (A) $2n + 1$ (B) $6n - 1$

   (C) $3n^2 + 1$ (D) $6n + 2$

7. Carlos's average driving speed for a 4-hour trip was 50 miles per hour. During the first 2 hours, he drove 60 miles per hour. What was his average driving speed for the last 2 hours of his trip?

   (A) 35 miles per hour

   (B) 40 miles per hour

   (C) 45 miles per hour

   (D) 50 miles per hour

8. Two rectangles have areas given by the polynomials $x^2 - x$ and $x^2 - 3x + 2$. What is the ratio of the areas reduced to lowest terms?

   (A) $\dfrac{x - 1}{x + 3}$

   (B) $\dfrac{-x}{3x + 2}$

   (C) $\dfrac{x}{x - 2}$

   (D) $\dfrac{1}{(x - 3)(x + 2)}$

9. $\dfrac{5ab^2}{3b(a - 2)} \div \dfrac{25ba^2}{(a - 2)(a + 3)} =$

   (A) $\dfrac{5(a + 3)}{b^2}$ (B) $\dfrac{a + 3}{15b}$

   (C) $\dfrac{5}{3ab}$ (D) $\dfrac{a + 3}{15a}$

10. To eliminate the denominators in $\dfrac{1}{2x} - \dfrac{1}{x - 2} = \dfrac{1}{x + 2}$, each fraction must be multiplied by

   (A) $2x(x^2 + 4)$

   (B) $x^2 - 16$

   (C) $2x(x^2 - 4)$

   (D) $x^2 + 16$

11. A train travels 48 miles in 45 minutes. What is the train's average speed per hour?

Ⓐ 44 miles per hour

Ⓑ 94 miles per hour

Ⓒ 84 miles per hour

Ⓓ 64 miles per hour

12. Which of the following expressions is equivalent to the expression below?

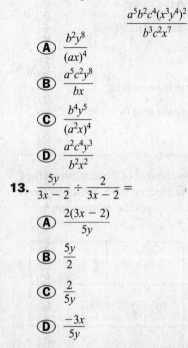

$$\frac{a^5b^2c^4(x^3y^4)^2}{b^3c^2x^7}$$

Ⓐ $\dfrac{b^2y^8}{(ax)^4}$

Ⓑ $\dfrac{a^5c^2y^8}{bx}$

Ⓒ $\dfrac{b^4y^5}{(a^2x)^4}$

Ⓓ $\dfrac{a^2c^4y^3}{b^2x^2}$

13. $\dfrac{5y}{3x-2} \div \dfrac{2}{3x-2} =$

Ⓐ $\dfrac{2(3x-2)}{5y}$

Ⓑ $\dfrac{5y}{2}$

Ⓒ $\dfrac{2}{5y}$

Ⓓ $\dfrac{-3x}{5y}$

14. What is the common factor of the denominator and numerator in the expression below?

$$\frac{5x^2y - 10x}{xy - 2}$$

Ⓐ $x^2 - 2$

Ⓑ $y - 2$

Ⓒ $5xy$

Ⓓ $xy - 2$

15. Two triangles have areas given by the polynomials $x^2 - 9$ and $x^2 - x - 6$. What is the ratio of the areas of the triangles reduced to lowest terms?

Ⓐ $\dfrac{x-3}{x+2}$

Ⓑ $\dfrac{x+3}{x-3}$

Ⓒ $\dfrac{x+3}{x+2}$

Ⓓ $\dfrac{x+3}{x-2}$

16. Jim can pick 20 apples in 5 minutes and Sally can pick 25 apples in 5 minutes. Working together, how many minutes will it take them to pick 27 apples?

Ⓐ 2   Ⓑ 3

Ⓒ 4   Ⓓ 5

17. What is $\dfrac{2x^2 + xy - y^2}{2(x+y)}$ reduced to lowest terms?

Ⓐ $\dfrac{2x-y}{2}$

Ⓑ $\dfrac{x+y}{x-y}$

Ⓒ $\dfrac{2x+y}{2}$

Ⓓ $\dfrac{2x+y}{x+y}$

18. $\dfrac{x^2 + 2x - 24}{3(x+6)} \cdot \dfrac{x^2 - 36}{x^2 - 10x + 24} =$

Ⓐ $\dfrac{x+6}{3(x-4)}$

Ⓑ $\dfrac{x-6}{3(x+4)}$

Ⓒ $\dfrac{x+6}{3}$

Ⓓ $\dfrac{x-6}{3(x+6)}$

19. A chemist mixed some 15% saline solution with some 20% saline solution to obtain 75 milliliters of a 17% saline solution. How much of the 15% saline solution did the chemist use in the mixture?

Ⓐ 30   Ⓑ 35

Ⓒ 40   Ⓓ 45

California Standards
Algebra 16.0, 18.0

Relations and Functions

Example   ### Determine Whether a Relation is a Function

a. Determine whether the relation $\{(2,6), (-1,3), (4, 2), (6, 2)\}$ is a function.

Solution

Because each input is assigned to exactly one output, the relation is a function.

b. Determine whether the rule $y = \dfrac{2}{\pm\sqrt{x}}$ represents a function for the domain of real numbers greater than 0.

Solution

When $x = 4$, $y = \pm 1$. Therefore, one input is paired with more than one output.

So, $y = \dfrac{2}{\pm\sqrt{x}}$ is not a function for the domain of real numbers greater than 0.

Exercises

1. Which of the following is a function?

Ⓐ $\{(3, 5), (6, 9), (9, 6), (3, 9)\}$

Ⓑ $\{(-7, 4), (4, -7), (8, 2), (2, 8)\}$

Ⓒ $\{(0, 0), (1, 1), (1, 2), (0, 1)\}$

Ⓓ $\{(4, 9), (6, -2), (5, 9), (6, 4)\}$

2. If x is the independent variable and the domain is the set of real numbers, which of the following is *not* a function?

Ⓐ $y = |x|$ Ⓑ $|y| = x$

Ⓒ $y = |\sqrt{x}|$ Ⓓ $y = |x^2|$

3. Write a rule for the function below.

$\{(1, 12), (2, 24), (3, 36), (4, 48)\}$

Ⓐ $y = 12x$ Ⓑ $y = 3x$

Ⓒ $y = 12x + 3$ Ⓓ $y = 5x - 1$

4. Write a rule for the function shown in the table.

Hours Worked	1	2	3	4
Pay (dollars)	9	18	27	36

Ⓐ $y = x$ Ⓑ $y = 9x$

Ⓒ $y = 9x + 2$ Ⓓ $y = 6x$

5. The table shows the cost of various amounts of dried fruit at the grocery store. Which of the following best describes the information in the table?

Amount (pounds)	7	8	9	10
Cost (dollars)	49	56	63	70

Ⓐ not a relation

Ⓑ function

Ⓒ not a function

Ⓓ not enough information

6. Write a rule for the function below.

$\{(1, 6), (2, 12), (3, 18), (4, 24)\}$

Ⓐ $y = -8x$ Ⓑ $y = 3x$

Ⓒ $y = 7x - 1$ Ⓓ $y = 6x$

7. Which of the following is *not* a function?

Ⓐ $\{(2, 6), (-4, 5), (-2, -2)\}$

Ⓑ $\{(6, -6), (5, -3), (-3, -2)\}$

Ⓒ $\{(-5, 2), (-4, 6), (-5, -3)\}$

Ⓓ $\{(-6, 12), (5, -1), (6, -2)\}$

California Standards
Algebra 17.0

Domain and Range

Example   **Find the Domain and Range of a Function**

Find the domain and range of the function $y = \sqrt{x}$.

Solution

Because the square root of a negative number is undefined, x must be nonnegative. So, the domain D is the set of all real numbers greater than or equal to 0 or $D = \{x: x \geq 0\}$.

The range R is the set of all real numbers greater than or equal to 0 or $R = \{y : y \geq 0\}$.

Exercises

1. What is the domain of the relation
$\{(-8, 6), (7, -3), (12, 10), (-4, 5)\}$?

(A) $\{6, -3, 10, 5\}$

(B) $\{(-4, 6, 5, 8)\}$

(C) $\{-8, 6, 7, -3, 12, 10, -4, 5\}$

(D) $\{-8, 7, 12, -4\}$

2. What is the range of the relation
$\{(-3, 8), (4, -2), (6, 14), (-10, 12)\}$?

(A) $\{-3, 12\}$ **(B)** $\{3, 8, 10, 12\}$

(C) $\{8, -2, 14, 12\}$ **(D)** $\{-3, 4, 6, -10\}$

3. The table shows Delaney's pay for various numbers of hours worked. What is the range of the function?

Hours worked	6	12	18	24
Pay (dollars)	42	84	126	168

(A) $\{6, 12, 18, 24\}$ **(B)** $\{42, 84, 126, 168\}$

(C) $\{6, 24\}$ **(D)** $\{42, 168\}$

4. What is the range of the function $y = 4x + 2$ if the domain is $\{3, 2, -6, 4\}$?

(A) $\{10, 6, -26, 14\}$

(B) $\{3, 2, -6, 4\}$

(C) $\{-12, -10, 22, 18\}$

(D) $\{14, 10, -22, 18\}$

5. Identify the domain of the function $y = 4x$ if the range is $\{160, 200, 240, 280\}$.

(A) $\{40, 50, 60, 70\}$ **(B)** $\{50, 60\}$

(C) $\{30, 40, 50, 60\}$ **(D)** $\{30, 40\}$

6. What is the domain of $y = \sqrt{|x|}$?

(A) $\{x : x < 0\}$

(B) $\{x : x > 0\}$

(C) set of all real numbers

(D) $\{x : x \geq 0\}$

7. What is the range of $y = x^2$?

(A) $\{y : y \geq 0\}$

(B) $\{y : y < 0\}$

(C) $\{y : y > 0\}$

(D) $\{y : y \leq 0\}$

8. Which rule is *not* a function for the domain $\{x : x > 0\}$?

(A) $y = \sqrt{x}$ **(B)** $y = x^3$

(C) $y^2 = x$ **(D)** $y = \dfrac{1}{x + 1}$

9. What is the domain of the function $y = 4x - 5$?

(A) $\{4\}$

(B) $\{5\}$

(C) all real numbers

(D) $\{6, 2, 3, 9\}$

California Standards
Algebra 16.0, 17.0, 18.0

Mixed Review

1. The table shows the cost of different amounts of trail mix from the same jar at a bulk foods grocer. What is the domain of the relation?

Amount (ounces)	6	9	14	16
Cost (dollars)	1.87	2.81	4.37	4.99

   (A) 6, 9, 14, 16

   (B) 1.87, 2.81, 4.37, 4.99

   (C) 15

   (D) 3.51

2. What is the domain of the relation $\{(-5, 7), (3, -2), (-5, 14), (-8, 24)\}$?

   (A) $\{7, -2, 14, 24\}$

   (B) set of all real numbers

   (C) $\{-5, 7, 3, -2, 5, 14, -8, 24\}$

   (D) $\{-5, 3, -8\}$

3. What is the range of the relation $\{(-6, 8), (2, -5), (7, 14), (-12, 10)\}$?

   (A) $\{8, -5, 14, 10\}$

   (B) $\{-6, 8, -12, 10\}$

   (C) $\{-6, 8, 2, -5, 7, 14, -2, 10\}$

   (D) $\{-6, 2, 7, -12\}$

4. Which relation is a function?

   (A) $\{(3, 9), (4, 3), (3, -2), (4, 5)\}$

   (B) $\{(5, 6), (4, 3), (3, -2), (2, -3)\}$

   (C) $\{(-5, 10), (4, 3), (4, -2), (3, 7)\}$

   (D) $\{(-6, -12), (-5, -1), (-6, -2), (1, 0)\}$

5. In the equation $y = -9x - 3$, which variable is the independent variable?

   (A) -3 (B) -9

   (C) y (D) x

6. In the equation $b = -4a + 12$, which variable is the dependent variable?

   (A) b (B) a

   (C) -4 (D) 12

7. Which relation is *not* a function?

   (A) $\{(3, 12), (-4, 3), (6, -2), (5, 4)\}$

   (B) $\{(5, 6), (4, 3), (3, -2), (6, 3)\}$

   (C) $\{(-5, 10), (-4, 3), (4, -2), (-6, 4)\}$

   (D) $\{(-6, 12), (5, -1), (-6, -2), (2, 7)\}$

8. What is the range of the function $y = 4x + 2$ if the domain is $\{4, 6, -3, 5\}$?

   (A) $\{18, 26, -10, 22\}$

   (B) $\{16, 24, -12, 20\}$

   (C) set of all real numbers

   (D) $\{10, 12, 3, 11\}$

9. Which set of ordered pairs is generated by the function $y = 2x + 1$ when the domain is $\{3, -6, 5\}$?

   (A) $\{(7, 3), (-11, -6), (11, 5)\}$

   (B) $\{(3, 7), (-6, -11), (5, 11)\}$

   (C) $\{(3, 6), (-6, -10), (5, 10)\}$

   (D) $\{(7, 4), (-11, -5), (11, 6)\}$

10. Write a rule for the function shown in the table.

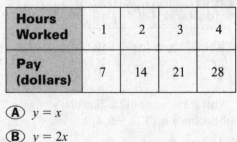

Hours Worked	1	2	3	4
Pay (dollars)	7	14	21	28

   (A) $y = x$

   (B) $y = 2x$

   (C) $y = 7x + 2$

   (D) $y = 7x$

California Standards
Intensive Review

11. Which of the following is the dependent variable in the equation $y = 4x - 6$?

  Ⓐ 4

  Ⓑ -6

  Ⓒ y

  Ⓓ x

12. Which of the following is the independent variable in the equation $b = -5a - 6$?

  Ⓐ b

  Ⓑ a

  Ⓒ -5

  Ⓓ -6

13. Identify the domain of the function $y = 2x$ if the range is $\{8, 12, -4, 14\}$.

  Ⓐ $\{16, 24, -8, 28\}$

  Ⓑ $\{16, 24, 8, 28\}$

  Ⓒ $\{4, 6, -2, 7\}$

  Ⓓ $\{-4, -6, 2, -7\}$

14. The table shows the weight of a puppy at different months of age. What is the domain of the relation?

Age (months)	3	6	9	12
Weight (pounds)	12	24	36	48

  Ⓐ $\{12, 24, 36, 48\}$

  Ⓑ $\{36\}$

  Ⓒ $\{3, 6, 9, 12\}$

  Ⓓ $\{9\}$

15. What is the domain of the relation $\{(12, 6), (12, -1), (4, 14), (-3, 12)\}$?

  Ⓐ $\{12, 4, -3\}$

  Ⓑ $\{12, 6\}$

  Ⓒ $\{12, 6, -1, 4, 14\}$

  Ⓓ $\{6, -1, 14, 12\}$

16. Identify the range of the relation $\{(-8, 4), (3, 4), (7, 4), (-4, 4)\}$.

  Ⓐ $\{4\}$

  Ⓑ $\{4, -4\}$

  Ⓒ $\{-8, 3, 7, -4\}$

  Ⓓ $\{-8, 4, 3, 7, -4\}$

17. Which relation is a function?

  Ⓐ $\{(3, 9), (3, 3), (5, -2)\}$

  Ⓑ $\{(2, 6), (5, 1), (2, -2)\}$

  Ⓒ $\{(-8, 2), (5, -2), (5, -4)\}$

  Ⓓ $\{(-6, -12), (-5, -1), (-4, -2)\}$

18. Which relation is *not* a function?

  Ⓐ $\{(2, 10), (-4, 5), (-8, -3)\}$

  Ⓑ $\{(5, 10), (-9, 3), (5, -2)\}$

  Ⓒ $\{(-8, 15), (-2, 3), (4, 12)\}$

  Ⓓ $\{(15, 11), (5, -8), (-6, -1)\}$

19. What is the range of the function $y = -3x + 5$ if the domain is $\{-2, 4, 7, -3\}$?

  Ⓐ $\{6, -12, -21, 9\}$

  Ⓑ $\{-1, 17, 26, 2\}$

  Ⓒ $\{11, -7, -16, 14\}$

  Ⓓ $\{2, -4, -7, 3\}$

20. Write a rule for the function $\{(1, -7), (2, -14), (3, -21), (4, -28)\}$.

  Ⓐ $y = 10x$

  Ⓑ $y = -7x$

  Ⓒ $y = 7x + 2$

  Ⓓ $y = 2x$

21. Identify the domain of the function $y = 3x$ if the range is $\{6, 15, -24, 12\}$.

  Ⓐ $\{6, 15, -24, 12\}$

  Ⓑ $\{2, 5\}$

  Ⓒ $\{2, 5, -8, 4\}$

  Ⓓ $\{6, 15, -24\}$

California Standards
Posttest

DIRECTIONS

Read each question. Then, on your answer sheet, fill in the bubble for the correct answer.

1. If $-y = -2$, then $y =$

(Alg. 2.0)

Ⓐ $-\dfrac{1}{2}$

Ⓑ -2

Ⓒ 2

Ⓓ $\dfrac{1}{2}$

2. Which of the following best explains why the graph below is a function? *(Alg. 18.0)*

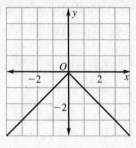

Ⓐ The vertical line $x = 0$ intersects the graph.

Ⓑ The vertical line $x = -1$ intersects the graph once.

Ⓒ The vertical line $x = 1$ intersects the graph once.

Ⓓ Every vertical line intersects the graph exactly once.

3. What is the y-intercept of the graph of $9x = 12 - 3y$? *(Alg. 6.0)*

Ⓐ -3

Ⓑ 4

Ⓒ 3

Ⓓ -4

4. Which inequality is shown on the graph below? *(Alg. 6.0)*

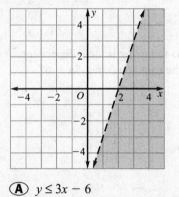

Ⓐ $y \le 3x - 6$

Ⓑ $y \ge 3x - 6$

Ⓒ $y < 3x - 6$

Ⓓ $y > 3x - 6$

5. What is the equation of the line that has a slope of -2 and passes through the point $(4, -4)$? *(Alg. 7.0)*

Ⓐ $3x + 6y = 6$

Ⓑ $2x + 3y = 12$

Ⓒ $6x + 3y = 12$

Ⓓ $3x - 2y = -6$

6. Joe parachutes from a plane. His height h above the ground is given by the equation

$$h = -16t^2 + 6400$$

where t is the time he is in the air in seconds. How long is Joe in the air? *(Alg. 23.0)*

Ⓐ 10 seconds

Ⓑ 15 seconds

Ⓒ 20 seconds

Ⓓ 25 seconds

California Standards
Posttest *continued*

7. Which of the following is an example of deductive reasoning? *(Alg. 24.1)*

Ⓐ If the first three terms of a sequence are 4, 8, and 12, the fourth term is 16.

Ⓑ Amy left for school at 7:30 on Monday, Tuesday, and Wednesday. You conclude that she will leave for school at 7:30 on Thursday.

Ⓒ If the first row of an orchestra has 5 seats and the second row has 7 seats, you conclude that the third row has 9 seats.

Ⓓ If the side of a square is 12 inches, you conclude that the perimeter is 48 inches.

8. Identify the property being illustrated. *(Alg. 1.0)*

$$6(-3 + r) = -18 + 6r$$

Ⓐ Associative property

Ⓑ Distributive property

Ⓒ Commutative property

Ⓓ Transitive property

9. Which of the following is an example of the product of powers property? *(Alg. 2.0)*

Ⓐ $q^2 \cdot q^3 = q^5$

Ⓑ $(x^2)^3 = x^6$

Ⓒ $(mn)^3 = mn^3$

Ⓓ $\dfrac{2d^3}{5d^5} = \dfrac{2}{5d^2}$

10. What is the hypothesis of the statement "If Steve gets up at 6:00 in the morning, then it must be a weekday"? *(Alg. 24.2)*

Ⓐ It must be Sunday

Ⓑ Steve gets up at 6:00 in the morning

Ⓒ It must be a weekday

Ⓓ It must be the morning

11. What is the conclusion of the statement "If x is a real number and x is not irrational, then x is a rational number"? *(Alg. 24.2)*

Ⓐ x is a real number

Ⓑ x is not irrational

Ⓒ x is a rational number

Ⓓ x is an integer

12. Which of the following is an example of the power of a power property? *(Alg. 2.0)*

Ⓐ $x^3 \cdot x^4 = x^7$

Ⓑ $(x^{1/5})^5 = x$

Ⓒ $2a^2 + 3a^2 = 5a^2$

Ⓓ $\dfrac{p^3}{p^5} = p^{-2}$

13. Solve $|x + 4| \geq 3$. *(Alg. 3.0)*

Ⓐ $-1 \leq x \leq 7$

Ⓑ $-7 \leq x \leq -1$

Ⓒ $x \leq 1$ or $x \geq 7$

Ⓓ $x \leq -7$ or $x \geq -1$

14. Which property of equality is illustrated by the statement "If $4x + 5 = 13$, and $13 = 3x + 7$, then $4x + 5 = 3x + 7$"? *(Alg. 25.1)*

Ⓐ Addition property

Ⓑ Symmetric property

Ⓒ Reflexive property

Ⓓ Transitive property

15. Which of the following correctly completes the statement "If $y = mx + 5$, then the graph is _?_ " *(Alg. 25.3)*

Ⓐ always a vertical line

Ⓑ sometimes a horizontal line

Ⓒ never a vertical line

Ⓓ always a horizontal line

California Standards
Posttest *continued*

16. What is the solution of $|p - 8| = 6$? *(Alg. 3.0)*

 Ⓐ $\{2, -8\}$

 Ⓑ $\{2, 14\}$

 Ⓒ $\{-14, -8\}$

 Ⓓ $\{-8, -2\}$

17. Which inequality is equivalent to $9x + 2 \geq -3 + 2x$? *(Alg. 4.0)*

 Ⓐ $11x \geq -5$

 Ⓑ $7x \geq -5$

 Ⓒ $11x \leq -5$

 Ⓓ $7x \leq -5$

18. What is the solution of $9x - 6 = -4 + 4x$? *(Alg. 5.0)*

 Ⓐ $x = \dfrac{5}{2}$

 Ⓑ $x = -\dfrac{5}{2}$

 Ⓒ $x = -\dfrac{2}{5}$

 Ⓓ $x = \dfrac{2}{5}$

19. Which of the following is *not* equivalent to $6x - 2 = 3(5 - 9x)$? *(Alg. 4.0)*

 Ⓐ $-33x + 15 = -2$

 Ⓑ $33x = 17$

 Ⓒ $17x = 33$

 Ⓓ $6x - 2 = 15 - 27x$

20. What is the x-intercept of the graph of $\dfrac{3}{2}x - \dfrac{7}{2}y = -6$? *(Alg. 6.0)*

 Ⓐ -4

 Ⓑ $\dfrac{12}{7}$

 Ⓒ $-\dfrac{12}{7}$

 Ⓓ 4

21. Which point lies on the line defined by $-8 + 2x = 4y$? *(Alg. 7.0)*

 Ⓐ $(4, 3)$

 Ⓑ $(5, -2)$

 Ⓒ $(-3, 4)$

 Ⓓ $(2, -1)$

22. Which of the following points lies in the solution set of the system $y \leq 2x$ and $y > -5x + 1$? *(Alg. 9.0)*

 Ⓐ $(-4, 3)$

 Ⓑ $(2, 1)$

 Ⓒ $(-2, -1)$

 Ⓓ $(2, 10)$

23. What is the solution of the system shown below? *(Alg. 9.0)*

$$2x - 3y = 6$$
$$4x - 3y = 1$$

 Ⓐ $\left(\dfrac{5}{2}, \dfrac{7}{6}\right)$

 Ⓑ $\left(-\dfrac{5}{2}, -\dfrac{11}{3}\right)$

 Ⓒ $\left(-\dfrac{5}{2}, \dfrac{11}{3}\right)$

 Ⓓ $\left(\dfrac{5}{2}, -\dfrac{11}{3}\right)$

24. $(x^2 - 5x + 1) - (-2x^2 - 2x + 3) =$ *(Alg. 10.0)*

 Ⓐ $3x^2 - 3x + 4$

 Ⓑ $3x^2 + 3x - 2$

 Ⓒ $-x^2 - 3x - 2$

 Ⓓ $3x^2 - 3x - 2$

25. Simplify the expression below. *(Alg. 10.0)*

$$\dfrac{2x^4 - 2x^3 + 6x^2}{2x^2}$$

 Ⓐ $x - 3$

 Ⓑ $x^2 - 3x$

 Ⓒ $x^2 - x + 3$

 Ⓓ $x^2 + x + 3x^2$

California Standards
Posttest continued

26. Simplify the expression below to lowest terms. *(Alg. 12.0)*

$$\frac{x^2 - 9}{x^2 - 9x + 18}$$

(A) $\frac{x + 3}{x - 6}$

(B) $\frac{x + 3}{x + 1}$

(C) $\frac{x - 3}{x - 6}$

(D) $\frac{x + 3}{x + 6}$

27. Write as a product of two factors. *(Alg. 11.0)*

$$4(x - 2) - x(x - 2)$$

(A) $(x - 2)(4 + x)$

(B) $(2 - x)(x - 4)$

(C) $(2 - x)(4 - x)$

(D) $(x - 2)(x + 4)$

28. What number should be added to both sides of $x^2 - 8x = 4$ to complete the square? *(Alg. 14.0)*

(A) 12

(B) 16

(C) 8

(D) 4

29. Which is a solution to the equation $x^2 - 4x = 12$? *(Alg. 14.0)*

(A) 2

(B) 4

(C) −6

(D) −2

30. Which relation is a function? *(Alg. 16.0)*

(A) $\{(-3, 3), (-2, 3), (-1, 3), (0, 3)\}$

(B) $\{(3, -3), (3, -2), (3, -1), (3, 0)\}$

(C) $\{(4, 5), (5, 4), (4, 6), (3, 5)\}$

(D) $\{(-3, 0), (2, 7), (1, 7), (2, 3)\}$

31. $\frac{2x}{x} - \frac{3x}{x + 3} =$

(Alg. 13.0)

(A) $\frac{-5x^2 + 6x}{x(x + 3)}$

(B) $\frac{-x^2 + 6x}{x + 3}$

(C) $\frac{-x^2 + 6x}{x(x + 3)}$

(D) $\frac{x^2 + 6x}{x(x + 3)}$

32. Roger's average biking speed on a 3-hour trip was 25 miles per hour. During the first hour his speed was 30 miles per hour. What was his average speed for the last two hours of the trip? *(Alg. 15.0)*

(A) 18 miles per hour

(B) 20 miles per hour

(C) 22.5 miles per hour

(D) 25 miles per hour

33. Let x be the independent variable. Which of the following statements best explains why $-x = |y|$ is *not* a function? *(Alg. 18.0)*

(A) There is a minus sign before the x.

(B) The x is on the left hand side of the equal sign.

(C) For the output of 0, there is exactly one input, 0.

(D) For the input of −1, there are two outputs, 1 and −1.

California Standards
Posttest *continued*

34. Which of the following graphs is *not* a function? *(Alg. 18.0)*

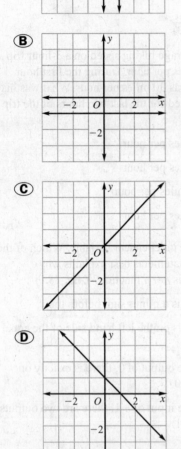

35. Which point lies on the line represented by the equation $3x - 6y = 2$? *(Alg. 7.0)*

- (A) $(0, -1)$
- (B) $(0, 1)$
- (C) $\left(0, -\frac{1}{3}\right)$
- (D) $\left(-1, \frac{5}{2}\right)$

36. Which of the following expressions, when simplified, gives the correct solutions to $5x^2 + 10x = -25$? *(Alg. 19.0)*

- (A) $\dfrac{-5 \pm \sqrt{5^2 - 4 \cdot 10 \cdot 25}}{2(5)}$
- (B) $\dfrac{5 \pm \sqrt{5^2 - 4 \cdot 10 \cdot 25}}{2(5)}$
- (C) $\dfrac{-10 \pm \sqrt{10^2 - 4(5)(-25)}}{2(5)}$
- (D) $\dfrac{-10 \pm \sqrt{10^2 - 4(5)(25)}}{2(5)}$

37. What is the solution set of the quadratic equation $x^2 + 3x - 7 = 0$? *(Alg. 20.0)*

- (A) $\left\{\dfrac{-3 + \sqrt{37}}{2}, \dfrac{-3 - \sqrt{37}}{2}\right\}$
- (B) $\left\{\dfrac{3 + \sqrt{37}}{2}, \dfrac{3 - \sqrt{37}}{2}\right\}$
- (C) $\left\{\dfrac{-3 + \sqrt{18}}{2}, \dfrac{-3 - \sqrt{18}}{2}\right\}$
- (D) $\left\{\dfrac{3 + \sqrt{18}}{2}, \dfrac{3 - \sqrt{18}}{2}\right\}$

38. The graph of which equation has *x*-intercepts at $(3, 0)$ and $(-2, 0)$? *(Alg. 21.0)*

- (A) $y = (x + 3)(x + 2)$
- (B) $y = (x - 3)(x - 2)$
- (C) $y = (x + 3)(x - 2)$
- (D) $y = (x - 3)(x + 2)$

39. Identify the error (if any) between Steps 2 and 3. *(Alg. 25.2)*

Step 1: $(5x - y)^2 = 3x^2 + 6y - 4$
Step 2: $5x^2 - y^2 = 3x^2 + 6y - 4$
Step 3: $-y^2 = 8x^2 + 6y - 4$

- (A) There was no error made.
- (B) The inverse property of addition was violated.
- (C) Unlike terms were combined.
- (D) The additive property of equality was violated.

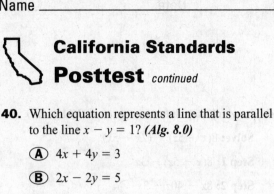

California Standards
Posttest *continued*

40. Which equation represents a line that is parallel to the line $x - y = 1$? *(Alg. 8.0)*

- (A) $4x + 4y = 3$
- (B) $2x - 2y = 5$
- (C) $7x + 7y = 13$
- (D) $-6x - 6y = 2$

41. Line A has a slope of $\frac{1}{2}$. Which equation represents a line that is perpendicular to line A? *(Alg. 8.0)*

- (A) $-4x + y = -2$
- (B) $-4x - y = 2$
- (C) $-4x + 2y = 1$
- (D) $-4x - 2y = -1$

42. $\frac{3x^6}{21x^2} =$

(Alg. 10.0)

- (A) $\frac{x^4}{7}$
- (B) $6x^3$
- (C) $\frac{2}{7x^5}$
- (D) $\frac{4x^{-5}}{7}$

43. What is the factored form of $2x^3 - 2x^2 - 12x$? *(Alg. 11.0)*

- (A) $2x(x + 2)(x - 3)$
- (B) $2x(x - 2)(x + 3)$
- (C) $x(x + 3)(x + 2)$
- (D) $2x(x + 2)(x - 2)$

44. Which is a factor of $x^2 - 36$? *(Alg. 11.0)*

- (A) $x + 6$
- (B) $x - 3$
- (C) $x - 9$
- (D) $x^2 + 3$

45. Which shows $9x^4 + 24x^2y^2 + 16y^4$ factored completely? *(Alg. 11.0)*

- (A) $(3x^2 + 4y^2)^2$
- (B) $(3x^2 + 4y^2)(3x^2 - 4y^2)$
- (C) $(3x^2 + y^2)(x^2 + 4y^2)$
- (D) $9x^4 + 24x^2y^2 + 16y^4$

46. Solve $3x^2 + 5x - 2 = 0$ by factoring. *(Alg. 14.0)*

- (A) $x = -\frac{1}{3}$ or $x = -2$
- (B) $x = \frac{1}{3}$ or $x = -2$
- (C) $x = -\frac{1}{2}$ or $x = -3$
- (D) $x = \frac{1}{2}$ or $x = -3$

47. Which of the following numbers is *not* in the domain of the function shown below? *(Alg. 17.0)*

$$\{(8, -4), (1, 1), (-2, 8), (0, 0)\}$$

- (A) -4
- (B) -2
- (C) 0
- (D) 1 and 0

48. Which function has no x-intercepts? *(Alg. 22.0)*

- (A) $y = x^2 - x - 9$
- (B) $y = x^2 - 4x + 12$
- (C) $y = 9x^2 - 2x - 11$
- (D) $y = x^2 - x - 24$

49. Which equation represents a line that is parallel to the line represented by the equation $y = -5$? *(Alg. 8.0)*

- (A) $x = -5$
- (B) $y = x$
- (C) $y = 5$
- (D) $x = 5$

California Standards Posttest

California Standards
Posttest *continued*

50. If the discriminant of $ax^2 + bx + c = 0$ is negative, what can you conclude about the graph of $y = ax^2 + bx + c$? *(Alg. 22.0)*

(A) The graph opens downward.

(B) The graph does not intersect the y-axis.

(C) The graph intersects the x-axis left of the y-axis.

(D) The graph does not intersect the x-axis.

51. Simplify $(-2)(8m - 2n)$. *(Alg. 1.0)*

(A) $16m - 4n$

(B) $10m + 4n$

(C) $-16m + 4n$

(D) $\frac{1}{4}m - n$

52. Which of the following is *not* an example of deductive reasoning? *(Alg. 24.1)*

(A) If the first three terms of a sequence are 7, 9, and 11, the fourth term is 13.

(B) If the length and width of a rectangle are 6 inches and 8 inches, you conclude that the perimeter is 28 inches.

(C) If the area of a square is 49 square inches, you conclude that each side is 7 inches.

(D) If the length of a rectangle is 9 inches and the area is 27 square inches, you conclude that the width is 3 inches.

53. Which of the following is an example of inductive reasoning? *(Alg. 24.1)*

(A) If the first term of a sequence is 6, you conclude that the last term is 100.

(B) If the first three terms of a sequence are 5, 10, and 15, you conclude that the fourth term is 20.

(C) If the first term of a sequence is 12 and the last term is 81, you conclude that the fourth term is 44.

(D) If the side of a square is 10 inches, you conclude that the area is 100 square inches.

54. In which step does an error occur? *(Alg. 1.1)*

Solve: $8(x - 5z) + (2x - 5x)$

Step 1: $8(x - 5z) - 3x$

Step 2: $8x - 40z - 3x$

Step 3: $11x - 40z$

(A) Step 1

(B) Step 2

(C) Step 3

(D) No error

55. Tell whether the statement is true or false. If it is false, select the choice that gives a valid counterexample. "If x is the square root of a prime number, then x is rational." *(Alg. 24.3)*

(A) false; $x = \sqrt{31}$

(B) false; $x = \sqrt{36}$

(C) false; $x = \sqrt{21}$

(D) true

56. Identify the statement that completes the argument. *(Alg. 25.1)*

3 is a root of $2x^2 - x - 15$ because

(A) $2(3)^2 - 3 - 15 = 0$.

(B) 3 is odd.

(C) $2x^2 - x - 15 = 0$.

(D) 3 is prime.

57. Solve for q. *(Alg. 5.0)*

$$\frac{3q - 4}{q} = 6$$

(A) $q = \frac{3}{4}$

(B) $q = \frac{4}{3}$

(C) $q = -\frac{3}{4}$

(D) $q = -\frac{4}{3}$

California Standards Posttest